Mindfulness *Workbook* FOR DUMMIES®

by Shamash Alidina and Joelle Jane Marshall
Foreword by Dr Shanida Nataraja

A John Wiley and Sons, Ltd, Publication

Mindfulness Workbook For Dummies®

Published by:
John Wiley & Sons, Ltd
The Atrium
Southern Gate
Chichester
West Sussex
PO19 8SQ
England

www.wiley.com

Registered office

John Wiley & Sons Ltd, The Atrium, Southern Gate, Chichester, West Sussex, PO19 8SQ, United Kingdom

For details of our global editorial offices, for customer services and for information about how to apply for permission to reuse the copyright material in this book please see our website at www.wiley.com.

Wiley publishes in a variety of print and electronic formats and by print-on-demand. Some material included with standard print versions of this book may not be included in e-books or in print-on-demand. If this book refers to media such as a CD or DVD that is not included in the version you purchased, you may download this material at http://booksupport. wiley.com. For more information about Wiley products, visit www.wiley.com.

Designations used by companies to distinguish their products are often claimed as trademarks. All brand names and product names used in this book are trade names, service marks, trademarks or registered trademarks of their respective owners. The publisher is not associated with any product or vendor mentioned in this book.

For general information on our other products and services, please contact our Customer Care Department within the U.S. at 877-762-2974, outside the U.S. at (001) 317-572-3993, or fax 317-572-4002.

For technical support, please visit www.wiley.com/techsupport.

A catalogue record for this book is available from the British Library.

ISBN: 978-1-118-45643-9 (pbk) ISBN: 978-1-118-45648-4 (ebk)

ISBN: 978-1-118-45644-6 (ebk) ISBN: 978-1-118-45645-3 (ebk)

Printed in Great Britain by TJ International Ltd, Padstow, Cornwall

WILEY

Contents at a Glance

Table of Contents

Foreword

*I*n a world filled with constant distractions, demands and stresses, an increasing number of people are earnestly searching for a way of life that brings focus, clarity, calm and, ultimately, fulfilment and happiness. Whilst there are numerous doctrines or disciplines that offer this way of life, mindfulness is a discipline that I am particularly drawn to as a neuroscientist, as it is supported by a rich and convincing scientific evidence base. Thanks to the work of Jon Kabat-Zinn and other researchers, we know that mindfulness-based stress reduction (MBSR) can boost well-being, reduce symptoms of stress and improve mood and coping strategies in a wide range of patients, including those suffering from chronic pain, those fighting cancer or those managing stress-related diseases. Through the research of John Teasdale and colleagues, we know that mindfulness-based cognitive therapy (MBCT) is an effective treatment for depression and anxiety in patients who are failing to respond to traditional treatments. And through the efforts of countless researchers, we know that mindfulness-based practices can boost work productivity, reduce work absenteeism and improve social interactions in the workplace. This compelling evidence suggests a clear role for mindfulness in maintaining health, as well as addressing ill health, in people of all ages, backgrounds and professions.

Over the last decade, science has also revealed what happens in the brain during the practice of mindfulness, and this exciting research suggests that mindfulness may have effects on the performance of our brains, as well as beneficial effects on our physical and mental well-being. On both the short- and long-term, mindfulness can elicit changes in our brain that improve our emotional resilience, enhance our ability to regulate our emotional states, fine-tune our concentration and problem-solving skills, and develop compassion and empathy, for ourselves and others. These changes allow us to realise more of the potential of our brains, better equipping ourselves to deal with the challenges of modern life. This evidence presents a strong rationale for incorporating regular mindfulness practice into our everyday lives: in our families; in our schools; in the workplace; as part of our healthcare systems; and in our prisons.

The *Mindfulness Workbook For Dummies* is an excellent introduction to mindfulness and the nuts and bolts of how to live a mindful life. Embarking on any journey can be daunting and the mindful journey is no different. Where should you start? What books should you read? Who is a good teacher? And what is mindfulness anyway? This book sheds light on what being mindful really means and uses practical exercises to escort the reader through the different stages of the mindful journey. Whether a short body scan exercise to raise awareness of bodily sensations or a breathing meditation to calm the mind in a stressful situation, Shamash Alidina and Joelle Jane Marshall provide readers with a series of tools to help them both understand mindfulness and incorporate it into their everyday lives. The *Mindfulness Workbook For Dummies* can be used both in conjunction with an eight-week mindfulness-based programme taught by an experienced teacher and as an aid to guide the reader through this programme in their own home through solitary practice. By providing helpful tips and tricks, addressing potential difficulties arising through mindfulness practice, and giving readers step-by-step instructions on how to do the various mindfulness exercises, Shamash and Joelle have created an invaluable resource for anyone wishing to embark on their own mindful journey.

Dr Shanida Nataraja

Neuroscientist and author of *The Blissful Brain: Neuroscience and Proof of the Power of Meditation* (Gaia Books).

Introduction

*W*elcome to the *Mindfulness Workbook For Dummies.* Mindfulness offers both a set of techniques and a way of living that can lead towards greater peace, wisdom and joy. Mindfulness is an ancient approach, but now scientific evidence from top universities worldwide shows its effectiveness in treating a range of conditions like depression, anxiety, chronic pain and much more.

Life is full of many challenges – everyone goes through some sort of difficulty over the course of their time on earth. Some difficulties may be physical or practical; others mental or emotional. Mindfulness offers a way of coping with all these difficulties in a harmonious way, so that you don't make those difficulties even more painful, but meet them with wisdom and dignity, allowing them space to dissolve in their own time.

Mindfulness also enhances your life when things are going well. You learn to notice the world around you, become more grateful for what you have, more kind and forgiving towards yourself and others, focus more effectively at work, home, and in your relationships and enhance your physical and emotional health and wellbeing.

We've written this book to make mindfulness a practical reality in your life. The written exercises and accompanying guided meditation audio tracks offer a way to practise and then reflect on your personal experience of mindfulness and deepen your insights, both for beginners and more experienced practitioners too.

About This Book

This book contains a range of different ways to practise mindfulness in your life. We give you a combination of some theory along with lots of exercises to try out. With mindfulness, you discover much more by trying out the exercises rather than just reading theory, so this workbook is an ideal format for exploring mindfulness.

You can use this book as a stand-alone way of developing your own mindfulness. We describe all the key methods of practising mindfulness, and together with the accompanying audio, you can take your first steps into a more mindful way of living.

You can also use this book with a mindfulness teacher or therapist to discover new insights, try new exercises and to keep a useful record of your progress. You can then look back at what you wrote in this book to see how things have changed for you in the weeks, months or years that you've been engaging in mindfulness.

This book contains the main ways in which you can use mindfulness to overcome common difficulties like stress, anxiety, depression and physical health conditions. But the exercises are helpful for everyone; improving creativity, focus and offering a fresh, new look at your own life.

How to Use This Book

You don't need to read this book from beginning to end. You can dip in and out of different chapters, choosing what's most relevant or interesting for you. We've done our best to cross-reference each chapter to other parts in the book, so you can delve deeper into any concepts or exercises that may be of help to you. Use the Table of Contents at the front of the book and Index at the back to locate specific information.

Please feel free to write in this book – that's how it's designed. Scribble in each table to your heart's content. And if you need more space, you may like to copy the tables for your own use or use your own notebook for further reflection.

Foolish Assumptions

If you're reading this book, we're assuming you're interested in learning mindfulness. We're guessing that you've heard about mindfulness and want to know more. As this is a workbook, we also assume, perhaps foolishly, that you want to get practical and do some mindfulness exercises and keep a record of your experience.

Perhaps you're a mindfulness teacher, coach or therapist looking for exercises to use with your students or clients. You may have a friend or relative suffering from a difficulty and want to know if mindfulness can help. Or you may already be an experienced mindfulness practitioner looking to deepen your awareness. Whatever the reason, we hope you find the book useful.

How This Book Is Organised

The *Mindfulness Workbook For Dummies* is divided into five parts:

Part I: Getting Started with Mindfulness

This part unlocks the treasure chest and gives you a basic overview of mindfulness. Chapter 1 is all about what mindfulness is and how mindfulness may unfold in your life. In Chapter 2 we explain all the benefits of practising mindfulness on a regular basis.

Part II: Preparing Yourself for Mindful Living

Part II is about ensuring that you have the best underlying approach and mind-set before you dive into practical mindfulness exercises.

Chapter 3 is all about engaging the right attitudes, so when you do the mindfulness practice, you have a good grounding. Without the right attitudes, you may easily get side-tracked or disheartened if your experience doesn't match your expectations. This chapter helps you to set things straight. Chapter 4 covers two modes of mind – 'doing' and 'being' mode. You explore the nature and importance of each of these modes, and how you can use mindfulness to identify and switch modes when necessary.

Part III: Practising Mindfulness

In this part we get down to detailed mindfulness practice. In Chapter 5 you learn all the core mindfulness meditations that you can continue to use for the rest of your life, if you like! Chapter 6 is all about how to integrate mindfulness into your everyday life. In this way, you don't just meditate, but live mindfulness, moment by moment. Chapters

7 and 8 offer you a detailed, evidence-based eight-week mindfulness programme that has been tested by tens of thousands of students for many years. You can use this to learn mindfulness in a methodical way – ideal for beginners to mindfulness. Chapter 9 helps to answer common questions that people have when first learning mindfulness. If you're having any difficulties in your mindfulness practice, Chapter 9 is the place to go.

Part IV: Enjoying the Rewards of Mindfulness

In this part, you discover how to use mindfulness to both increase your wellbeing and deal with common challenges. Chapter 10 is about happiness, and how mindfulness can help to enhance your long-term wellbeing. In Chapter 11 we offer ways mindfulness can relieve your stress and anger, and boost your energy. Chapter 12 explains the causes of anxiety and depression, and how mindfulness can help in these areas. Your physical health is covered in Chapter 13, along with how you can use mindfulness for conditions like chronic pain. And finally, Chapter 14 is about using mindfulness to improve your skills as a parent or teacher, and we share a range of specific mindful exercises to use with children.

Part V: The Part of Tens

Here in Chapters 15 and 16 you can pick up tips for living mindfully and ways to get yourself motivated to meditate. Online (at www.dummies.com/extras/mindfulnesswork bookuk), we give you an additional Part of Tens chapter with lots of resources and ways of creatively enhancing your mindfulness. Some people like to start by reading the Part of Tens – we encourage you to take a look at these mini chapters for instant inspiration.

Icons Used in This Book

We use icons throughout this workbook to bring different types of information to your attention and to clearly guide you through the book.

This icon is used to emphasise information worth bearing in mind.

The Tip icon alerts you to additional useful information that may help you to better understand a concept or to complete an exercise.

You'll see this icon next to exercises to encourage you to flex your mindfulness muscles.

This icon is an alarm denoting possible pitfalls, common errors or potential dangers.

Find pearls of wisdom and stories to get you thinking with this icon.

Where to Go from Here

This book offers a practical hands-on approach to mindfulness. Being a workbook, we devote more space to exercises and less to the underlying theory of mindfulness. If you'd like a more detailed description of the mindfulness exercises and to experience a different set of guided audio meditations, you may also like *Mindfulness For Dummies* by Shamash Alidina (Wiley). If you're looking for a variety of techniques to help you relieve stress, check out *Relaxation For Dummies* by Shamash Alidina (Wiley). For more suggestions of a range of books, audio, films, websites, retreats and more, go to www.dummies.com/extras/mindfulnessworkbookuk for an extra Part of Tens chapter: '(Nearly) Ten Ways to Expand Your Mindfulness Experience'. Head to www.dummies.com/go/mindfulnessworkbookuk to find the accompanying audio meditations mentioned in the book:

✔ **Track One:** Introduction (2 minutes)

✔ **Track Two:** Body scan meditation, Chapter 5 (25 minutes)

✔ **Track Three:** Sitting meditation (expanding awareness), Chapters 5 and 7 (20 minutes)

✔ **Track Four:** Mountain meditation, Chapter 9 (10 minutes)

✔ **Track Five:** Lake meditation, Chapter 3 (10 minutes)

✔ **Track Six:** Three-minute breathing space meditation, Chapter 6 (3 minutes)

Part I
Getting Started with Mindfulness

getting started
with
Mindfulness

web
extras

Go to www.dummies.com/go/mindfulnessworkbookuk to listen to audio meditations.

In this part . . .

✔ Explore the origins and benefits of mindfulness.

✔ Understand different types of meditation.

✔ Consider your goals and expectations for your mindfulness journey.

✔ Enjoy the many benefits of mindfulness, from the positive effect on your body to improving your concentration.

✔ Go to www.dummies.com/go/mindfulnesswork bookuk to listen to audio meditations.

Chapter 1

Beginning Your Mindfulness Journey

No matter how or why you decided to look into mindfulness, we believe that you've made a smart move. Everyone can benefit from the increased awareness and self-knowledge that practising mindfulness can bring.

So what do we mean by that phrase? *Practising mindfulness* means paying attention regularly and intentionally to your present-moment experience with mindful attitudes. Four of the most important attitudes of mindfulness are compassion, curiosity, acceptance and openness for yourself, other people and the surrounding world. You deepen and develop your mindfulness by practising mindfulness exercises and meditations and by living mindfully on a day-to-day basis.

Scientific studies confirm that practising mindfulness regularly allows you to begin to change the way you experience life. As a result your brain is less stressed, focuses better and reacts automatically less, becomes more resilient to future challenges and regulates your emotions more effectively. Your body also becomes better at fighting disease and your tension eases. Most likely your relationships improve and you're more engaged at work. You may well experience greater levels of happiness and peace in your life by living with mindfulness.

In this chapter we introduce you to the concept and practice of mindfulness and guide you gently into beginning your mindfulness journey.

Understanding Mindfulness

In some ways, mindfulness is simple. You pay attention to whatever's going on right now with the right attitude, whether it's an internal or external experience. But mindfulness is also much more subtle. The challenge is remembering to be mindful, rather than reacting automatically, and letting go of your self-criticism and doubt as you begin to practise.

The triangle in Figure 1-1 summarises the essence of mindfulness as proposed by Dr Shauna Shapiro and colleagues, and published in the *Journal of Clinical Psychology*.

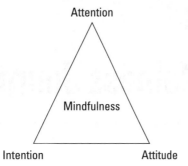

Figure 1-1:
Defining
mindfulness.

Locating the origins of mindfulness

Mindfulness isn't a new concept, although it's rapidly gaining popularity in the West, especially in the field of psychology. Mindfulness is now part of both traditional psychology, which aims to help alleviate conditions such as depression or anxiety, and modern positive psychology, which advocates scientifically sounds ways to raise levels of long-term wellbeing and satisfaction (Chapter 10 discusses how mindfulness can boost your happiness).

Many consider mindfulness to have its origins Buddhism, but even before the Buddha's birth some 2,500 years ago, Hindus practised a range of meditations, some of which involved mindfulness.

Mindfulness isn't inherently Eastern, just as electricity isn't inherently Western. Mindfulness is a quality of presence that's innate in all human beings. Awareness is a natural and beautiful quality of being human that can't be limited to one particular tradition or country.

Noticing what your judgements of the word *mindfulness* are before you delve into the practice more deeply is interesting. For the next minute, write down in Worksheet 1-1 all the words that pop into your head when you think of the word *mindfulness*. Don't think about the process. Time yourself for a minute and just write down what occurs to you.

Worksheet 1-1	What Mindfulness Means to Me

Mindfulness is for all

We aren't religious in the traditional sense, and Shamash, who teaches mindfulness, offers trainings in a completely secular way. Mindfulness certainly requires no belief and has no single teacher, guru or organisation. You can discover it from many teachers or just by picking up a book on the subject (oh, you have!). This is partly why we were attracted to the approach. The other main reason why we're so passionate about mindfulness is that it's scientifically based. Just as you expect your doctor to prescribe you medication that's been proven to work, so you should develop your mental health and wellbeing with proven techniques such as mindfulness.

The development of mindfulness in the West

One of the key people who popularised mindfulness in the West is Professor Jon Kabat-Zinn, together with some colleagues working at the University of Massachusetts Medical School. In 1979 he created an innovative eight-week course that eventually became known as Mindfulness-based Stress Reduction (MBSR). He tested the programme on chronic pain patients and found that not only their pain went down, but also their feelings of stress, anxiety and depression. Hundreds of research studies have been carried out on that eight-week course, showing positive outcomes for many physical and mental-health conditions. You can find out more about the eight-week course in Chapters 7 and 8.

In the years that followed, more and more medical institutions began researching mindfulness. Mindfulness is now researched in top university departments all over the world. For example, The University of Oxford in the UK has a whole centre dedicated to researching the health benefits of mindfulness for depression, anxiety, childbirth, parenting and more.

Afterwards, consider the words you're written. Are they positive, negative or neither? Some of them may be your unconscious judgements of mindfulness, and you may find that being aware of this is useful. Your judgements may be based on what someone else has told you or something you've read in a magazine, book or seen on television. After you've discovered your judgements, try to consciously set them aside and consider mindfulness afresh. Suspend your opinions and beliefs until you've learnt and practised mindfulness yourself for some time.

If you didn't get many words coming to mind, perhaps try drawing a picture or image instead. You may well be a more visual person.

Mulling over what mindfulness means

In this section, we take a look at each concept that makes up the following definition of mindfulness: *Intentionally paying attention to your present moment experiences with compassion, curiosity, acceptance and openness.*

- ✔ **Intention:** The process of being mindful requires an intention. Your intention is your reason to practise – this may be to reduce your stress, to manage your emotions or develop wisdom. Being clear about what you hope to get from mindfulness in the long term shapes the quality of your mindfulness experience. For example, if you go to your local supermarket with a clear intention to get milk, bread and eggs, you'll probably achieve it. But if you turn up not really sure what you're after, you may end up buying anything on special offer, even if you don't need it.

- ✔ **Paying attention:** Attention can be narrow or wide. Traditionally mindfulness is about developing a wide, open awareness, but most mindfulness exercises begin with a narrow, focused attention on something – for example, focusing your attention on your breath or a part of your body. Most meditations move on to encompass a wide, open attention too.

- ✔ **Present moment:** The here and now – whatever is happening in this moment. If you're paying attention to whatever is happening now, and you're aware that you're paying attention, you're in the now. Much of the time, your mind is focused on events of the past or concerns about the future. Mindfulness values experiences in the present moment, which ironically leads to a better future! Ultimately, the only moment that exists is the present moment – everything else just exists in your own mind.

  Your present moment experiences can be internal (such as thoughts or emotions) or external (such as whatever you perceive through your senses).

✔ **Compassion:** Kindness to yourself is the key here. When practising mindfulness, you're invited to be nice to yourself. Whenever you notice yourself judging yourself in a harsh way, mindfulness encourages you to be aware of this process and let the judgement go.

You probably have an inner critic within your mind that's often criticising you or others. Most people do. Mindfulness is about noticing this aspect of yourself and stepping back from it, rather than feeding or encouraging more criticism.

In the ancient Indian Pali language, the words for *mind* and *heart* are the same. And the Chinese character for *mindfulness* is a combination of two characters. One part means *now* and the other means *mind* or *heart*. So, when you hear the word *mindfulness* you can also consider it to mean *heartfulness*.

✔ **Curiosity:** Mindfulness is quite natural for children because they're naturally inquisitive and constantly asking 'why?'. Mindfulness is about rekindling your inner curiosity. If you're more curious about the world around you, you're immediately more mindful instead of behaving habitually and reacting to situations automatically. Even children can benefit from mindfulness though, as we explain in Chapter 14.

This dimension of curiosity is especially helpful when dealing with difficult thoughts and emotions. Instead of automatically trying to fight or run away from unhelpful thoughts or emotions, mindfulness encourages you to become curious about them. This in turn creates a different mind state and is more likely to allow your difficult inner experience to pass away.

✔ **Acceptance:** One of the most important and poorly understood attitudes in mindfulness. In fact, mindfulness is sometimes referred to as an acceptance-based therapy because this attitude is so important. Acceptance for some people has negative connotations of passivity, giving up or allowing someone to do wrong without taking action – acting like a doormat. But this isn't at all what acceptance means in mindfulness.

Acceptance is an active process of acknowledging your present-moment experience and is particularly important when dealing with emotions. This example may help. Imagine that you're travelling from London to Manchester. Before you can get to Manchester, you need to accept that you're in London. That makes sense. If you don't accept that you're in London, you're never going to get to Manchester. You need to begin where you are. In the same way, if you're feeling sad, you need to accept it. Pretending, denying, fighting or running from your feeling doesn't help – in fact, you're inadvertently giving the feeling more attention and so are more likely to strengthen it.

✔ **Openness:** Mindfulness encourages you to open up to your inner and outer experiences, as best you can. By *openness,* we also mean a sense of stepping back from your experiences, but not avoiding or running away from them. This stepping back is tremendously helpful when you're having relentless thoughts or difficult emotions. Mindfulness enables you to watch the thoughts arising and passing away without the need to cling or attach to them. You don't need to believe everything you think. A sense of detached openness also enables you to watch emotions come and go from a safe distance instead of being overwhelmed by your feelings. In this way, instead of suppressing emotions you deal with them.

For example, say you're nervous about an upcoming exam. You can watch your thoughts, such as 'I hate exams' or 'What if I fail?', as just thoughts and let them go. You can also be aware of the feeling of anxiety in your stomach with a sense of distance or perspective. You may then centre yourself by taking a few deep, slow breaths, feeling the sensation of your breath in your body. You then feel more effectively prepared to study for your exam.

Figure 1-2 summarises the four mindful attitudes. (We discuss maintaining healthy attitudes in Chapter 3.)

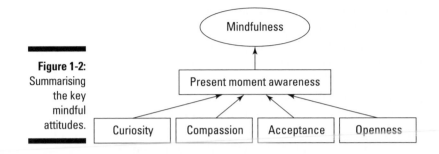

Figure 1-2:
Summarising
the key
mindful
attitudes.

Exploring Types of Mindfulness Meditation

Mindfulness, also called wise attention, helps us see what we're adding to our experiences, not only during meditation sessions but also elsewhere.

— *Sharon Salzberg*

One of the areas of common confusion is the difference between mindfulness and meditation. To clarify:

- **Mindfulness** is the act of being consciously aware with mindful attitudes. You can practise mindfulness over any length of time, for the duration of a single breath or for your whole life. You can practise it while waiting in a queue, talking to your partner or walking down the street.

- **Mindfulness meditation** is an activity where you make time deliberately and consciously for cultivating mindfulness (flip to Chapter 5 for some formal mindfulness meditations).

Clinically proven courses usually contain certain common mindfulness meditations such as:

- **Body scan meditation:** Often done lying down, but you can use any posture you like. This meditation involves becoming aware of your bodily sensations in a mindful way, step by step. You also begin to discover how easily your attention wanders off to other thoughts and how to be kind to yourself rather than self-critical when this happens. Check out Chapter 5 for more.

- **Movement meditation:** Usually yoga, t'ai chi, qi gong or another physical mind-body exercise (see Chapter 6). This type of meditation involves focusing on your bodily sensations, breathing and mindfully watching and perhaps letting go of whatever thoughts and emotions arise as you practise. Slow walking meditation is another possibility that's sometimes used. For how mindfulness can help with physical pain and illness, turn to Chapter 13.

- **Breathing space meditation:** A short, roughly three-minute, meditation that we describe in Chapter 6. We recommend that you do this practice a few times a day and whenever you experience a highly stressful situation or difficult emotion. The idea is to create a mindful awareness of your experience instead of avoiding it. This approach has been shown scientifically to be much more effective than avoidance. For more mindfulness approaches to stress and anxiety, check out Chapters 11 and 12 respectively.

- **Expanding awareness meditation:** Usually called sitting meditation, but it can be practised in any position. The meditation involves focusing, often in this order, on your breath, body, sounds, thoughts and feelings, and finally developing an open awareness where you're choicelessly aware of whatever is most predominant in your consciousness (see Chapter 5).

You can break down the expanding awareness meditation into separate meditations, each powerful and transformative in themselves:

- **Mindfulness of breath meditation:** Focusing your attention on the feeling of your in-breath and out-breath. Each time your mind wanders, bring your attention back non-judgementally.

- **Mindfulness of body meditation:** Feeling the physical sensation in your body from moment to moment. You can also practise this together with the awareness of breathing.

- **Mindfulness of sounds meditation:** Being aware of sounds as they arise and pass away. If no ambient sounds exist, you can simply listen to the silence and notice what effect doing so has for you.

- **Mindfulness of thoughts meditation:** Being aware of your thoughts arising in your mind and passing away and having a sense of distance between yourself and your thoughts. You allow the thoughts to come and go as they please, without judging or attaching to them.

- **Mindfulness of feelings meditation:** Noticing whatever feelings arise for you. In particular, you notice where you feel the emotion in your body and bring a quality of acceptance and curiosity to your emotions.

- **Open awareness meditation:** Sometimes called choiceless awareness, because you become aware of whatever's most predominant in your awareness without choosing. You may be aware of any of the above meditation experiences as well.

Another group of mindfulness meditations are more like visualisations. These meditations slightly expand the definition of mindfulness, which usually involves paying attention to present-moment experiences. However, many people are quite visual and find the meditations valuable. The two main visual meditations included in the audio of this book are:

- ✔ **Mountain meditation:** This meditation helps you to cultivate stability and groundedness and feel more centred. For details, flip to Chapter 9 and listen to Track 4 on the accompanying audio.

- ✔ **Lake meditation:** This meditation is about exploring the beauty of accepting and allowing experiences to be just as they are. Check out Chapter 3 and listen to Track 5 for more.

If you've already tried some form of meditation in the past, use Worksheet 1-2 to record your experiences and what you discovered.

Worksheet 1-2	**Recording My Past Experiences of Meditation**
Type of Meditation	*What Did I Think of the Meditation? How Was My Experience of It?*

Reflecting on any past meditation experience allows you to see what type of meditations seem to work well for you. If you've never practised meditation, don't worry. You're in a good position because you're starting with a blank slate.

Setting Off on a Mindful Journey

In the end, just three things matter: how well we have lived, how well we have loved, how well we have learned to let go.

— *Jack Kornfield*

Going on a holiday is similar to the journey into mindful living. In this section, imagine that you're going on a trip and reflect on how the journey is like the inner journey of mindfulness.

Taking the first steps: Choosing your learning method

The journey of a thousand miles begins with a cunning plan . . . and then a single step.

Like deciding to set out on a mindfulness journey, the start of an excursion is tremendously exciting! You're going on an adventure and aren't sure what you'll experience. So you need to have at least a rough idea of where you're going. And when you're planning your journey, you need to know what you hope to get from the trip. Here are the kind of questions you may consider:

- ✔ Are you interested in connecting with nature or finding adrenalin-rush activities?
- ✔ Will you have lots of free time or are you on a tight schedule?
- ✔ What's your budget?
- ✔ Will you be sleeping in a tent, a campervan or checking into a motel or 5-star luxury accommodation?
- ✔ What type of traveller are you? Do you like to go with the flow or prefer to have every day pre-planned?

For me (Shamash), I prefer planning trips by speaking to someone, and I don't like to pre-plan too much. So I just turn up to a tourist office when I arrive and have a nice chat with the representative and plan that way. You may prefer to read books. Others like asking all their friends or discussing the trip online. You can plan a trip in loads of different ways.

Discovering and integrating mindfulness into your life is similar. The first stage in the mindfulness journey is to find out about mindfulness. Do you prefer to learn from just reading a book such as this one or to complement the experience with further support? If so, you may consider:

- ✔ An online course.
- ✔ A workshop.
- ✔ A course in person with a teacher.
- ✔ One-to-one coaching with an expert, on the phone or in-person.

Your choice depends on what you've preferred in the past, your budget, how much time you have and so on. You may just decide to read this book and use the audio to begin with – that's a perfectly good way to start.

Go with whichever option you prefer and let the process unfold naturally. Just as planning a trip isn't the trip itself, so planning to practise mindfulness isn't mindfulness! Until you have a go and see what effect the mindfulness has, you haven't started. You're close if you're planning, but not quite there yet.

Mindfulness isn't something new for you to learn; it's the rediscovery of a world you used to live in as a child, with the added wisdom of experience. Mindfulness is an innate quality in every human being (check out Chapter 4), and you experience mindfulness from time to time in your daily life. Each time you really see a sunset, marvel at the beauty of your baby, take a deep conscious breath or listen to piece of music, you're being mindful.

Use Worksheet 1-3 to evaluate your experience of past learning methods. This exercise can help you to decide what would be the best method for you to learn mindfulness.

Worksheet 1-3	Deciding How I Want to Learn	
Method of Learning	*Have I Tried this Learning Method Before? If so, for Learning What?*	*How Effective was the Learning Method for Me?*
Online		
Weekly group course		
Half-day workshop		
Weekend workshop		
One-to-one coaching		
Audiobook		
Anything else		

Treading the path: Committing to practise mindfulness regularly

Life is what happens to you while you're busy making other plans.
— *John Lennon*

After you plan your trip, you need to go! You don't want to be an all-talk but no-action kind of person. So, pack your bag and go. As you're travelling you may stop in some unexpected places, just out of curiosity. Yesterday I (Shamash) was driving on a small road and noticed a beautiful turquoise lake. I stopped my car and asked a coffee-shop owner if she could recommend a walk. She did. I found myself walking up to an observatory at the top of local peak and seeing the lake from high above, with ice-capped mountains in the distance.

You need to practise mindfulness regularly. If possible you need to practise the mindfulness meditations every day, or at least make an effort to be mindful in your daily activities (as we discuss in Chapter 6) as best you can. Your reward is a brain that's more focused, creative, productive, emotionally resilient and peaceful. Not bad, eh? (To read about all the benefits that mindfulness can bring, check out Chapter 2.)

One of the challenges that most people have is remembering to be mindful. Drifting back into your usual habits on autopilot is just so easy. Therefore you need to think of ways to support yourself to keep going. For more help on your motivation, flip to Chapters 2 and 16.

Which of the approaches in Worksheet 1-4 do you think is going to help you stick to practising mindfulness regularly? You know yourself better than anyone else, so trust your intuition and see what answers you come up with.

Worksheet 1-4	Maintaining My Motivation
Method or Approach	*How I Can Use this Method to Help Practise Mindfulness Regularly*
Learning with a friend, putting mindfulness exercises in your diary, joining a class, reading more books on the subject.	

Overcoming difficulties along the way

'I have not failed. I've just found 10,000 ways that won't work.'
— *Thomas Edison*

To enjoy an excursion, you need to let go of your expectations and instead go with the flow. If you're obsessed with planning and something goes wrong, you may get upset rather than enjoy the adventure. The same is true for the journey into mindfulness. You need to practise the mindful exercises as best you can and just see what happens. Letting go of your goals, desires or specific outcomes makes the process work far more effectively. You may feel calm and peaceful, or you may release more emotion and feel a bit drained. Whatever happens, happens. That's the attitude you want to cultivate to keep your journey running smoothly.

Journeys are almost guaranteed to have difficulties. Without difficulty, you're probably too far inside your comfort zone. Sometimes you need to move out of that zone to experience something radically exciting and different. Figure 1-3 contains a great picture we saw online the other day.

Figure 1-3:
The benefits
of leaving
your com-
fort zone.

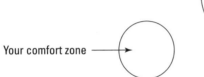

You need to take a chance sometimes and do things that feel slightly uncomfortable. Practising mindfulness can itself be outside your comfort zone. You may think that when you practise something scary could happen: difficult emotions might come up and overwhelm you, or thoughts that you've been suppressing may suddenly arise. Chapter 9 covers dealing with difficulties in your practice.

Meditation has been shown to be a very safe process and many people feel much better and happier through mindfulness practice. Consider it as a bit like flying in a plane: it may seem risky, but in fact travelling in a car is far more dangerous. Mindfulness is a very safe way to travel.

Staying flexible

Here's an example from a recent trip. I (Shamash) stopped at one scenic point and admired the view. As I was returning to my car, I spotted a few brown streaks on my bonnet. Just out of pure curiosity, I decided to look at the engine. To my astonishment, the oil cap had come off and engine oil had spilt all over the engine. If you're not mechanically minded, basically this isn't good. Fortunately I was in a mindful state and saw the whole thing as quite an adventure. I was grateful I'd spotted the problem before it got worse, and I managed to get myself to the nearest garage and have the problem fixed.

Journeys are only frustrating if you plan for an outcome and fixate on that desire. If I'd planned exactly what I was going to see and do that afternoon, I may have been quite upset and reacted negatively.

Your own thoughts may well be the biggest barrier to your mindful journey. 'I can't meditate. My mind never shuts up!' is an excuse we hear again and again. But mindfulness isn't about shutting your mind up; it's about becoming aware of your thoughts in a different way.

Nonetheless, when planning an excursion, expecting the worst and making sensible provisions for it is a good idea. You might have a first-aid kit and medical insurance in case you get ill. You can take a similar approach in anticipating difficulties in your mindful journey ahead.

Use Worksheet 1-5 to spell out what obstacles you expect to encounter when practising mindfulness and how you can handle them.

Worksheet 1-5	Problems I Expect and Their Solutions
Difficulties I Expect with Practising Mindfulness	*How I'm Going to Manage Them*
Examples: Lack of time, discipline, not sure what to do, lack of motivation, too excited about the process.	Examples: Use my mindfulness diary, learn with a friend, do a course after reading the book, reward myself after a month of practice, try and practise before I preach about the benefits to others.

Accepting that the journey is the destination

It's good to have an end in mind but in the end what counts is how you travel.
— *Orna Ross*

Mindfulness is all about the journey rather than the destination. In fact, getting caught up in fixed ideas of what you have to achieve almost certainly makes them harder to meet. See a personal experience in the nearby sidebar 'Seeking perpetual bliss: Simple!'.

Seeking perpetual bliss: Simple!

When I (Shamash) first started practising mindfulness, I was told that as long as I practised the process diligently, it would lead to a state of enlightenment without any worries or concerns – the end of suffering. I'd live in a state of perpetual bliss! This idea appealed to me greatly at that time. I practised for hours daily, diligently hoping to reach a state of enlightenment as soon as possible. 'If you're not enlightened in this life, don't worry, you'll reach the state in your next life,' my teachers reassured me. I had lots of blissful experiences but none ever lasted.

I began to understand and really benefit from my mindfulness practice only after I started to let go of my attachment to achieving perpetual bliss, or any other fixed, final state like perfect relationships, zero stress or no more anxiety.

Here are a few encouraging insights that we've discovered from years of mindfulness practice:

- ✔ **Seeking a particular, permanent state of mind, such as freedom from all suffering, or anything like that, is a form of 'spiritual ego'.** Just as someone obsessed with becoming a millionaire focuses on gaining riches and can miss out on living a fun, balanced life, so someone obsessed with being enlightened or being totally free of all difficulties can also miss out on life. Far healthier to just live a mindful, balanced life and fully participate in what life has to offer.

- ✔ **Mindfulness isn't a final destination.** Mindfulness is present-moment awareness and can't happen in the future. The very point of mindfulness is to be in the now; you can be mindful right now, or not! Dreaming of a mindful future is pointless – as the saying goes, tomorrow never comes!

- ✔ **Mindfulness isn't a special state of mind that you reach after reading lots of books or doing lots of courses.** Mindfulness is an ordinary, everyday awareness in many ways. Sometimes that awareness may seem special, peaceful or restful, and at other times it may feel like a struggle, a practice that you don't want to do, or even painful. This is what mindfulness is about. Rest assured, you're not doing the practice wrong. The idea is simply to be present and open up to whatever experience arises in your awareness. Actually, you can't do mindfulness wrong. As long as you're practising as best you can, you're going in the right direction.

- ✔ **Mindfulness is counter-intuitive in some ways.** It's not a goal to achieve, more effort doesn't necessarily get you closer, you don't get there in the future and in many ways, you already have it. You just need to water the seeds of mindfulness that lay latent within your being and see what unfolds.

Here's an example to illustrate what mindful living is about:

As I sit here, writing, I can see some horse chestnut trees out of the window, on the other side of a road, swaying in the wind. I notice as the sun eventually breaks through the clouds and makes the green, lush leaves even more vivid. Then, a few moments later, the sun is once again shielded by clouds. As I sit, a little slouched on my chair, I feel my right shoulder is a bit tense. I take a deep breath, sit up a little and enjoy the feeling of slowly breathing out. My shoulder eases a bit, but there's still some tightness. I turn back to my computer. I type a few more sentences before getting lost in thought. I eventually notice this and bring my attention back to the work in hand.

That's it! That's mindfulness: an awareness of whatever experience is arising for you. You're being mindful right now, as you're conscious of reading this book, or waiting for the bus in the cold or whatever you're doing, when you have a sense of curiosity, self-compassion and acceptance, or even if you're just trying to bring those attitudes to your awareness.

Letting go of your goals is partly what mindfulness is about. As Chapter 4 describes, mindfulness is about *being* rather than *doing*.

Use Worksheet 1-6 to identify what goals you have for mindfulness and see how they may help or hinder your progress.

Worksheet 1-6	Considering How Goals May Help or Hinder Me	
What I Hope to Achieve from Mindfulness	*How This Goal May Help My Progress*	*How This Goal May Hinder My Progress*
Peace of mind	The hope of greater peace will give me some motivation.	Whenever I find the mindfulness process stressful, I may get frustrated because I feel that I'm not moving towards my goal.

Chapter 2

Enjoying the Benefits of Mindfulness

Mindfulness is about waking up and living your life to the full. With regular practice, your awareness of the world and your life increases and you start to notice the benefits to your physical, mental and emotional wellbeing. We cover these subjects in this chapter.

Discovering these many benefits can help to motivate you to start out and continue with your mindfulness practice, but we encourage you not to get too caught up looking for certain outcomes and results. Many parts of your life are probably already about attaining goals, and so you benefit most from letting your time with mindfulness be a respite from the pressures of personal achievement.

Mindfulness is a time to rest your attention simply on your chosen object or activity for its own sake. As you consider the undoubted benefits of mindfulness, try not to seek them obsessively and instead enjoy mindfulness itself. Live mindfully, moment to moment, in an engaged and meaningful way as life unfolds before your eyes. If the benefits we describe do come, see them as a great bonus.

Connecting with Your Body

Mindfulness can have a huge, positive effect on your physical body. Although this may seem strange, because many people think of mindfulness as a mental process, the body and mind are closely linked, and easing mental anxiety through mindfulness leads to a range of healthy physical outcomes, such as boosting your immune function and helping digestion among many others. For example, mindfulness is effective for managing chronic pain (see Chapter 13), psoriasis and tinnitus.

Mindfulness is not designed to replace any existing medical treatments. Always check with your health professional before using mindfulness to help manage your condition.

Feeling more in tune with your body

When Shamash teaches mindfulness to groups of people, one of the most common positive observations is 'I feel more connected to my body'. Being more effectively aware of and tuned into your bodily sensations provides the following benefits:

- ✔ You can begin to calm your mind. Awareness of your body is always in the present moment and offers you an anchor to rest your attention.

- ✔ You can deal with suppressed emotions. By feeling emotions in your physical body, you make it easier to process feelings like anxiety, anger or sadness.

- ✔ You can be more aware of any minor injuries or illnesses and take appropriate action if necessary.

- ✔ You can more effectively ease physical tension that wastes energy and feels uncomfortable.

- ✔ You feel more grounded, centred and present.

- ✔ You become less automatically and negatively reactive to your emotions – if somebody says something hurtful, you notice the feeling in your body and choose your words and action carefully rather than automatically, which is often an unhelpful reaction.

You can use this five- to ten-minute mini body scan meditation before going to sleep, although you can try it anytime of day to help you connect with your body:

1. **Sit or lie down in a comfortable position and take five deep, slow breaths.** Be aware of the physical sensation of each breath as it enters and leaves your body.

2. **Notice the sensations in your feet during one full in-and-out breath.**

3. **Be aware of the physical sensations in your lower legs for the next in-and-out breath.**

4. **Continue moving your awareness up your body in this way: upper legs, hips and pelvis, lower torso, upper torso, upper arms, lower arms, shoulders, neck, head. 'Feel' each body part for one full breath cycle (in and out).**

5. **Your mind is bound to wander off to other thoughts. When you realise this is happening, kindly and gently, with a smile, bring your attention back to where you left it, moving through your body.**

6. **Finish by 'feeling' your body as a whole, for a few breaths. Experience a sense of affection towards your own body if you can. If you can't, that's okay – you can only do your best and see what happens.**

Now answer the questions in Worksheet 2-1.

Worksheet 2-1   **Reflections on Experiencing the Mini Body Scan Meditation**

Did you notice any sensations that you hadn't noticed before? If so, what?

Do you feel more or less connected with your body?

What emotions, if any, did you feel in your body?

_____

Did you dislike any sensations? Can you be a bit more accepting of them? Can you make more space for them to just be there, even though you don't like them, and see what happens?

_____

What's your relationship to your body? Through this exercise did you feel a bit more loving towards your body? Or a bit more caring or accepting? Consider whatever words work for you.

_____

Boosting your immune function and digestion

Mindfulness is being increasingly used to treat a range of clinical conditions. In some cases, such as chronic pain and psoriasis, good evidence for its success has been reported. In other areas, the research is at very early stages. Here's a list of some physical conditions for which mindfulness is being researched as a treatment:

- Cancer
- Chronic pain
- Diabetes
- Fibromyalgia
- Heart disease
- Hepatitis/HIV
- Hypertension (high blood pressure)
- Immune system-related illnesses
- Irritable bowel syndrome
- Recovering from surgery
- Psoriasis
- Tinnitus

If you suffer from one of the above conditions, ask your doctor whether mindfulness may be a helpful treatment – together with whatever other treatment you're already receiving of course.

We believe that one reason why mindfulness is an effective treatment for physical conditions is because it boosts your immune system and allows your digestion to work more effectively.

Here's how. When you're stressed, a part of your automatic bodily function turns on the stress response. The physical changes that take place are hard-wired into your nervous system, and in fact into the nervous system of most other animals too. It's the fight-or-flight mechanism and creates a range of changes in your body designed to prepare you physically to avoid danger by fighting, freezing or running away. The changes also prepare you mentally for danger by heightening your senses and causing you to see any small disturbances as possible threats.

But the main physical changes that take place in the stress response are unhelpful if you're chronically stressed:

- ✔ Heart rate and blood pressure rise.
- ✔ Glucose (sugar) gets released into your bloodstream.
- ✔ Muscle tension increases.
- ✔ Digestion and your immune system almost shut down.

Mindfulness reduces the stress response. When faced with a stressful situation, you don't feel quite so stressed and are able to let go of unhelpful thoughts more easily because you're aware of your negative thoughts and can step back from them. You see the big picture and so are less likely to react automatically to situations. Mindfulness also seems to reduce activity in the part of the brain responsible for turning on the stress response, so your background level of stress in everyday life goes down too.

With greater awareness and less stress, your digestion works better, as does your immune system. If you're suffering from a stress-related illness, consider using mindfulness alongside other treatment. And even if your disease isn't stress-related, the chances are that mindfulness can help you to get better, quicker.

Calming Your Mind

Many people come to mindfulness to help manage their racing minds and inability to concentrate. They're looking to create some inner space and clarity in their heads and hope that mindfulness can tame their thoughts and give themselves a break.

If your mind just never stops, rest assured that you're not alone. You have billions of connections in your brain, so you're bound to be thinking a lot. You don't need to give yourself a hard time about it. In this section, you find out how mindfulness helps to calm your mind, even though the process doesn't aim to do this directly.

Coming to your senses

One of the simplest ways to practise mindfulness and calm your mind is to connect with one of your senses. Have a go at the following exercise:

1. **Breathe in slowly through your nose and allow your belly to fill with the breath.** Hold your breath for a few moments and slowly breathe out through your mouth, as if you're blowing through a straw. Repeat a few times.

2. **Notice five objects you can see around you.** By all means label each item, but also remember to view them in detail as they really are. Spend a few moments looking curiously at each object, as if seeing it for the first time. See if you can notice whether your mind judges each object, and if it does, let that judgement go. Feel a breath (as we describe in the earlier section 'Feeling more in tune with your body') if doing so helps.

3. **Repeat Step 2 but this time with five sounds.** Notice each sound and label it in your mind as you do so. For example, your thoughts may go 'music, road traffic, my breathing, rustling bag, people talking'. Listen to each sound for a few moments, with a sense of freshness and interest and without judging it.

4. **Do the same process again but with five different scents.** You may not have many scents around, so just notice what you can; or make a point of noting the smell of your next meal in a café, restaurant or your own kitchen.

5. **Try the process this time with five different tastes.** This aspect works particularly well while you're having a meal or a drink.

6. **Repeat finally for touch.** Notice how your body feels: for example, the sensation of your body touching the chair, a tightness in your shoulders, warmth on your arm, cool wind against your ankles or a belt slightly tight around your waist.

Complete Worksheet 2-2 by noting down what you notice for each sense when you first try this exercise. Writing down what you observed helps you to consolidate your experience and makes you more curious and focused as you go about your daily activities. This effectively makes you more mindful.

Worksheet 2-2	Connecting with My Senses
Sense	*What I Notice*
Sight	
Sound	
Scent	
Taste	
Touch	

If you're wondering how connecting with your senses can calm your mind, good job you kept reading because here's how:

✔ Your conscious attention can be on only one thing at a time. If you're focusing on one of your senses, your attention isn't feeding your circling worries and concerns. As a result, they begin to lose a bit of their strength. Without your attention on your worries, they effectively don't exist.

✔ You're training your mind to be more focused on the present moment. With time, you find that living in the now is easier and you become less lost in thoughts unnecessarily.

All mindfulness practices lead to a gradual calming of your mind, but the key word is *gradual.* If you aim directly to calm your mind, you end up frustrated and probably give up. Instead, accept that your mind is going to wander, and just keep bringing your attention back when it does so, perhaps with a little smile on your face to remind you not to be self-critical. Mindfulness is about awareness: by noticing how your mind wanders, what it focuses on and how to manage it, you grow in wisdom – and that's what you're aiming for. Figure 2-1 shows the difference between how many people imagine mindfulness to be, and the reality.

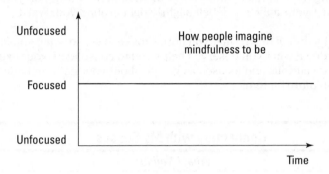

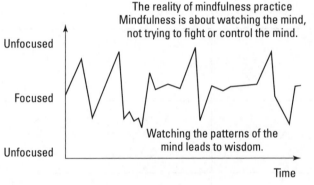

Figure 2-1: Mindfulness is about awareness of your mind wandering; not fighting or controlling your mind.

Expect your mind to be rather wild and if you have a few moments of calm focus in the meditation, accept that as a bonus rather than a sign that you're doing the process right or wrong.

Stepping back from your thoughts

Human beings tend to have what's called a *negativity bias*. In other words, you're designed to give more weight to negative thoughts, emotions and experiences than positive ones. This tendency may be due to an evolutionary strategy (see the nearby sidebar 'Being negative: it comes naturally' for more). Therefore, stepping back from experiences, especially negative ones, is helpful. Seeing the big picture is often considered a wise way of living, and mindfulness certainly helps you to do that.

Imagine your face is pressed right up against a television screen and all you can see is a bunch of blurred colours. You can't possibly follow the programme. In fact, you can't even tell whether an action film or a wildlife documentary is on. Your whole experience is just of colours changing. But as you take a step back you begin to see the whole of the screen, and if you continue to watch you start to understand what's going on. When you're too close, you may think that the television screen is the only thing in the room. But when you step back, you notice the furniture, other people and when you look out of the window, you see a whole world outside with other things going on. You're now able to see the big picture – the wider context.

Being negative: it comes naturally

Have you noticed that your mind finds it easier to focus on negative things rather than positive ones? Even if you consider yourself a positive person, if something frustrating happens during the day that event is more likely to pop into your head in the evening rather than any of the positive ones that also happened. This tendency is called *negativity bias* and here's why it happens.

Humans have evolved to survive, and, therefore, to avoid danger to do this. If your brain didn't focus on potential dangers, you could easily make a mistake and end up dead, to put it bluntly. The humans that survived in ancient times were the ones who could best focus on danger and avoid it. Any humans that simply focused on the positive and didn't worry about the tiger that might eat them got eaten by tigers. We humans are the result of that evolution – we're the survivors who were extra careful. So even

though the dangers nowadays may not be directly life-threatening, such as a long queue at the shops, an aggressive boss or concern about a global recession, your brain still focuses on them.

Here is where mindfulness comes in to help. Instead of simply reciting positive thoughts to drown out negative ones, it's more effective to become aware of those negative thoughts and put them into perspective. Okay, the queue at the supermarket is long, but hey, at least you can afford to buy food. The boss is aggressive, but then again, he's always in a bad mood. And the recession – well, it will pass, like everything else. Worrying about it won't make the problem go away. Mindfulness helps you to manage your negativity bias and prevents you from getting stuck in repetitive negative thinking. There's hope for you if you worry too much!

In the same way, when you're up close with your thoughts, noticing only them, you're not seeing the big picture. You're stuck or fused with your thoughts. So if they're judgemental, self-critical and self-limiting, that's what you take to be true as that's all you know. But stepping back from your thoughts and emotions allows you to see them for what they are and reduces their control over you.

You're not trying to stop your thoughts; that just doesn't work in the long term. Instead, you're shifting your relationship with your thoughts, discovering how to see thoughts as just thoughts: ultimately, they're sounds and pictures in your mind.

The benefits of stepping back from thoughts are:

- **Greater choice and wisdom.** Say that you're fixated on your to-do list, frantically going through the items one after the other. If you don't step back, you keep going through that list until you're exhausted. But if you can step back, you give yourself a choice. Maybe some of those things aren't necessary and can wait till tomorrow. Or perhaps you just deserve a break now. Stepping back provides a choice and allows the wise part of your mind to make an appropriate decision.

- **Greater ability to overcome self-limiting beliefs, such as 'I'm not good enough', 'I can't do that' or 'That person's much better than I can ever be'.** Taking these thoughts as facts stops you moving forward in that area, but stepping back allows you to see the situation from a distanced perspective.

- **Greater sense of control and calm.** Imagine that you're having a nightmare while sleeping. It seems very real even though the ghosts, goblins, monsters or whatever are figments of your imagination. When you wake up from the nightmare, you're free of it. If you knew within the dream that it was a dream, you wouldn't have been so scared. In the same way, stepping back from thoughts gives you a sense of control. You no longer have to believe the thoughts and can move your attention somewhere else.

Here are a few great ways to step back from your thoughts:

✔ **Practise mindfulness of thoughts:** See Chapter 5 and work through the Mindfulness of Thoughts exercise, which is part of the Sitting Meditation.

✔ **Ask yourself questions such as:** What are my underlying beliefs? Is this thought true? Can I be absolutely certain that this thought is true? Is this thought helpful for me?

✔ **Change the way the thought speaks to you, to get some distance:** Imagine an actor or cartoon character saying those thoughts or hearing the thought in a really deep, high-pitched or funny voice; try slowing down and speeding up the thought.

✔ **Say to yourself, 'Thank you, mind,' whenever you notice an unhelpful thought.** Just smile and feel a couple of breaths before continuing with your day. Doing so puts a positive spin on focus rather than battling with your mind. And feeling your breaths helps to anchor you in the now.

✔ **Do a breathing space meditation to help you step back:** See Chapter 6 for details.

Consider a problem that you're going through at the moment. Notice the thoughts and feelings in yourself that are associated with the problem. Now try and step back from those thoughts and see them as part of the bigger picture. Notice what effect doing so has. Use Worksheet 2-3 to help you out.

Worksheet 2-3	Recording the Effect of Stepping Back from Thoughts
Problem or Challenge	*After Practising a Stepping Back Exercise, How Do I See the Problem Differently?*
I keep thinking, 'I'm so tired' all day.	After doing a breathing space meditation for 3 minutes, I can see it's just a thought. And I feel like I have a bit more energy too!

Improving your focus and concentration

Being able to pay attention to one task at a time is so important; underestimating the value of this ability is all too easy.

As William James, often called the father of psychology, said:

The faculty of voluntarily bringing back a wandering attention, over and over again, is the very root of judgement, character, and will. No one is compos sui [master of himself] if he have it not. An education which should improve this faculty would be the education par excellence.

Fortunately, you have in your hands a book that helps you to develop just that ability – how to bring back your wandering attention.

Think for a few moments of the kind of tasks that would be impossible to do effectively without the ability to focus: writing, reading, driving, having a conversation, taking a shower, listening to a lecture – pretty much everything that you do. And also consider the amount of time you'd save and the sense of satisfaction you'd achieve with higher levels of attention on important tasks.

List a few tasks in Worksheet 2-4 that you did well today because you were able to focus on them: for example, getting dressed, making a phone call and so on.

Worksheet 2-4 **Tasks I Focused on Doing Today**

Mindfulness meditation trains your brain to be better at concentrating because each time you notice that your mind wanders off from whatever you're focusing on, you intentionally bring your attention back to the object of your attention.

Attention doesn't mean that you need to put a massive amount of effort into achieving focus. The idea is to make a balanced effort, just like when you're drawing with a pencil on a sheet of paper: press too lightly and the pencil makes no line; press too hard and the pencil keeps breaking.

Experiment by trying quite hard, not trying hard at all and then find the sweet spot in the middle. Sometimes, you can almost let go of effort altogether and your mind stays focused quite happily, although this may never happen to you. As always with mindfulness, no rules exist, so experiment and see what works for you.

Feeling the flow

Mihaly Csikszentmihalyi, who wrote the fabulous book *Flow,* discovered that people are most happy when fully engaged in a task: the more fully engaged, the more likely they are to be in a *flow state* that's deeply satisfying and probably quite nourishing for the mind. People who often experience flow states are happier and thereby more creative and successful in their work and relationships. Through regular mindfulness practice, you enhance your ability to focus and probably experience more regular and deeper flow states in more tasks.

Focus on the research

Researchers at the University of North Carolina found that just 20 minutes of mindfulness meditation a day for four days had a positive effect. Those who meditated were ten times more effective at a challenging concentration task compared to a non-meditating control group and better in a task testing deadline stress too.

Another study by mindfulness researcher Amishi Jha found that mindfulness meditation improved the participants' ability to avoid distractions and improved short-term (working) memory. Even just 12 minutes of meditation a day did the trick. With these improvements, you're better able to focus and achieve your daily goals, improving your accuracy and reducing your wandering mind.

Mindfulness is also being used to help people with ADHD (attention deficit hyperactivity disorder). For example, researchers at the Mindful Awareness Research Center at the University of California, Los Angeles taught a modified version of a mindfulness course to a small group of adolescents and adults. They found that after doing the training, the participants were better at doing tasks without being distracted.

Psychology professor Marsha Linehan offers this unique five-minute meditation for improving your focus:

1. **Sit on a park bench or any other public place, every day, for five minutes.**

2. **Practise just looking ahead as people walk past for those five minutes (even if you're tempted to look at the people, just keep looking ahead).**

3. **Do this daily for a couple of weeks and see what effect it has on the rest of your life.**

One client who tried doing this exercise for a few weeks found that she focused better at work and no longer dreaded doing tasks such as washing the dishes or cleaning the house.

Try out the effect of practising mindfulness immediately before doing a daily activity or task. Assess how focused you are, practise any mindfulness exercise you like for five to ten minutes before the activity and then assess your focus again afterwards. Use Worksheet 2-5 to record how you get on.

Worksheet 2-5	Effect of Mindfulness on My Ability to Focus		
Activity	*How Focused I am at the Moment (scale 1–5)*	*My Chosen Mindfulness Exercise*	*How Focused I am After Doing the Mindfulness Exercise (scale 1–5)*

Here are some other tips for improving your focus:

- ✔ When at work, help yourself to be focused by turning off your email and, if possible, your phone, even for short periods of time. The lack of distraction boosts your productivity, focus and sense of satisfaction immensely.

- ✔ The next time you find yourself multi-tasking, stop. Take a deep breath. Then say to yourself: 'Let me have a go at focusing on just one task as mindfully as I can today.' Multi-tasking reduces productivity and increases stress – avoid it when you can.

- ✔ Every day, look out for one thing that you find beautiful, such as your child or partner, a flower, a piece of architecture or the sky, and see whether you can watch and be with that beauty for a few minutes, without distraction. Your mind wanders off as usual of course, but just gently and kindly bring your attention back.

If you're new to meditation, you may think that your attention seems to be getting worse as you practise. This isn't true – you're just discovering how easily your mind can get distracted! Persevere even if you feel you aren't focusing well at all. Trust in the process and ease away from thoughts such as 'I can't focus', 'I'm rubbish at this', 'I can't do it' and so on. They're only thoughts and not helpful statements to believe.

Making better decisions

You make decisions all day long: whether to have toast or cereal, to exercise or watch TV, to check your emails or make a phone call. And yet the majority of these decisions are probably unconscious, habitual and automatic.

Becoming mindful in your choices

Mindfulness takes a radical stand against habitual decisions and is all about making your decisions more conscious and considered – especially the important ones. Good quality decisions require your brain to be in the right state. If you're stressed, anxious or experiencing a strong emotion, you're thinking is heavily influenced by this fact. This fact is particularly worrying when you're making tremendously tricky decisions with lots of factors to consider, such as deciding whether to change your job, get married, have children or move to a new country.

Consider this example of a small decision and how easily you're affected. You just won a holiday, and your son asks if he can have that new computer game; you're likely to agree. But if you had a tough day at work and your boss gave you a hard time, you feel irritated. Your son asks the same question and you say no.

Emotions affect your decisions, and if you're not aware of this process happening, your decisions are likely to be compromised and perhaps irrational.

Here's the way mindfulness helps you to make decisions more consciously. Imagine going into a coffee shop and choosing what to buy:

> You look at the wide range of foods on offer: chocolates, biscuits, salads, sandwiches and more.

> The waitress asks, 'What would you like today?'

> If you're operating automatically, you may go for the big coffee and chocolate cake without even thinking. But today, you're mindful, so you don't rush into a decision.

> You decide to just order the coffee, and if, after 15 minutes, you're still hungry, you'll order some food.

> Finishing your coffee you feel quite full up already, and go on your way.

Intuition saves racing car driver's life

A Formula One racing car driver's life was saved when he was approaching a sharp bend and had an overwhelming urge to stop his car. He said his urge to stop the car was even stronger than his urge to win. As it turned out, an accident had happened farther ahead, and if he'd continued at his normal speed, he may have crashed and died. When asked how he knew, the driver couldn't explain. A team of psychologists asked him to watch the footage and relive the moment again. On watching the film, he noticed that the crowd weren't looking at him as he was racing – they were looking in a different direction. This was the clue that had entered his unconscious brain and urged him to brake.

Some scientists believe that all intuitive experiences are based on deciphering clues from things happening within your thoughts and emotions and the world around you. Sometimes you're not consciously aware of these clues, but your brain has processed the information and worked it out. If you're not mindful at all, you don't take note of the information and so are less intuitive.

Mindfulness doesn't mean that you have to make sensible decisions all the time and can't be a bit naughty in your dessert choices! Mindfulness is about making conscious decisions – and sometimes those decisions include treating yourself to some guilt-free pleasures. In fact, mindfulness can help to heighten the pleasure if you're able to focus fully on your chosen treat!

Tuning in to intuition

Mindfulness helps you tune in to your intuition and so helps you make choices; instinct or gut feelings can be a powerful way of making decisions. Intuition isn't a spooky force: decisions based on what you feel access a powerful part of your unconscious brain, although scientists haven't yet come to any definite conclusions about this process. Sometimes your intuitive side is worth listening to, at other times it may be inaccurate. Mindfulness can help you decide when to follow your intuition.

Often you feel intuition in your body, perhaps a gut feeling to follow your heart or the sensation of shivers at the thought of a particular choice. These bodily signals probably come from neurons connected to your brain that are located all over your body. In fact, your gut contains 100 million neurons! Even your heart is linked to the brain by many thousands of neurons. These brain connections through your body can be signalling subtle clues about what's the best step for you to take next.

Mindfulness helps to deepen your intuition through its focus on your physical experiences from moment to moment. Through mindfulness, you become more sensitive to and in touch with the sensations that your body is sending you. This practice can result in a greater ability to be intuitive – you notice your intuitive feelings earlier and can therefore decide whether to base your decisions on them.

In Worksheet 2-6, write about a time where you had an intuition about something: perhaps about a relationship with someone, a business partnership or just being wary of danger. Note down whether you feel you made a wise decision or not – not an easy thing to do, but have a go if you feel like the challenge!

Worksheet 2-6	Recording My Past Experiences of Intuition and Decision-making	
Situation and My Intuitive Feeling	*Did I Follow My Intuition?*	*Did the Decision Turn Out to be Helpful?*
Had a chat with a stranger in a bookshop and felt I should keep in touch. The feeling was of warmth in my chest.	Yes, I kept in touch.	Yes it was; we got on really well!

Soothing Your Emotions

Positive emotions can be a wonderful feeling. Joy, elation, excitement and happiness all feel great. But how can you deal with so-called negative emotions?

In this section you discover the mindful way to manage emotions – the steps to take when you're feeling low, excessively angry or uncomfortably anxious.

Using mindfulness for emotional health

Mindfulness is becoming a powerful, vital part of many psychological treatments. Experts are researching mindfulness in the areas of anxiety, bipolar disorder, depression, eating disorders, post-traumatic stress disorder and relapse prevention for addiction.

The evidence for mindfulness as a treatment for recurring depression is so strong that it's the recommended and supported approach by the UK's National Health Service. Evidence for the other conditions is in early stages, but looks promising.

Mindfulness also raises your subjective wellbeing – commonly known as happiness! Even a few weeks of mindfulness practice has been shown to create positive changes in the brain and long-term meditators display levels of wellbeing far higher than average.

Understanding the nature of emotions

Experiencing emotions is completely natural. For some people, the experience of emotions is mild – they don't feel emotions strongly –whereas other people have wild fluctuations of emotion from one moment to another.

Consider for a moment how you relate to your emotions: do you think of them as an experience to be embraced or do you shy away from them; perhaps you try to fight or push away some emotions, yet cling to others.

Mindfulness encourages you simply to be aware of your emotions with mindful attitudes, such as compassion, curiosity, acceptance and openness (we describe the central importance of these four attributes to mindfulness in Chapter 1).

Imagine that you're feeling anxious at the moment. You can even try evoking some anxiety right now by thinking about something you're a bit concerned about. Now go through each attribute to see how it can help you cope with your emotions:

- ✓ **Awareness:** Helps you feel the emotion in your body. Notice in what part of your body you feel the emotion itself. Without the awareness, your emotional response is automatic and can't change.

- ✓ **Self-compassion:** Helps you to be understanding of the fact that you're feeling anxious. If a friend was feeling anxious, what soothing words would you say? Now say those words to yourself. Perhaps gently place your hand on the area of the emotion in your body in a caring, loving way.

- ✓ **Curiosity:** Helps you to shift your attitude from unhealthy avoidance to a healthier approach state. Become aware of its size, shape, possibly associated colour, scent and texture. Notice whether the bodily emotion is getting bigger or smaller with each breath you take.

- ✓ **Acceptance:** Helps you process the emotion. See whether you can allow your emotion to be just as it is, in this moment. Try saying to yourself, 'The feeling is already here . . . it's okay . . . let it be.' Also try feeling your breathing and the emotion together.

- ✓ **Openness:** Helps you shift your perspective. As best you can step back from your emotion and make space for it to just be there. Become a curious but dispassionate observer (as we discuss in the later section 'Meeting your observer self'). Imagine yourself as being distanced from the emotion. Try saying, 'I'm watching this anxiety . . . I'm the observer . . . the witness . . .'.

Overall, this process helps to switch off your unhelpful avoidance mode of mind and switch on your approach mode.

In Worksheet 2-7 write down how any emotion affects you. Write down what you're feeling and how you're likely to behave while feeling like it. Be as honest as you can; try not to write what you think you should do, but what you actually do.

Worksheet 2-7		Recording My Mindful Approach to Emotions			
Emotion	*Thoughts*	*Where I Feel It in My Body*	*The Feeling in My Body*	*The Action I Take While Feeling That Emotion*	*The Effect of a Mindful Approach*

Being Yourself

Your sense of self, of who you are, is something most people take for granted. You probably think of yourself as a fixed entity that goes through the world thinking, feeling and doing things. But in fact your sense of self is a lot more fluid. For example, when you're lost in a daydream or fall into a deep sleep at night, your sense of self seems to disappear altogether.

Meeting your observer self

In mindfulness, you come to see that a part of you is a watcher or witness of everything you think, feel and do. Although English has no word for this dimension of yourself, we call it *the observer self* because it enables you to observe and notice your thoughts, feelings and bodily sensations. It's a core part of your being.

Ultimately people enjoy mindfulness because it allows them to rest in this deeper, ever-present dimension of themselves with a sense of being, presence, heartfulness, mindfulness and restful observation. In this inner space, you aren't thrown around quite so easily by life's ups and downs. You have a place to retreat to: a refuge. A place inside that's never touched, no matter what you do, how ill you are or how wrong things seem to be going. The observer is just that – non-judgementally watching your thoughts, feelings, bodily sensations and your life around you. When you step back from your thoughts and emotions, you're stepping back into your peaceful, ever-present observer self.

The main benefits of this ability to observe without judgement are: you feel freer, better able to cope with difficulties and have a deeper sense of connection with yourself.

Letting go of unhelpful identification

Identification in this context is when you feel deeply interconnected with something and it can be a real problem. Here are some sentences that you may say to yourself when you're in a state of identification:

- ✔ I'm sad.
- ✔ I'm happy.
- ✔ I'm stressed.
- ✔ I've been hit (for example, when you're in a car accident).
- ✔ I'm useless.
- ✔ I'm brilliant.

All these statements imply that you *are* that thing, whether it's a feeling, a group, a philosophy, a state of mind, a judgement and so on.

Seeing the mask itself rather than through the mask

The practice of personal development usually focuses on changing your thinking. You're told to think positively, optimistically, bigger and differently; to let go of negative thoughts and think yourself happy. The belief is that if you change your thoughts *you* change yourself, implying that you *are* your thoughts.

Mindfulness offers a different perspective. Note that the word 'personal' comes from the Latin *persona*, meaning 'mask' (referring to the masks actors used in theatre to represent different characters) and 'development' comes from the old French word *developer*, meaning 'to unveil'. So, interestingly, personal development is about unveiling your mask to reveal your true self. You wear different masks every day: mother or father, husband or wife, teacher or writer, footballer or driver. But underneath all that is another dimension that's easily missed – the fact that you're able to observe all these different roles implies that you're separate from them. We call this the *observer self*.

'I want to tell you a story'

Researchers at the University of Toronto identified two different ways in which your brain constructs your sense of self – of who you are. These two ways seem to involve different pathways of the brain:

✔ **Narration:** Your brain is constantly telling you a story of what's going on and who you are. Your brain is effectively using thinking to create your sense of self.

✔ **Direct connection with your senses:** Your brain is observing the world around and using that to create a sense of 'you-ness'. This identity is created by living in the present moment and is what mindfulness does well.

These two aspects are interlinked, with one triggering the other. This explains why, while practising mindfulness, you're connected with the feeling of your breath or the sounds around you (senses) and before you know it, your brain is recalling a story from your past (narration).

Research on the mindfulness meditation group found that the meditators were better able to connect with the present moment without automatically going into story-telling mode, perhaps suggesting that mindfulness reduces unhelpful self-centred thinking. In other words, be more mindful and kiss your neurotic self goodbye!

The problem with identification is that you become *less flexible* because your identity is fixated on one particular idea. Without flexibility, you're less likely to be able to create a shift or change when necessary. Here are some mindful ways in which you can alter your language to let go of identification for each of the above thoughts:

✔ I notice a feeling of sadness in my body at the moment.

✔ I'm feeling happy at the moment. My body feels light.

✔ My shoulders feels tense and my heart's racing; stress is showing up – hello stress!

✔ My car's been hit . . . not me!

✔ I didn't manage to finish the project on time. I notice some negative thoughts coming up. Let me feel my breathing to help manage myself.

✔ I completed that project on time and feel a sense of satisfaction. I'm grateful for the help of those who assisted me.

Identification is usually unhelpful, whether it's positive or negative:

✔ **Negative identification** is unhelpful because you become fixated on that thought or feeling. You act as if it's true, thus strengthening the difficulty.

✔ **Positive identification** can be unhelpful too. Imagine your boss thinks he's brilliant. If you try and tell him that his team is unhappy or that he needs to change something, he probably disagrees, because he believes that whatever he does is perfect and he can't display any flexibility.

For Worksheet 2-8, read the phrases and then complete the sentences as quickly as you can. By doing this written activity, you're immediately stepping back from the identification as you're taking the thoughts out of your head and putting them onto a piece of paper. This exercise can lead to a more flexible sense of self.

Worksheet 2-8   Working on Breaking Down Identification

I am . . .

I am . . .

I am . . .

I am . . .

I am . . .

Now for each state, reduce the level of identification by changing the sentences to:

I feel . . .

I think . . .

My body is . . .

My brain is . . .

I'm aware of . . .

In this way you're stepping back and letting go of the identification.

By practising mindfulness, you begin to understand your observer self. Then you're better able to watch yourself identifying with thoughts and feelings, and so let them go, or make space for them to be there, without clinging on to them.

Part II
Preparing Yourself for Mindful Living

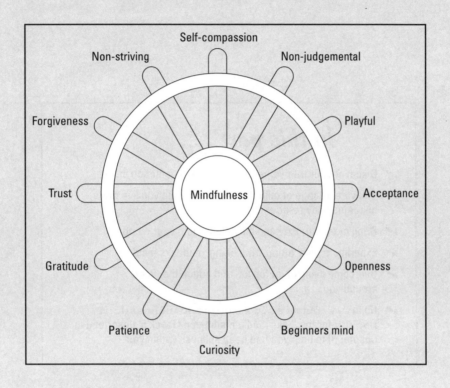

Go to www.dummies.com/go/mindfulnessworkbookuk to listen to audio meditations.

In this part . . .

- Discover your true values to find more satisfaction in life.
- Cultivate a range of mindful attitudes to help you live more peacefully day-to-day.
- Bring more curiosity and playfulness into your world.
- Experiment with 'doing' and 'being' modes of mind.
- Overcome living on autopilot, and notice the world around you.
- Go to www.dummies.com/go/mindfulnesswork bookuk for the 'Lake' audio meditation (Track 5; described in Chapter 3) to help you find deep stillness within you.

Chapter 3

Setting a Healthy Intention and Mindful Attitude

*W*henever I (Shamash) wake up and it's raining, instead of groaning and hauling myself out of bed, I think of all the benefits that rain has. By being appreciative of the rain, I automatically change my attitude towards it. And that grateful attitude is more conducive to developing mindfulness. In London, I get lots of practise!

In this chapter, you explore your intention – what you really hope to get from mindfulness and how it can fit with your values. You discover what your underlying and perhaps unconscious attitudes to mindfulness are, and then explore some helpful attitudes to develop to enhance your experience of mindfulness.

Mindfulness isn't positive thinking. However, mindfulness also isn't being more aware in a neutral way either. Mindfulness is about developing a greater awareness of your present moment experience *with* certain attitudes that help to gently nurture a greater sense of well-being and openness to learning new things.

Exploring Your Intentions

You may wonder why intention is so important in mindfulness. Well, the origins of the word give a clue. 'Intention' comes from the Latin meaning to 'turn one's attention' and so intention is about pointing your attention towards something, and the reason for doing so. Imagine a surgeon making an incision in someone's chest with the intention of helping to make the patient better. Now imagine a murderer making the same incision. The action is the same, but the intention is quite different – the intention is everything in this case.

Therefore exploring your own intentions is central for increased mindfulness. Clear intentions help you to engage more fully in the practice of mindfulness and move in your desired direction.

Clarifying your intentions

Here are some typical outcomes that people want from practising mindfulness. See how many tie up with what you want:

✔ Reduction of a medical symptom.

✔ Stress reduction/increased sense of resilience.

✔ Better relationships.

✔ Greater emotional awareness and management.

✔ Greater sense of meaning in life.

✔ Deepening of your spirituality.

✔ Peace of mind/clarity/wisdom/stillness.

✔ Greater sense of subjective wellbeing/happiness.

✔ Feelings of calm or peace.

Mindfulness is ultimately about the intentions of being, allowing and letting go. A great idea is to consider these intentions as qualities you *already have*. You then stop striving to reach them. A central aspect of mindfulness is to help you ease off from the striving for, running after and obsessing about goals. In other words, hold your intentions lightly, without clinging or attaching.

Discovering your deepest intentions

Here's a great visualisation that helps you to discover your deep core intentions for practising mindfulness. Make sure that you have ample time to do this exercise (at least 15 to 30 minutes), so that you go deep into it:

1. **Find a comfortable position.** You may be in your favourite room at home, sitting on the sofa curled up with a blanket, or perhaps in the bath if you don't mind getting this book a little damp! Wherever you feel calm and peaceful is perfect.

2. **Take a few deep, conscious breaths.** Remember to breathe in slowly through your nose all the way down so that your belly expands and hold it for a few moments before slowly breathing out through your mouth. Notice the sensation of your breath entering and leaving your body. Doing this a few times may begin to relax you. Then just breathe as you normally do.

3. **Close your eyes gently if that feels natural for you.**

4. **Check in with your body.** Shift and move around till you find the most comfortable position for you today. Take your time – there's no rush. Let go of any tension you feel.

5. **Imagine a place that you find peaceful.** It can be somewhere you've visited, a place you make up or a combination of the two. Take your time, but after you decide, stick to that place. It can be in nature or indoors, with other people or on your own. You decide where you feel most calm, secure and serene.

6. **Become mindful of what you can see in this peaceful place.** Notice the actual tone of the colours, the shadows, the distance of the scene from you. Pick one object for a few moments and really notice it – for example, if you're at the beach, really notice the colours and shells on the sand near you. Enjoy looking around in your peaceful place.

7. **Move on to hearing the sounds in your peaceful place.** Notice the quality of the sounds, how they arise and go back to silence, and their volume and pitch. Immerse yourself in the experience of these sounds.

8. **Continue in the same way, noticing scents, physical feelings in your body and imagine yourself eating something to really notice tastes.**

Intention GPS

Think of your intention as being like the location you enter into the GPS in your car, helping to direct you to a city you haven't visited before. If you don't programme in the right location, you're not going to get there. But the GPS isn't the actual journey. It can't put you in the car, fasten your seatbelt and steer you through the traffic – you need to take the necessary action.

The irony is that in mindfulness practice, the action is often physical *inaction*. You may sit quietly more often and observe your breathing, or just reflect mindfully at the end of the day.

9. **Ask yourself the following question: 'What do I hope to get from mindfulness?'** Don't try and force any answers. Just ask the question and see whether any thoughts, feelings or images arise for you.

10. **Allow some time to pass and then ask yourself: 'What do I really, really hope to get from mindfulness?'** Let the question drop from your head, into your heart, as if you're asking yourself something deep within your being.

11. **Go from this inner place back to the outer world when you're ready.** Slowly take a few deep breaths, have a stretch and gently open your eyes if they were closed (to avoid tripping over the cat and ruining your peaceful vibe!).

Write down your experiences and observations in Worksheet 3-1. What did you notice? What happened when you asked yourself what you hope to get from mindfulness?

Worksheet 3-1	Discovering My Deep Intention For Mindfulness

Whatever answers you come up with may be your deep intentions for mindfulness. Keep them handy in your purse or wallet or perhaps stick them up on a wall or on the fridge where you see them regularly. If nothing comes up for you, not to worry. You're probably just a different type of learner.

Unveiling Your Values

Values are the things that you believe are important in your life – your heart's deepest desires about how you want to act. Identifying your values and moving towards them causes you to feel more satisfied.

Values aren't goals but rather directions you want to move in. You can think of a value as being like a direction on a compass. Not knowing your value is like not knowing the direction you want to travel in. Thinking of values as directions and not goals also reminds you that you never reach a direction. If you're going north, you can keep heading north, wherever you are. Similarly, values represent a way of living that you're continually travelling in.

Being aware of your values and having a sense of direction is helpful. The following quote from *Alice in Wonderland* illustrates this nicely:

> *'Would you tell me, please, which way I ought to go from here?'*
> *'That depends a good deal on where you want to get to,' said the Cat.*
> *'I don't much care where –' said Alice.*
> *'Then it doesn't matter which way you go,' said the Cat.*
> *'– so long as I get SOMEWHERE,' Alice added as an explanation.*
> *'Oh, you're sure to do that,' said the Cat, 'if you only walk long enough.'*

Your values aren't always fixed and can change throughout your life. They may shift after reading this book, for example, you may value mindfulness more. As you go through life and acquire new facts, gain insights, engage in conversations and have different experiences, your values change.

Being clear about your values is an act of mindfulness. To be aware of what's important to you, what you deeply care about, gives your life a meaningful direction. If instead you live habitually, you act automatically without thinking whether your actions are in line with what you feel is important in life.

Therefore clarifying your values from time to time is a useful exercise, especially when life doesn't feel satisfying. You can clarify your values in different ways and we describe two methods in this section.

Selecting values that work for you

Look though the values in Worksheet 3-2 and circle those that you feel are very important for you. Put a star next to the ones that are quite important and cross out any values that aren't important to you at all. We provide some empty boxes where you can add your own chosen values too. Don't think about the process too much – trust your instinct and see what results you get.

Worksheet 3-2		Discerning My Common Values	
Adventure	Gratitude	Openness	Strength
Beauty	Hard work	Peace	Success
Calmness	Happiness	Perfection	Teamwork
Creativity	Health	Pleasure	Tolerance
Cleanliness	Improvement	Power	Tradition
Community	Independence	Preservation	Trust
Curiosity	Integrity	Progress	Truth
Determination	Justice	Punctuality	Variety
Diversity	Kindness	Respect	Wellbeing
Enjoyment	Knowledge	Safety	Wisdom
Fairness	Learning	Self-reliance	
Family	Love/romance	Sensitivity	
Freedom	Mindfulness	Service	
Friendship	Money	Simplicity	
Generosity	Nature	Spirituality	

This is just a selection of values – take your time to think of and add any other values that are important for you.

Using memory to uncover your values

Here's another method to help you clarify your values.

Think back to a time in your personal or work life when you felt really happy. Then answer the questions in Worksheet 3-3.

Worksheet 3-3   **Remembering a Time When I Felt Happy**

What were you doing?

What precisely made you feel so happy?

If anyone else was present, how did that person contribute to your happiness?

What were the underlying values in this situation? Look at the list of values in the earlier Worksheet 3-2 to help you decide.

Now consider a time in your personal or work life when you felt really satisfied. Perhaps you had a strong sense of achievement.

Answer the questions in Worksheet 3-4 about this time or event.

Worksheet 3-4   **Remembering a Time When I Felt Satisfied**

What were you doing?

What precisely made you feel so satisfied?

If anyone else was present, how did that person contribute to your satisfaction?

What were the underlying values in this situation? Look at the list of values in the earlier Worksheet 3-2 to help you decide.

Mindfulness, values and goals

Mindful living is about being awake and present to your life, with mindful attitudes. But in addition, we also believe that mindful living is about being clear what's important to you in your life, your values and taking action to fulfil those values with awareness. This way you move your life in a direction that results in deep levels of wellbeing and satisfaction. The journey isn't necessarily easy, but mindfulness offers you the tools to manage the change by making space for difficult emotions and seeing thoughts for what they are – just thoughts.

From your values, you can begin to set some new goals. Mindfulness isn't traditionally about goal-setting, but that doesn't mean you need to shy away from goals altogether. Denis Waitley puts it well: 'Learn from the past, set vivid, detailed goals for the future, and live in the only moment of time over which you have any control: now'.

So, tune in to your values and set some goals if you want to, but don't cling on to them too tightly – and most importantly, live in the present moment.

Listing your top five values

Having completed the activities in Worksheets 3-2, 3-3 and 3-4, now compile your top five values in Worksheet 3-5. Choose values that most resonate as your heart's deep desires.

Worksheet 3-5	My Top Five Values

1.

2.

3.

4.

5.

Use this list to remind yourself of what's most important in your life – the direction you want to move in. You may like to keep a copy of the list handy and look at it from time to time.

With your values uncovered through the exercises in this section, answer the questions in Worksheet 3-6 to discover whether you're on the right track.

Worksheet 3-6	Assessing My Direction

Do you feel that your life is moving in your valued direction? What's going well in your life? What areas need clearer direction?

_____

_____

What small changes can you make to help you move in the direction of your heartfelt values?

_____

_____

How determined are you to making these small changes? If you have any doubt, consider who can help you or what other support you can seek.

_____

_____

Unleashing the Power of Attitude

Attitude is predominantly about choice. You're in control of your attitude; that's what makes it so empowering. Attitude is an important part of not only practising mindfulness, but also having a happier life.

Whatever attitudes you decide to bring to an activity shape your experience. And this includes practising mindfulness. If you decide mindfulness is too difficult, you'll struggle to discover a potentially life-changing approach to living. If you accept your experience of mindfulness, whatever that is, and trust in the process, you may begin to undergo a subtle yet profound transformation.

Uncovering your attitudes to mindfulness

Attitudes, like habits, are either helpful or unhelpful. They're not always easy to change, but a starting point is to discover what your underlying attitudes are, and then work on cultivating more helpful attitudes. Worksheet 3-7 can help to uncover your attitudes to mindfulness.

Worksheet 3-7	Uncovering My Attitude to Mindfulness

What do you hope mindfulness will give you?

_____

What experiences do you expect to arrive at through practising mindfulness?

_____

How long are you willing to practise mindfulness before deciding if it works for you?

_____

(continued)

What physical sensations do you expect during or after a mindfulness meditation?

_____

What are your past experiences of meditation?

_____

How much effort are you willing to put into the practice? Will you meditate several times a day or once a day, or once a week, or whenever you feel like it?

_____

What's the great thing about mindfulness for you?

_____

Are your attitudes primarily negative, neutral or positive? The human mind can be quick to criticise, so don't worry if your answers seem quite negative. Just notice them and see if you can be a bit less judgemental. If you hold neutral or positive attitudes, observe them too to see if they may hinder your journey into a more mindful life by creating unrealistic expectations. As you read through this chapter, notice if your attitudes begin to shift and change.

Fill in the previous questions again after reading this chapter or after a few weeks of mindfulness practice to see if any of your attitudes have changed.

Nurturing a non-judging attitude

The human mind is almost always judging things, people and experiences, probably without you even noticing. Try the following exercise to put your mind to the test!

1. **Look around the room or wherever you are now.**

2. **As you look at the objects or people around you, notice how your mind may begin to judge them.** For example, you may have thoughts like 'I like that', 'Her shoes are nice', 'That needs tidying up' or 'My table's always messy; I should be more organised'.

3. **Continue for a few minutes and notice if the judging stops or continues.**

4. **Fill out Worksheet 3-8.**

Worksheet 3-8	Reviewing Judging Thoughts
Object/Person Seen	_Thought/Judgement_

Being mindful doesn't mean you stop judging. Your mind is designed to think and judge, so don't judge yourself for judging! Instead, the idea is to *notice* that you're judging. To make judgements is an important part of everyday living. For example, you can't go to work and look at a report by your co-worker and then say nothing. You need to say what you like and identify areas for improvement. However, to be mindful means to notice when you're judging. And practising mindfulness meditation is a time to be aware of your mind making judgements and step back from them.

Mindfulness means being a witness to your experience. To be impartial to fleeting thoughts, emotions and bodily sensations as best you can. This means *noticing* your attitude to an experience rather than trying to control or force a change in your attitude.

Exploring Mindful Attitudes

In this section, you discover a range of useful attitudes to consider, both when practising mindfulness exercises and in your daily life.

Mindfulness is a way of living, not just a set of techniques. So, bring these mindful attitudes to your work, home and relationships, and see how they help you.

Figure 3-1 summarises the key mindful attitudes that you can cultivate along with mindfulness. They're all inter-related and feed into each other. Through mindfulness, they grow and strengthen each other within your being, leading to a life of deeper wellbeing and balance.

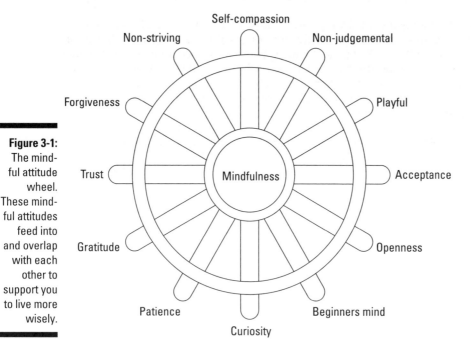

Figure 3-1: The mindful attitude wheel. These mindful attitudes feed into and overlap with each other to support you to live more wisely.

Fostering acceptance

Acceptance is a core attitude of mindfulness. Acceptance means allowing your experience to be just as it is, whatever it is, rather than fighting it. Acceptance doesn't mean complacency or giving up. It means taking your experiences one at a time and acknowledging them as your present-moment reality, as best you can. If you prefer, use a different word to 'accept', such as 'acknowledge', 'allow' or 'let be'.

The poisoned prince

A prince was out hunting one day and was shot in the heart by a poisoned arrow that appeared from nowhere. His doctors arrived immediately, but before they were allowed to administer medicine, the prince said, 'Tell me what kind of poison is on this arrow!' After the poison was identified and the doctors started to administer the medicine, the prince then asked, 'What is the arrow made of?' After he was told, he then demanded to know who might have made the arrow. All the while, the poison spread through his body. The prince began to weaken, but asked to know who had shot him and for the assailant to be found. He then requested his spiritual advisor so he could find out why he had been shot. Eventually the prince died with an arrow in his heart.

In this story, you are the prince, trying to avoid your pain or discomfort. The doctors are your acceptance. The prince's eventual death is the outcome of long-term avoidance causing emotional and mental discomfort.

If you feel upset or hurt, the natural urge is to fight it immediately to try to feel better. This avoidance tactic may work for a short while, but in the long run it does just the opposite of what you wanted – you end up feeling more tense and hurt because you're in denial.

When you're preparing to meditate, sometimes you may feel as if your mind is full of thoughts that keep dragging you away from your meditation. If you don't accept these thoughts and allow your experience to be just as it is, you may find yourself frustrated, angry and stressed. You are trying to focus but you just can't.

Remember that judgement is learnt and not innate or natural. You judge yourself or your behaviour as good or bad, right or wrong. With this judgement, there can then be little acceptance. Judgement causes your lack of acceptance and openness. Difficult feelings become stuck to you if you try hard to constantly fight or avoid them. Feelings want to be felt rather than pushed away – if you can accept them, they'll ease off in time. In mindfulness you are encouraged to skilfully welcome, accept and explore your emotions.

If acceptance of your experience seems impossible, start with baby steps. For example, if you're experiencing pain, try feeling the sensations and moving towards them slowly. Be as courageous as you can in your baby steps. Even the tiniest beginning of acceptance can start a chain of events that can lead to an eventual transformation. Think of acceptance as having a positive snowball effect.

Acceptance of your current experience is the starting point for transformation.

This exercise helps you to move towards accepting a situation, circumstance or sensation that you just can't change. Have a go by following the steps below:

1. **Consider your current 'unacceptable' thoughts, feelings and sensations, and write them in the first column of Worksheet 3-9.** In the second column, consider how accepting you are of the experience.

2. **Gently state the label of the experience you aren't accepting.** For example, if you're fighting feelings of anger, say to yourself, 'I'm feeling angry at the moment. I'm feeling angry'. In this way, you begin to acknowledge your feeling.

3. **Notice which part of your body feels tense and imagine your breath going into and out of the area of tightness.** As you breathe in and out, say words that help you move towards acceptance. For example: 'The feeling of X is already here. Let me feel X with gentleness. I can be okay with feeling X, moment by moment.' Replace X with whatever you're feeling. Feel the experience you're avoiding slowly and gently. If the feeling is overwhelming, like rage or depression, see Chapters 11 and 12 for dealing with strong negative emotions.

4. **Become really curious about your experience.** Ask yourself: 'Where did this feeling come from? Where do I feel it? What's interesting about it? How is it changing as I breathe?' Complete the third column.

5. **Now consider how much you accept or acknowledge your current thoughts, feelings or sensations on a scale of one to ten.** Ask yourself what you need to do to increase your acceptance by one, and then do it as best you can. Write how accepting you are of the situation in the fourth column of Worksheet 4-1.

6. **Notice what effect the exercise has on your level of acceptance of difficult emotions day to day.**

Worksheet 3-9	Experiencing Acceptance		
Thoughts, Feelings and Bodily Sensations Before the Mindful Exercise	*How Genuinely Accepting Am I of This Experience? (1 = Not Accepting, 10 = Totally Accepting)*	*Thoughts, Feelings and Bodily Sensations After the Mindful Exercise*	*How Genuinely Accepting Am I of This Experience? (1 = Not Accepting, 10 = Totally Accepting)*

Lake meditation

Track 5 on the audio (at www.dummies.com/go/mindfulnessworkbookuk) is the lake meditation, which can encourage feelings of acceptance.

Lie on a bed or floor, or wherever feels comfortable for you, and close your eyes.

Picture a lake and visualise it as clearly as possible, noticing the colours of the lake, and its natural surroundings. Notice how the lake changes all the time and yet in some ways the lake is always the same. Some days the lake is still and perfectly reflects the clouds, birds, trees and sun during the day, and the moon and stars at night. On other days the lake may be quite choppy; the reflections not so clear. You can see sparkles like diamonds dancing off the surface as the water catches the light of the sun.

As the seasons change, the lake also changes. During winter, the surface may freeze over, though underneath, the water is still there; that's the nature of the lake.

Have the idea that your being can merge with the lake. You experience changes just like the lake does; your mind is sometimes calm and reflective; sometimes choppy and unstable.

So perhaps, even on those days when your mind is agitated on the surface, you can go deeper, underneath, to the stillness of the water beneath the surface, just by remembering the lake.

Practising patience

Meditation isn't guaranteed to bring you joy and peace every time you practise. Like riding a bike or learning to drive, it's a skill you develop. Patience is an attitude that can help you with mindfulness. Patience can be challenging to cultivate, especially when you live in a world where everything is available now – fast food, fast communication, instant shopping and instant results!

Try these ways of cultivating the attitude of patience:

✔ When you feel impatient, ask yourself, 'Why am I feeling impatient?' After you ask that question and start considering possible answers, you change your state of mind from impatient to curious – a more mindful place to be in.

✔ Being on a tight schedule or multitasking can lead to impatience. Consider reducing your work load, delegating some of your tasks and just saying no more often when people ask for help. Being too busy is synonymous with impatience.

✔ Identify triggers that get you feeling impatient in your life. Make a list of them. Now reflect on why these situations make you feel impatient. What's the underlying cause of the feeling? Perhaps you keep thinking 'I must do more' or 'I'm being lazy'. Let go of those underlying sneaking thoughts and experience some freedom from the feeling of impatience. Who says you have to be busy all the time? You don't.

✔ Keep a journal for a couple of weeks, recording when you feel impatience, what you were doing and what thoughts and other feelings you were having. See if you can notice any patterns. Begin to notice if impatience is more related to your state of mind rather than outer circumstances. Insights like this can lead to a reduction in impatience.

Do one activity every day for a week that requires patience and record your progress in Worksheet 3-10. Be creative and choose a different thing every day. Whatever you choose, notice what effect it has and see if you become a little bit more patient as the week goes on. If you notice no improvements, try it for a couple more weeks.

Worksheet 3-10		Exercises in Patience
Day	*Patience Exercise*	*How Did I Feel as I Did the Exercise?*
Monday	Walked home a longer route and looked at the trees.	Frustrated at first but began to enjoy it towards the end.
Tuesday		
Wednesday		
Thursday		
Friday		
Saturday		
Sunday		

Easy like Sunday morning . . .

Thich Nhat Hanh, a renowned mindfulness teacher, has 'lazy days' on his retreats. On lazy days, you're encouraged to do nothing! You don't have to meditate if you don't want to, or write or read too much, or do anything too strenuous. Just eat, sleep, go for the occasional walk if you feel like it . . . and that's it! Lazy days can be difficult for people who are always busy and on the go, but the experience is deeply restful. Plan for a lazy day at home and see what happens!

Being non-striving

Doing nothing brings about quality of being, which is very important. So doing nothing is actually something.

– Thich Nhat Hanh

You could call this attitude of being non-striving being 'lazy', 'carefree' or 'easy-going'. They all point to letting go of trying to *achieve* something from practising mindfulness. Today, much of what people do is goal-orientated – doing and achieving and becoming something better.

Mindfulness is different. Mindfulness is more about *being* rather than doing and allowing things to be just as they are. So, if you feel more tense or stressed out at the end of a mindfulness meditation, that's okay. That's just the way it was for you today. Don't be too worried. You're learning to let go of a frantic need to get a certain feeling or experience out of mindfulness. Mindfulness is a unique activity where you can watch and see what happens – and then let go.

Mindfulness doesn't mean you stop doing all activity and vegetate. Instead, you find a healthy balance in your life between doing and achieving, and finding times for non-doing and being with thoughts, emotions, sensations and situations just as they are.

Cultivating beginner's mind

In the beginner's mind there are many possibilities. In the expert's mind there are few.

– Suzuki Roshi

Seeing afresh or seeing with 'beginner's mind' is a useful approach that can make you view life in a new way. The personal physician to His Holiness the Dalai Lama says, 'Empty your bowl of yesterday's rice.' This means letting go of your perceptions, ideas and concepts and allowing yourself to look at life with new eyes.

As a child, you saw things afresh, but as you grew up, things became familiar and no longer exciting. A rainbow doesn't get you jumping for joy, washing the dishes isn't a fun task and you ignore a plane flying past. Mindfulness encourages you to reinvigorate the miracle of being alive and see things with a beginner's mind. The fact that you're alive is a huge mystery itself. By being mindful, you can begin to live in this exciting way, as if everything is miraculous.

1. **Sit or lie down in a relaxed and comfortable position and close your eyes.**

2. **Notice the sensation of your breathing and the feel of your body against the surface you're sitting or lying on.** Prepare to see things as if for the first time when you open your eyes. Prepare to be amazed at the experience of colour entering your eyes.

3. **When you're ready, gently open your eyes.** Notice colours with a sense of wonder. Notice the range of different colours, the shades and hues, the shadows or bright light.

4. **Continue to operate this way as you go about your daily activities and see what happens.**

Living with beginner's mind is fun. You can't live every single moment with wonder, but by doing mindfulness exercises regularly, you're more likely to experience how special it is just to be alive.

The beginner's mind attitude isn't easy to develop, but it is fundamental to practising mindfulness.

Try filling out Worksheet 3-11 by jotting down some daily activities that you do without really paying attention to them. Notice what happens and what you discover when you do them as if for the first time.

Worksheet 3-11	Doing Activities with Beginner's Mind
Activity I Do Habitually	*What I Observed When I Did the Activity as If for the First Time*
Making a sandwich.	I noticed that I usually just start thinking about other things. I enjoyed the smell of the cheese and the softness of the bread. I've never noticed that before. My sandwich turned out tastier too!

Building trust

Trust is important in mindfulness because you can't expect mindfulness to give instant results. You need to trust in the process for anything between a few weeks to a few months before you notice any benefits. Without that genuine trust, you may not put your heart into the process and thereby reduce the chance of enjoying your journey into mindful living.

After you trust your ability to engage in mindfulness, you develop patience, dedication, willingness and regular practice. These attributes are likely to lead to some positive outcomes and your trust will grow.

Trust is the thread that helps you to maintain your meditation practice when you face the feeling that it's not working for you. If you start to feel frustrated when you meditate, you need to trust that this is just a feeling to observe as part of the process.

Where you place your trust is where you place your power and therefore your entire attitude. Many religions talk about the importance of faith. When you can let go of your critical mind and have some faith in a particular approach, even just for a few weeks, you allow time and energy for the process to work. Scepticism is healthy, but a total lack of trust prevents you from trying out the mindfulness approach in the first place. Balance your scepticism with trust and see what happens.

Here are some ways of building your trust:

- ✔ Decide on the length of time you wish to practise mindfulness every day and stick to your decision. If you just stop whenever you feel like stopping, the process doesn't really work. You need to work through your feelings in the mindfulness practice.

- ✔ Research the benefits of mindfulness to help you to see how others have benefited from mindfulness and to help you trust the approach.

- ✔ Meditate with someone more experienced in mindfulness practice. Just being close to someone with more experience can have a positive effect, showing how you can change as you deepen your commitment to mindfulness.

- ✔ Ask yourself: 'What needs to change so that I fully trust in mindfulness, for the next few weeks or months?' Jot down your answers on a piece of paper and consider adopting some of them.

Staying curious

> *Curiosity is one of the great secrets of happiness.*
>
> – *Bryant McGill*

Curiosity is at the heart of any learning process. If you're curious about something, you want to find out more about it. When you feel curious, you ask lots of questions, listen intently and get excited by new information and new concepts.

You can bring an attitude of this curiosity to your mindfulness practice. Ask yourself questions like 'Where do thoughts come from?' and 'What happens if I move towards my frustration and try to breathe into it?'

If you bring curiosity to your daily life, you find that mindfulness spontaneously arises. You're paying attention, noticing what's happening and find it easier to be in the present moment.

To cultivate a natural attitude of curiosity, ask yourself questions. Worksheet 3-12 lists some questions. As you continue to practise mindfulness, put in your own questions too.

Worksheet 3-12	Questions to Stimulate Curiosity
Questions to Ask in My Next Mindfulness Practice	*What did I Discover?*
What happens if I meditate every day for 20 minutes for four weeks, whether I feel like it or not?	

Questions to Ask in My Next Mindfulness Practice	What did I Discover?
What effect does putting more effort into my meditation have? What happens if I put in less effort?	
What happens if I sit or lie really still, even if I have the urge to move?	
Where in the body do I feel positive emotions? Where do I feel negative ones? What shape and colour do the emotions have, if any?	
What effect does having a gentle smile whilst meditating have on my practice?	
A question of my own:	

Ask questions about the way you think and feel, and bring a sense of wonder with your questioning. Doing so helps you to understand yourself, including your thoughts and feelings, better. An attitude of curiosity also helps you to understand others better, as humans are all made in a similar way.

Remaining playful and light-hearted

Mindfulness is also play. It is too serious to be taken too seriously!
– Jon Kabat-Zinn

A lovely attitude to have towards mindfulness and life in general is playfulness and light-heartedness. If a meditation doesn't work for you first time or doesn't feel right for you, don't panic but think of the experience as an experiment that you can try again later. Approach mindfulness as you would a new game or trying something new for fun. This way, you can take the practice as it comes without holding on to any concepts or ideas you have about how things *should* be.

The next time you have to do a boring task, see how long you can feel your breathing at the same time. Each time your mind wanders off, crack a big smile and a fake laugh. Then try again.

A playful attitude isn't limited to mindfulness. If you get bored at work, ask yourself what you could do to make things more interesting. Offer to make cups of tea for the entire team? Listen to some funky music on your headphones? Plan a lunch with your colleagues and have a good laugh at a local restaurant? The sky's the limit.

Many research studies show the positive benefits of fun and play on the brain: you become less frustrated, more creative and better able to find solutions to problems.

Have a go at filling in Worksheet 3-13 and see what effect it has.

Worksheet 3-13		Practising Playfulness		
Time of Day	*Activity*	*What Did I Do to Make It More Playful and Mindful?*	*How Did I Feel Afterwards?*	*My Thoughts of the Experience*
Morning				
Mid-morning				

Time of Day	Activity	What Did I Do to Make It More Playful and Mindful?	How Did I Feel Afterwards?	My Thoughts of the Experience
Afternoon				
Early evening				
Evening				

If you find this exercise difficult, start doing just one activity a day in a more playful way. Or do one thing every day, just for fun, like watching an episode of a sitcom or tickling a stranger . . . okay, maybe not!

Developing self-compassion

How often are you kind or compassionate to yourself? Do you give yourself a treat from time to time? If you've been working hard and make a mistake, do you give yourself a break or do you criticise yourself?

If, like many people, you're self-critical and overly harsh to yourself, self-compassion is a particularly important attitude to cultivate.

A mindful approach is to notice the self-critical thoughts and the physical sensations and emotions that go with them. Then, take a step back from the thoughts and allow them to pass, without believing them to be true or factual – just see them as thoughts. (See Chapter 5 for more on stepping back from thoughts.)

Sometimes seeing things in a wider context and then offering yourself some kinder thoughts is helpful. For example, if you didn't get the drink you ordered at the restaurant and felt overly upset, consider why you felt this way. Maybe you had a tough day at work or hadn't eaten all day and were tired. Worksheet 3-14 can help you to begin to develop self-compassion.

Worksheet 3-14	Developing Self-Compassion		
Difficult Situation, Event or Activity	*My Thoughts, Feelings and Bodily Sensations*	*In What Ways Was My Reaction Common to All Human Beings?*	*What Compassionate Attitude Can I Adopt Right Now?*
Received negative feedback from my boss.	T: I'm no good. F: Upset. B: Tense shoulders.	Most people feel stressed with negative feedback. I don't need to be perfect at the end of the day. Nobody is.	It's okay to feel a bit upset. I'll have a nice hot bath tonight and call my friend to chat about it. It's not the end of the world.

If you found this worksheet too challenging to complete, simply practise being aware of any self-critical or harsh thoughts that you have about yourself and notice their effect. Just being aware of them and letting them pass is beneficial.

An attitude of compassion towards yourself and others has been shown in a range of studies to be one of the healthiest attitudes to develop. See Chapter 5 to practise a loving kindness meditation.

Tuning in to an attitude of gratitude

You're grateful when you're aware of what you have rather than what you don't. Mindfulness is the starting point for gratitude. Without mindfulness, you can't be aware of all the things that are going well in your life. A grateful person is therefore a mindful person. Mindfulness with gratitude gives a sense of being more fully alive. As Thornton Wilder said: 'We can only be said to be alive in those moments when our hearts are conscious of our treasures.'

With practice you can develop gratitude the way you can with any skill, such as cooking or learning an instrument. The more you practise, the easier feeling grateful becomes. The more grateful you are for everything in your life, the more things you find to be grateful for! You begin to notice more and thereby strengthen your mindful awareness.

If you feel frustrated or low, try working on gratitude. With gratitude, the most difficult of days can be lit with hope and joy.

In the science of positive psychology, gratitude has been shown to be amongst the most positive attitudes to cultivate. Recent studies are beginning to show that gratitude has a uniquely powerful relationship with wellbeing. Over time you can change the programming in the brain by practising gratitude. You automatically focus on what's going well in your life and notice those things more often in a positive feedback loop.

Here's a simple mindfulness exercise to get you started with gratitude.

Think of something you don't yet feel grateful for. Perhaps you feel resentful or ungrateful about your job, a particular relationship or your commute to work.

Now think of all the things that are good about that particular thing. Give yourself two minutes and challenge yourself to come up with as many good things as possible. For example, if you have a long commute to work in the car, you could feel grateful that you can afford a car; that you have a job to drive to; that you have the ability to drive; that you have some time to be by yourself, listening to the radio. Think of as many positive aspects for which you are grateful. Try to list at least ten things.

In Worksheet 3-15, write down three things you're grateful for. It can be anything: 'It's a sunny day', 'I have a roof over my head' or 'I met my friend today'.

Commit to doing this on a daily basis for a week and you many find yourself being grateful for all sorts of other things too!

Worksheet 3-15	My Gratitude Journal
Date	*What Am I Grateful for Today?*
Monday	1. 2. 3.
Tuesday	1. 2. 3.
Wednesday	1. 2. 3.
Thursday	1. 2. 3.
Friday	1. 2. 3.
Saturday	1. 2. 3.
Sunday	1. 2. 3.

Buy yourself a nice little journal and place it by your bed. Every evening, before going to sleep, jot down a few things you're grateful for. You'll probably find that you sleep better and wake up with a little more positivity and freshness.

Letting go through a forgiving attitude

The truth is, unless you let go, unless you forgive yourself, unless you forgive the situation, unless you realise that that situation is over, you cannot move forward.
– Steve Maraboli

Forgiving others or yourself is a difficult thing to do. Being annoyed and angry with someone for a prolonged time isn't beneficial for your wellbeing; to paraphrase Nelson Mandela, it's like drinking poison and expecting the other person to feel the effects. Keeping anger locked in can cause resentment, which may lead to you feeling depressed.

A forgiving attitude toward someone doesn't mean that the action the other person did was right. You're forgiving the person, not the action. Forgiveness benefits you more than the other person. You're learning to let go of the corrosive negative emotions that you're walking around with. Instead, you're giving yourself permission to let all that negative baggage go, so that you can live your life in a wise and harmonious way.

Try this approach to cultivating a forgiving attitude:

- Understand that not forgiving someone else doesn't actually hurt that person at all.

- Be compassionate with yourself. If you've been ruminating over a problem for some time, perhaps now's the time to let it go. You don't deserve all this hurt you're carrying around with you.

- Feelings of hurt may be repeating themselves in your mind through a story ('My boss knew I deserved that promotion, so why did my colleague get it?'). Try letting go of the story or seeing the story from another person's perspective. Something may shift to help you to forgive.

Fill in Worksheet 3-16 to encourage an attitude of forgiveness. Try talking the questions through with a close friend who may have a different point of view.

Worksheet 3-16	Encouraging an Attitude of Forgiveness
Who do I want to forgive?	
What are the benefits that have emerged from this difficult situation? (Try to see the situation from a totally different perspective, at least for a few moments)	
How do I think I'll feel if I manage to forgive?	
If someone has hurt you, try the forgiveness meditation (following). Wish the person well just as you wish or a friend well. What effect does this have?	

Only practise this meditation if you're ready to adopt a forgiving attitude towards someone. If you don't want to forgive, give this a miss and come back to it when you're ready.

1. **Sit in a comfortable and relaxed position.** Let your eyes close if that's okay with you and breathe naturally. Imagine your breath going into your heart, as best you can.

2. **Consider the person who you want to forgive.** Recall what they did to hurt you. If possible, gently feel the sense of hurt that you experienced. Notice any other feelings that you have towards the person, such as anger, frustration or disappointment.

3. **Notice that the other person doesn't experience these feelings at this moment, but you do.** You are carrying the feelings. And holding on to the difficult feelings doesn't help you or affect the other person. Reflect on this.

4. **See the situation from the other person's perspective.** What sort of moods are they affected by? What's their willpower like? What's their character like? Understand that their actions are strongly influenced by their upbringing and circumstances.

5. **Finally, be compassionate with yourself.** Understand that the process of forgiveness takes time, but leads to a happier and more peaceful you.

Dealing with Unhelpful Attitudes

When you first learnt to ride a bike, you probably didn't go cycling off into the horizon balanced perfectly first time. When a baby is learning how to walk, he doesn't just suddenly get up and start walking. He falls over a lot, but keeps trying to walk until he can.

In order to practise mindfulness, you need to begin to let go of any perfectionist or impatient attitudes you may have towards it. If you struggle with the mindfulness meditation, you fall asleep or your mind wanders, try not to get angry or frustrated with yourself. Meditation is a practice you can cultivate over time. Develop an attitude of kindness towards yourself (refer to the previous section 'Developing self-compassion').

You don't need to wait until your life is one hundred per cent perfect to start mindfulness practice.

Here are examples of common experiences that people think mean they've failed at meditation, and answers to them. See if any of them apply to you. Understanding and dealing with a perfectionist attitude can make a big difference to your experience of mindfulness.

- ✔ **'I couldn't concentrate. My mind was all over the place. I did it wrong!'** No one can concentrate continuously. Sooner or later your mind goes into thoughts, dreams, ideas or problems. The nature of the mind is to wander off. Lack of focus is an integral part of meditation experience. See Chapter 2 for more on concentration in meditation.

- ✔ **'I couldn't sit still.'** Your body is designed to move. However, through training, slowly but surely you're able to sit still for longer. If sitting really isn't for you, remember you can still do mindfulness when you move – that's the beauty of it! Try exercises that integrate awareness such as yoga and t'ai chi, or any other action you choose in a mindful and therefore meditative way. Chapter 5 has more on mindful moving.

✔ **'I felt bored/tired/frustrated/angry/annoyed/jealous/excited/empty.'** You're going to feel a variety of emotions in your meditation, just as you do in your everyday life. The difference is, instead of reacting to them automatically, you have the valuable opportunity to watch them come and go. In the long run, these emotions will probably calm down a bit, but in the meantime you need simply to be aware of them. If you can, enjoy the show!

✔ **'I had a negative experience.'** People have both pleasant and unpleasant experiences in meditation. The experience may be anything from deep sadness to feeling as if you're disappearing, or your arms may feel as if they're floating. Your mind may be releasing emotions from your unconscious into your conscious mind. This is part-and-parcel of mindfulness meditation. Let the process unfold by itself as much as you can.

Try not to think of meditation experiences as good or bad. Instead, see all experiences as opportunities to learn something new about yourself.

If you feel yourself becoming very concerned or frightened and these feelings are on-going, you may need professional support, so contact your doctor or therapist.

Have a go at filling in Worksheet 3-17 to get you reflecting on this topic.

Worksheet 3-17	Examining Unhelpful Attitudes
My Current Unhelpful Attitude to Mindfulness	*Exploring Alternative Attitudes to Help Me Practise Mindfulness*
I must do my mindfulness perfectly.	No one's perfect. It's better for me to try to practise as best I can and see what happens. And whatever happens will be a learning experience.

Chapter 4

Discovering a Mindful Mode of Mind

What is this life if, full of care, We have no time to stand and stare.

– William Henry Davies

All over the world, people are incessantly busy doing things. Buying, selling, washing, eating, walking, driving, talking, typing . . . Being constantly on the move, whether physically or mentally, can mean you have difficulty just *being*; taking time to stop your activities and rest in your own inner sense of existence. This chapter shows you a way to connect with yourself in a state that isn't frantic or rushing. And that is simply to *be*. Everyone can access this being way of operating and this chapter shows you how.

Science backs up this aim. Research by leading neuroscientists including Professor Mark Williams and colleagues from the University of Oxford discovered two specific modes of mind that the brain can be in: *doing mode* and *being mode*. In this chapter, you're going to find out the benefits and drawbacks of each mode, how to switch between them and why you may need to use more being mode in your life.

To Be or Not to Be: Understanding Two Modes of Mind

As a busy person, falling into doing mode of mind for almost 100 per cent of the time is very easy. Doing mode of mind is often a useful practice to have a constructive day – you need to remember to brush your teeth, pay that bill, post that gift, call your sister, arrange that meeting and remember to put the cat out. Multitasking can be very useful, but if you're in doing mode too much, you end up living your life on autopilot.

To be able to effectively shift from one mode of mind to another, you need to be able to recognise the hallmarks of two different modes of mind. When you know that you're in doing mode, you can decide if you want to stay that way for the time being or take steps to shift into being mode.

Nothing's inherently bad about doing mode or good about being mode. They're just different mind states that are helpful in different ways.

Discovering the elements of doing mode

Here are the key elements of doing mode:

- ✔ **Your attention is on the past or the future.** When in doing mode, you're concerned about how you want things to be in the future. And you may reflect on or regret the way your life has gone in the past.

- ✔ **You strive to try to fix things.** Doing mode is goal-oriented. So you're constantly trying to fix problems and make things better. You're not accepting the way things are at the moment at all.

- ✔ **You act and think habitually.** Your thoughts and actions arise automatically from habit rather than as a conscious choice. You're doing things the way you are because you're in a less reflective state.

- ✔ **You avoid difficult thoughts, feelings or situations.** Doing mode is also marked by a state of *avoidance*. Your attitude is one of avoiding difficulties rather than facing up to their reality.

- ✔ **You take thoughts to be real.** For example, if you think 'I always mess up Sunday roast dinner', then you take that thought to be a fact. In reality, many people may have admired your Sunday lunch offering, but as you're in an unreflective state, you are unable to see this.

Time to put your thinking cap on! Answer the questions in Worksheet 4-1 as honestly as possible to get an idea of how often you're in doing mode.

Worksheet 4-1	Evaluating How Often I'm in Doing Mode
Question	**Yes/No/Maybe**
Do I find focusing on what's happening in the present moment difficult?	
Do I tend to travel to my destination without focusing on what's along the way?	
Do I feel as if I'm running on autopilot?	
Do I rush through things, not paying great attention to what I'm doing?	
Do I get so focused on a goal that I lose concentration on what I'm doing right now to get there?	
Do I think a lot about the future and the past and less about the present moment?	
Do I become easily stressed and frustrated?	

If you answered yes or maybe to four or more questions, then you may be in doing mode of mind too often.

Although doing mode is useful for humans in some ways (such as tying your shoelaces, or brushing your teeth on autopilot), this mode has its downsides. You can start to live your whole life in doing mode and you lose awareness of what's around you. You miss the blackbird in the tree outside your office window, the blessing that you have access to clean water, the feel of the wind in your hair as you walk down the street.

If you find yourself trapped in an endless cycle of doing, don't feel disheartened. It's quite common, and the nice thing is, mindfulness can help you to get out of this rut.

Finding out about being mode

Being mode is an uplifting and supportive state of mind that's always available to you, even in the midst of busy activity. You can be in the middle of a very challenging time at work and still very aware of your physical, emotional and psychological state of mind – this state is being mode.

Here are six key qualities of the being mode of mind:

- ✔ **You're connected with the present moment.** When you're in being mode, you're mindful of the here and now. You're not thinking about the past or the future. You're living moment to moment, as best you can.

- ✔ **You're non-striving.** You're less goal-oriented. You have less of a burning desire for situations to change. You accept how things are before moving to change anything. Being mode doesn't mean being resigned to a less-than-ideal situation, it means active acceptance of the way things are at the moment. If you're lost, the only way of getting anywhere is by knowing where you are to start with. Being mode is about acknowledging where you are.

- ✔ **You're willing to approach difficulties instead of avoiding them.** You're willing to open up to painful and unpleasant sensations or emotions without trying to run away from them. You understand that avoiding an emotion just locks you into it more tightly. (Head to the later section 'Dealing with Emotions in Being Mode' for more about dealing with painful emotions.)

- ✔ **Seeing thoughts as just thoughts, not necessarily facts.** Through mindfulness, you become aware of your thoughts but don't take every thought as an absolute truth. Just because you may have the thought 'I'm useless' or 'I'm a failure' doesn't mean it's true – it's just a thought. You see that thoughts are just sounds and images in the mind, not necessarily true reality. Being mode is about awareness of thoughts and the ability to decide if they're helpful or not.

- ✔ **You experience life through your senses.** You experience life in a more sensory, direct way. If you feel annoyed, you actually feel the physical sensation within your body, perhaps as tightness of the muscles in your chest or belly. You're better able to listen to people when they're speaking to you. You see all the different elements in a room when you walk inside a building.

- ✔ **You act consciously rather than automatically.** You're aware of and pay attention to your experience in an intentional, conscious way rather than being unaware, automatic and habitual. You're more awake to your moment-by-moment experience.

In Worksheet 4-2 write down what you notice when you carry out routine activities in being mode. To do this, follow the key qualities of being mode described in the previous list. Just do your best and see what happens.

Worksheet 4-2		Trying Out Being in Being Mode		
Routine Activity	*Thoughts That Popped into My Mind*	*How I Felt Emotionally*	*Sensations I Noticed*	*How Was the Whole Experience Different to Usual?*
Taking a shower.	Lots of thoughts about the meeting I have today.	Anxious at first, but then relaxed.	Warmth of shower, smooth soap on my skin, fresh scent of perfume in shampoo.	Started off rushing but managed to slow down and enjoy it a bit more.

Acceptance: Key to self-development

Acceptance is not submission; it is acknowledgement of the facts of a situation. Then deciding what you're going to do about it.

– *Kathleen Casey Theisen*

Accepting a situation or emotion just to make it go away doesn't really work and misses an important point. If you feel sad and you try and acknowledge it, secretly hoping your sadness will go away, you haven't fully accepted it yet. Instead, accept an emotion wholeheartedly if you can – emotions are true teachers. Listen to your emotions with kindness and see what they have to say. Chapter 3 explores acceptance in further detail.

Balancing Doing and Being in Your Life

Everyday life sometimes requires doing mode and sometimes being mode, as shown in Figure 4-1. Mindfulness helps you to become more aware of what is best for you in each situation and to apply the appropriate mode of mind. If you have a habit of always using doing mode, you need a bit of practice applying being mode in your life.

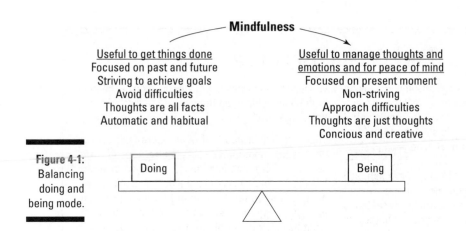

Figure 4-1:
Balancing
doing and
being mode.

An easy way to change modes of mind is to bring your attention to . . . your feet! Although simple, having an awareness of the contact of your feet with the floor, whether you're sitting still or walking, is a powerful step (see what we did there?) into being mode and the present moment.

Enjoying more being in everyday life

The sense of being, of presence, is your natural state of mind. Children are usually in being mode, living in the moment and unconcerned about achieving long-term goals or worrying about the past. To enjoy more being mode, simply begin to let go of the habitual tendency to constantly *do* all the time.

Here are some mindful practices that help to engage you in being mode:

- When waiting in a queue, rather than killing the time, engage your awareness. Notice the colours and sounds around you. Or challenge yourself to see if you can maintain the awareness of your feet on the floor for ten full breaths.

- When you've stopped at a red traffic light in the car you have a choice. You can feel frustrated and impatient, or you can do traffic light meditation! Nourish yourself with three refreshing, mindful breaths (refer to Chapter 5 for more on mindful breathing).

- The next time the phone rings, let it ring three times. Use that time to breathe and smile. Telesales companies know that you can 'hear the smile' on the phone and ask employees to smile when they're on a call. You're in a more patient and happy state of mind when you speak.

- Change your daily routine. If you normally drive to work, try walking or cycling for part of the journey. Go a slightly different route on the school run. Speak to different friends or colleagues.

- Take up a new hobby. When you change your habits, you engage different pathways in the brain. You instinctively wake up to the moment and just are.

Take a look at Worksheet 4-3. Make a list of all the things that you need to do today. Then prioritise. Ensure that you put mindfulness on the list too! That goes at the top!

WISE WORDS

The mindful fisherman

A young fisherman spent his days fishing and taking tourists out on his boat. One day he took a business-man out to sea who said to him, 'You could run a great business here. You could start to sell the fish you catch and buy a bigger boat.' The young fisher-man replied, 'What would I do then?' The business man replied, 'Then you could catch more fish, sell them and buy an even bigger boat. If you worked hard, you could eventually buy a whole fleet of boats and hire people to do the work for you.' 'What would I do then?' asked the young fisherman. The business-man replied, 'Well, then you could spend your days fishing and lying in the sun whenever you want.' The young fisherman smiled from his position on the front of the boat soaking up the sun and replied, 'Aren't I doing that now?'

This story illustrates that doing more isn't always necessary. Sometimes, simplifying your life and spending more time just being, can be what you're looking for. You can want more, but you don't always need it. The young fisherman had enough fish to eat, was happy and earning a decent living doing what he was doing right at that moment. Try not to get dragged into the rat race of doing just because everyone else is.

Put some things on your to-do list that aren't urgent but fun, such as reading a novel or taking the kids to the cinema. Non-urgent activities give you a chance to have a breather from energy-draining doing mode. Try doing some of the fun or pleasant activities without feeling guilty for doing so!

Worksheet 4-3	My To-Do and To-Be List
To-Do List (Things I Have to Do)	*To-Be List (Pleasant, Fun Activities That I Enjoy)*

REMEMBER

You can be in being mode when you're doing something. In fact, this is a major ben-efit of mindfulness. You can be busy working hard at cleaning the house and if your attention is right in the moment, you're in being mode. Fill in Worksheet 4-4 to identify places where you can encourage being mode in your life.

Worksheet 4-4	Encouraging Being Mode in My Life	
Way of Encouraging More Being in My Life	*When Will I Try It?*	*What Did I Notice? (Thoughts, Feelings and Bodily Sensations)*
When walking from place to place, take the opportunity to feel my feet on the floor, see the range of different colours in front of me and listen to the variety of sounds.		
When moving from one activity to another, take a moment to rest. Feel three complete in-breaths and out-breaths or more if I have time.		
Establish a regular meditation routine using formal mindfulness meditation practices every day for a week (Chapter 5 explores meditation).		
Use the three-minute mini meditation (described in Chapter 6) several times a day. Whenever I catch myself becoming excessively emotional, use the mini meditation to move towards being mode, opening up to the challenging experience rather than trying to avoid it.		
Do a hobby or sport mindfully. These activities tend to involve connecting with the senses, which immediately cultivates being mode. Painting, listening to music, playing football, working out at the gym, playing an instrument, dancing, singing and many more activities all offer a chance to be with my senses.		
Avoid multitasking for a whole day. If that's too much, try one hour. Doing one thing at a time with my full and undivided attention can engage being mode.		
Treat myself to a day of mindfulness. Wake up slowly, feel my breath frequently and connect with my senses and the world and people around me as much as I can.		
When taking a bath or shower, use the time to feel the warmth of the water and the contact with my skin. Allow all my senses to be involved in the experience; enjoy the sounds and breathe in the scent of my favourite soap.		
When I'm eating, pause before my meal to take a few conscious breaths. Then eat the meal with my full attention. Try chewing each bite about twenty times so I can really savour the flavour and take my time.		

Have an entire day once a week where you're relatively technology free. A flashing mobile phone light and constant Internet connection just encourages you to be back in doing mode. If you work a normal nine to five week, maybe choose Sunday as your day to be without. Take the kids for a walk in the park, play a game or read a book if it's raining. If anyone urgently needs to call you that day, give them your landline number. I (Shamash) like to have regular little breaks from being connected to technology, so I leave my phone at home while I'm supermarket shopping. I can be mindful of my walk to and from the shops and the shop itself. As I'm not distracted, I find I buy healthier food and make better decisions for meals!

Discovering key ways to just be

Are you a busy person? Do you have too much to do to have time to just be? One of the attractive things about mindfulness is that you don't have a fixed amount of time that you're supposed to practise for. Your daily practice can be meditation for one minute or one hour – it's up to you. The other great thing about mindfulness is that you can be mindful of your normal everyday routine and in that way build up your awareness and being mode. That takes no time at all; in fact, it can save time because you're more focused on your activities. In this section we explore three highly effective strategies for bringing being mode into your everyday life.

Act consciously rather than habitually

Being aware of your choices and actions instead of unconsciously behaving out of habit is a hallmark of being mode. So, when you type, feel the contact between your fingers and the keyboard. When you drive, give it your full attention instead of allowing your mind to wander. When drinking tea, do so mindfully. Feel the sensations as the cup comes towards your mouth and enjoy the refreshing taste of tea. Living in the present is trickier than it sounds but each time you try, you get a little bit better. Slowly but surely, you really start living in the moment.

Changing your habits is a great way to be mindful. Consider the following questions:

- ✔ What habits could you change that take you out of the present moment?
- ✔ What could you do today to encourage moment-to-moment living?

To help you focus on certain activities, fill in Worksheet 4-5:

Worksheet 4-5	Bringing Mindfulness to Everyday Activities
Habitual Activity	*Bringing Curiosity to that Activity, What Do I Discover?*
Brushing teeth (other examples you could use include: showering, getting dressed, talking to your partner, playing with your children, walking to work).	Tasted really minty, feeling of wanting to rush, body felt tense at first but after being mindful, I started to relax and enjoy it. Noticed how much I think about when just brushing my teeth!

Reduce activities that hijack your attention

Computers, televisions and mobile phones can easily capture your attention. You can end up spending hours in an energy-draining state of mind, where you go from website to website without purpose or satisfaction. Control your use of these devices by switching off the Internet or phone for periods of time, or even getting rid of your television!

I (Joelle) used to start my day with a meditation practice on waking up, then reached for my laptop and started working without getting out of bed! Hours would go by and I'd be distracted by social networking sites and emails, and still hadn't started writing properly! Nothing's wrong with these activities, but they don't encourage moment-by-moment living and lead to a passive state of mind. I now wake up, have my daily mindfulness practice and make sure I get out of bed straight afterwards. I sit up at the table to write in a separate room from my bedroom, and it makes me much more mindful and aware. Think about your own daily routine and reduce focus-draining activities like watching lots of television or surfing the Internet.

In Worksheet 4-6, list activities that draw you out of the present moment and list what you could do instead.

Worksheet 4-6 My Attention-Hijacking Activities and Their Replacements

Unhelpful Activities that Hijack My Attention	Alternative Activity
Television channel hopping, checking email endlessly, Internet surfing, talking to negative people.	Read a good book, go for a walk, meet up with a good friend, meditate, do some exercise, tidy up the cupboard, attend an adult course, do a hobby.

Find moments in your day to be mindful

Do mini mindfulness exercises whenever you have pockets of time. This habit can really help you to come back into the present moment and simply be. We describe mini meditations in Chapter 6.

Be creative and see when you can find a moment to practise every day, such as on the loo, in a boring meeting or waiting in a queue.

Use Worksheet 4-7 to record your mini meditation practice every day.

Worksheet 4-7	Mini Meditation Record		
Day	*Did I Do a Mini Meditation?*	*When Did I Do It?*	*What Effect Did It Have?*
Monday			
Tuesday			
Wednesday			
Thursday			
Friday			
Saturday			
Sunday			

You're always in the present moment. You've never been in any other moment. Don't believe us? Every time your mind worries about the past, when does it do it? Only in the present moment. Every plan you've ever made for the future is only made in the present moment. Right now, as you're thinking about what you're reading and comparing it to your past experience, you're doing so in this moment, right now. Your plans for tomorrow can only be thought about now. Now is all you're ever in. The question is how you can connect with bringing your mind into the here and now. That's where the mindfulness exercises and attitudes come in.

Dealing with Emotions in Being Mode

Emotions aren't problems to be solved, but experiences to be accepted.

Living on autopilot can cause negative thoughts to sneak into your mind. You could be thinking negative thoughts such as 'I'm lazy', 'I'm unlovable' or 'I can't do that' without even noticing. Thoughts have a huge effect on emotions, especially if you believe the thoughts to be true. Automatic thoughts can lead to unhelpful emotions. All you notice is that you're suddenly really tired, low or angry. However, if you're conscious of these negative thoughts, you have the choice to believe them or not.

When you use doing mode to try to manage your emotions, your challenging mood can deepen. Here's an example of how this happens:

1. You feel unhappy. But you want to feel happy. So you decide to 'fix' your emotion. (You're engaging doing mode.)

2. Emotions can't be fixed so easily. You notice your sadness hasn't gone away. So, you feel unsuccessful. You feel like a failure. You may call yourself a failure, useless. That makes you feel sadder. Your mood worsens.

3. You think 'I must try harder to be happier. I'm not trying hard enough.' (Doing mode again.) So you continue to avoid the sad feeling and fight it. Fighting your feeling puts you into an aggressive, stressed state of mind.

If you have an uncomfortable feeling like sadness, try this exercise to get into being mode and accept the emotion:

1. **Find a quiet, comfortable place and set your intention.** Let your intention be to engage in being mode. Feel the emotion and its effects as best you can with a gentle curiosity. You're not doing so as a clever way to get rid of it. You're just giving yourself space to learn from the emotion instead of running away from it.

2. **Breathe.** Simply feel your breath. Be with each in-breath and each out-breath. Notice how each breath is unique, different and vital for your health and wellbeing. Allow your breath to be natural, as best you can.

3. **Accept the emotion in your body.** Feel the emotion with care, kindness and acceptance, as best you can. Open up to it. Move in close to the emotion if you can, within your body. Notice where the emotion manifests itself in your body. Breathe into that part of your body and stay with it. Allow the emotion to be as it is. You don't need to fight or run away. Be with the experience as precisely as you can. It's not easy, so just try your best.

4. **De-centre from your thoughts and emotions.** Simply notice that you're having a thought or experiencing an emotion. As soon as you do this, you de-centre from them. Notice that you can be aware of the emotion without being the emotion itself. Be aware of a space between you and the feeling. The same goes for your thoughts too. As you observe the thoughts or feelings, you're separate from them in a sense, because you're watching them. It's like sitting on a riverbank as the water rushes by rather than being in the river itself. As you watch the water (emotion or thought) pass by, you may sometimes feel like you've been sucked into the river and washed downstream. But you're not the river itself. You can simply step back out of the river again. De-centring is an important aspect of mindfulness.

5. **Breathe.** Finish by feeling your breathing again. Notice if your breath has changed or stayed the same. Rest your attention on your breath for a few moments.

All emotions, no matter how strong, have a beginning and an end. Mindfulness teaches you to be with the emotion rather than push away, judge or fight it. Being with the emotion prevents a spiralling down into deeper, challenging emotions.

Use Worksheet 4-8 to experiment. Notice the next time you feel angry, sad, anxious or lonely. Then, use doing or being mode to notice what effect they have on the emotion. Remember, doing mode is about avoiding or fixing the emotion whereas being mode is about allowing, accepting and being with it with a sense of kindness and curiosity.

Worksheet 4-8	Exploring Doing and Being Mode on Emotions	
Emotion	*Effect of Using Doing Mode to Fix the Emotion*	*Effect of Using Being Mode to Gently Explore the Emotion*

We hope you'll discover that doing mode causes you to fall deeper into the emotion, whereas as being mode, although uncomfortable and counter-intuitive at first, leads you to stop fighting with the emotion and that it dissipates with time.

Part III
Practising Mindfulness

In this part . . .

✔ Try out a range of mindfulness exercises from mindful breathing to mindful movement.

✔ Enjoy the many benefits of the body scan meditation.

✔ Get an instant pick-me-up with mini meditations.

✔ Improve your relationships with mindfulness.

✔ Complete the eight-week structured mindfulness course.

✔ Overcome challenges and difficulties in your mindfulness practice.

✔ Go to www.dummies.com/go/mindfulnessworkbookuk for the body scan meditation (Track 2; described in Chapter 5) and the 'Mountain' audio meditation (Track 4; described in Chapter 9) to help you deal with strong emotions and challenging experiences.

Chapter 5

Engaging in Mindfulness Meditation

*I*n this chapter, you get into the detail of formal mindfulness meditation practice. We explore the core meditations that lie at the heart of mindfulness here, so if you want to get straight into some extended mindfulness practice, you've come to the right place.

Don't be put off by the word 'formal' by the way – it simply means a daily practice that you make time for. No posh outfits required! You decide how long to meditate for, and when to meditate.

A daily practice helps you to have a consistent mindful way of living. Without a routine of regular meditation, you may struggle to be mindful in your daily life. If you want to be a good runner, you need to run regularly and for a decent length of time. Similarly, if you want to develop a mindful brain, we recommend that you meditate regularly and for at least 15 to 20 minutes a day. Evidence suggests that about 20 minutes of daily meditation practice is long enough to positively rewire your brain to be more mindful and flexible. However, if you only have time for a few mindful breaths every day, those few breaths are valuable too. If you read the story 'The mindful cuppa' in the nearby sidebar, you'll see what we mean.

You'll find lots of mindfulness meditations in this chapter. We recommend you try each one for two weeks before moving on to the next one. Then you have some time to get the hang of the method and experience the meditation fully.

The mindful cuppa

I (Shamash) was talking to a mindfulness teacher, and he told me his path into meditation. After suffering from high levels of anxiety working in the corporate sector, he found himself suffering from depression. He tried various methods to manage the illness, and one route he tried was mindfulness meditation. He attended a local meditation group, but due to his high levels of stress, he couldn't do a full sitting meditation. His mindfulness teacher told him to simply drink one cup of tea mindfully every day. He had to look at the tea, notice the aroma and steam, become aware of the weight of the cup as he prepared to take a sip, taste the tea in his mouth and notice the experience of swallowing it. With time, he began to practise longer mindfulness exercises, including sitting meditation. And now, ten years later, he is a mindfulness teacher himself.

Focusing on Mindful Breathing Meditation

Mindful breathing is the most basic mindfulness meditation. But basic doesn't mean easy or shallow. Mindfulness of breath is a tremendously powerful practice. If all you gain from this book is how to do this breath meditation, you have learnt something enormously valuable for your life. Long-term practice of this meditation leads to all sorts of insights about how your mind works, a greater ability to focus in the present moment, less worry, a higher sense of wellbeing, greater emotional balance and a calmer state of mind. Don't take our word for it – practise the mindful breathing meditation and see what happens for yourself.

1. **Find a comfortable, straight sitting position.** You could be sitting up in a chair (with your back away from the back of the chair) or cross-legged on the floor. Keep your spine straight if you can. Close your eyes if that feels okay to you. Ensure that you won't be disturbed for the next ten minutes or so and are in a place with a comfortable temperature.

2. **Set your intention to focus on your breathing as best you can.** Remind yourself that if your mind drifts off to other thoughts, you don't need to criticise or judge yourself. Let go of any ideas of achievement or success. Whatever happens, happens.

3. **Focus on your breathing.** Close your eyes. Feel your breath going in and out of your nostrils, or passing through the back of your throat, or feel your chest or belly rising and falling. Try placing your hands on your belly and feel the breath moving in and out. After you've found the place that you can feel your breath comfortably, let your hands rest and try to keep your attention there. Allow your breath to flow at its natural depth and speed. Just accept your breathing as it is. It may gradually slow down or deepen, or it may not – either way is fine.

4. **Gently bring your mind back to your breathing.** Your mind may wander off into different thoughts, ideas, dreams, plans and fantasies. This behaviour is perfectly normal and what minds do. Without judgement, notice what you were thinking about and gently guide your mind back to your breath. Your mind drifting off and you bringing it back is an integral part of your meditation process. If you start to get frustrated or annoyed with yourself, try gently smiling and take a deep breath. Then guide your attention back to your breathing.

5. **After ten minutes, gently open your eyes.** Notice how you're feeling. Have a little stretch if you need to and mindfully continue with your day.

Try to accept the experience of your meditation, whatever it is. Avoid thinking 'I'm doing it wrong' or 'I can't get it' if possible. Each experience is different. Be with things just as they are, from moment to moment.

Practise this mindful breathing exercise for ten to twenty minutes every day. You can try it at different times of the day to see what effect it has. After each practice, record your experience in Worksheet 5-1.

Worksheet 5-1	My Mindful Breathing Meditation Log			
Day	**Time and Length of Practice**	**Posture I Adopted**	**Feelings Before the Practice**	**Thoughts, Feelings and Bodily Sensations During the Mindful Breathing**
Monday				
Tuesday				
Wednesday				
Thursday				
Friday				
Saturday				
Sunday				

Exploring Mindful Movement Meditation

Your body doesn't have to be physically still in order to practise mindfulness meditation. I (Shamash) find some of my clients struggle with being physically still for extended periods of time. However, almost everyone enjoys moving their body in a mindful way.

Making time to do mindful movements, with your attention fully in the activity with mindful attitudes, *is* meditation. Meditation doesn't mean you have to be physically still. Meditation is simply intentionally focusing your awareness on a chosen object for a designated period of time.

Many of the traditional martial arts as well as the ancient practices of yoga and t'ai chi emphasise a mindful awareness of the discipline. They sometimes include sitting still and meditating as part of the training.

Have a go at this simple mindful movement meditation sequence and see how you find it. Wear loose, comfortable clothing for the exercise.

If you suffer from a physical health condition, please check with your doctor before doing these exercises. Some may be inappropriate if you suffer from high blood pressure or back problems, for example.

1. **Begin with mindful standing.** Simply stand up straight with your feet about hip-width apart. Allow your knees to be slightly loose. Have your shoulders back and down and your chest comfortably open. Allow your arms to hang by the sides of your body. Check that your head is balanced on your neck and shoulders. Imagine a helium balloon is attached to the top of your head gently pulling you upright. Keep your eyes closed if you can maintain your balance safely that way.

2. **Feel sensations in your body.** Notice the sensation of your own breath. Feel the weight of your body upon your feet. Become mindful of areas in your body that feel tense or uncomfortable without trying to relax them.

3. **Move your arms up and down.** When you're ready, move your arms upwards in front of you as you breathe in and back down again as you breathe out. Notice the physical sensations in your arms and hands as you do this about ten times. See Figure 5-1a.

4. **Move your arms up and out, in and down.** The next time you breathe in, raise your arms in front. Then, as you breathe out, open your arms outwards. As you breathe in, bring your arms together in front of you again. As you breathe out, bring your arms back down to your sides again. Do this about ten times if you can. See Figure 5-1b.

5. **Stretch your arms.** Raise your arms above your head and feel the stretch. See how far you can comfortably reach. Hold that stretch until you begin to feel some discomfort and see if you can stay with the feeling of discomfort for a few moments before bringing your arms down again. Repeat if you wish. Keep breathing as you do so – no need to hold your breath!

6. **Rotate your shoulders.** Rotate your shoulders slowly several times in both directions. Feel any tension that may be there. At the same time, feel your breathing if you can.

7. **Gently rotate your head from side to side.** Be careful with this one and do it slowly. Gently drop your left ear towards your left shoulder. Then rotate your head round in front of you and then let your right ear move towards your right shoulder before going back into the centre again.

8. **Shake your arms and legs.** You may like to finish by shaking your arms and legs for about half a minute and then stand upright again and feel the sensations throughout your body.

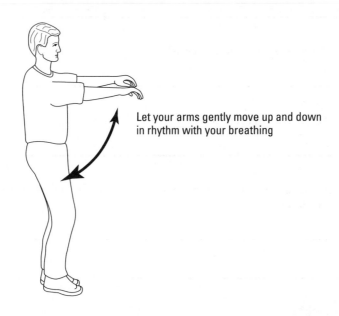

Let your arms gently move up and down in rhythm with your breathing

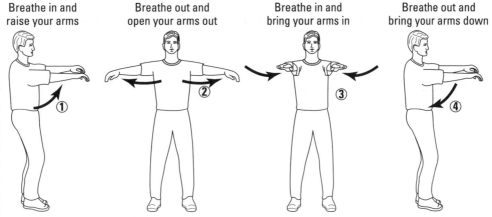

| Breathe in and raise your arms | Breathe out and open your arms out | Breathe in and bring your arms in | Breathe out and bring your arms down |

Figure 5-1: a and b: Diagram showing the directions to move your arms.

Use Worksheet 5-2 to write down your experiences of the mindful movement meditation. By reflecting on your experience, you generate more mindfulness as you'll be more curious about exactly what you notice next time you do the practice.

Worksheet 5-2 **My Reflections on Mindful Movement Meditation**

Write down a sequence of mindful movements or stretches that you'd like to try. Then try them!

_____

_____

How energised and mindful did you feel at the beginning?

_____

How energised and mindful did you feel at the end?

_____

What did you notice about your bodily sensations? Be as specific as you can – this writing exercise can be a mindful practice in itself.

_____

_____

What emotions arose for you?

_____

What thoughts crossed your mind?

_____

Engaging with the Body Scan Meditation

I (Shamash) guided this meditation with a group of executive coaches in London, and one of the participants said, 'That was a deeply _healing_ experience.' The root meaning of the word _heal_ means 'to make whole'. No matter what people have been through, meditation can make them feel a sense of wholeness again.

Introducing the body scan

One of the unique features of the body scan meditation is that you do it lying down, making it an ideal meditation for you to begin with, as you don't need to hold your body upright for long periods of time.

The body scan slowly shifts your attention through your body, usually beginning with the toes and finishing with the top of your head. You may prefer to use the audio accompanying this book, as it helps you to pace the length of your practice and if your mind wanders off, the recording reminds you to refocus your attention.

Practising the body scan meditation on a regular basis has many benefits. The body scan can:

- ✔ Help your mind become more focused.

- ✔ Train your attention to shift from one place to another at will.

- ✔ Shift your attention away from your thoughts.

- ✔ Indirectly help process latent emotions that may be trapped within your body (see the nearby sidebar 'Unlocking emotions from your body' for more on using mindfulness with difficult emotions).

- ✔ Move you from doing mode to being mode (refer to Chapter 4).

Find a place to practise when you won't be disturbed (turn off your phone!) and where you feel warm and comfortable.

You can practise the meditation at any time of day, but if you do it too late in the evening, you may fall asleep. Having said that, the body scan can help overcome insomnia.

Practising the body scan meditation

The best way to experience this mindfulness meditation is to listen to the audio accompanying this book (Track 2 at www.dummies.com/go/mindfulness workbookuk).

The experience takes between 15 and 45 minutes, depending on how intensively you wish to practise.

1. **Rest into the position.** Lie on your back with your legs a little apart from each other and your arms slightly away from the sides of your body with your palms facing upwards. Cover yourself with a blanket if you need to, as your body temperature may drop in the practice. If this position is too uncomfortable, try raising your knees to release tension in your lower back, or choose any position that feels right for you.

2. **Become aware of your inner attitude.** Let it be. Allow and accept whatever happens in the experience as best you can. Let go of any ideas about self-improvement or personal development – mindfulness is about simply allowing yourself to be as you are in a deep and authentic way.

3. **Breathe.** Focus your attention on your breathing for a few minutes.

4. **Move your attention through your whole body, step by step.** Shift your attention from your breathing down to your toes. Feel whatever sensation you can feel. If you can't feel any sensation, just be aware of the absence of a sensation. Gradually move your attention up through your feet, lower legs, upper legs, pelvic area, lower torso, upper torso, shoulders, upper arms, lower arms and hands. Then up to your neck, face, back of your head and finally the top of your head. This whole process can take 15 to 30 minutes. Each time your mind drifts, notice what it was focusing on and bring your attention back to your breathing. Imagine your breath going into and out of each part of your body as you're being mindful of it.

5. **Imagine that your breath is sweeping up and down your body.** As you breathe in, imagine your in-breath starting at your toes and reaching the top of your head. As you breathe out, your out-breath sweeps from the top of your head down to your toes. This sensation can feel healing or relaxing.

6. **Just be.** For the last few minutes of this meditation, try letting go of all effort to be mindful and just be. Rest in your own inner sense of aliveness, of presence, of being.

7. **Stand up slowly.** Gently bring the meditation to a close. We hope this has been a deep and nourishing experience, so avoid jumping up straight away or you may feel dizzy. Get up gradually and mindfully, feeling the sensations in your body as you do so.

Record your experiences of the body scan meditation in Worksheet 5-3.

Worksheet 5-3		Body Scan Meditation Log			
Day	**Time I Practised**	**Did I Use the Audio, and If So, All of It?**	**How I Felt Before the Practice**	**Thoughts, Feelings and Bodily Sensations I Noticed During the Body Scan**	**How I Felt After the Body Scan**
Monday					
Tuesday					
Wednesday					
Thursday					

Day	Time I Practised	Did I Use the Audio, and If So, All of It?	How I Felt Before the Practice	Thoughts, Feelings and Bodily Sensations I Noticed During the Body Scan	How I Felt After the Body Scan
Friday					
Saturday					
Sunday					

In Figure 5-2, use the label *A* to indicate areas that felt relaxed or comfortable during the body scan meditation, *B* for areas of discomfort or pain and *C* for areas where you felt no sensation at all. This exercise helps you to reflect more deeply about your experience and can make you more mindful next time you practise.

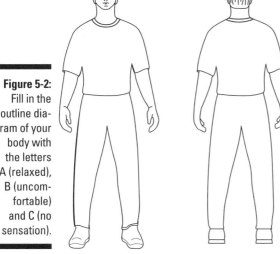

Front   Back

Figure 5-2: Fill in the outline diagram of your body with the letters A (relaxed), B (uncomfortable) and C (no sensation).

Unlocking emotions from your body

If you've experienced strong emotions in the past due to a loss, a highly stressful event or other circumstances, you may have automatically suppressed the emotions to protect yourself from the feeling. Some therapists believe that emotions get locked within certain parts of your physical body. Some even believe this can lead to disease in the part of your body that the emotion is locked in. For example, suppressing the pain of the loss of a loved one may have been followed with long-term discomfort in your abdomen area, or difficulty in digestion.

The body scan (explained in the earlier section 'Practising the body scan meditation') is a gentle way of approaching your body with mindful awareness,

allowing yourself to feel any sensations you may have suppressed. Tension is naturally released along with some emotions and past memories. This release of tension certainly isn't the aim of the body scan meditation, but can be a positive long-term side-effect. You may then find any physical tension has reduced and that you generally have a more positive outlook on life.

If you find the experience of mindfulness too emotional to cope with, seek the help of a professional therapist or mindfulness teacher who can support you through the experience in a way that you're comfortable with.

Overcoming common obstacles with the body scan

Here are some of the common difficulties that arise with the body scan. Look through the list to see if any of them apply to you. This may help to put your mind at rest if you had an unusual experience, which can happen, but is nothing to be alarmed about.

- ✔ **You fell asleep.** Doing so is very common. The idea is to 'fall awake' (become more aware) rather than asleep, but don't be hard on yourself if you end up snoozing. To overcome sleep, try practising at a different time of day, practise the body scan with your eyes open or have a cool shower before the practice. If you still keep falling asleep, try doing the meditation in a seated upright position, with your back supporting itself. If you *still* keep falling asleep, just accept it for now. With time, your body will learn to stay awake – it just takes practice. The most important thing is to keep practising, whether you fall asleep or not.

- ✔ **You couldn't feel any sensation.** This is another common experience. If you can't feel sensation in a particular part, or large parts of your body, that's okay. Just acknowledge and accept this – that's what mindfulness is all about. With time, you may feel more sensation, as the part of your brain that detects physical sensation begins to naturally strengthen. But if not, it doesn't matter.

- ✔ **You felt more anxious or stressed.** That's okay. Mindfulness isn't relaxation spelt differently. Sometimes you may not find the body scan relaxing. If you find it stressful, you may be trying too hard or hoping to achieve a certain experience. Just let that idea go if you can. If the anxiety keeps coming, explore the feeling within your body. Notice where you specifically feel the sensation and gently allow your attention to rest there. Don't be harsh or critical with yourself.

- ✔ **You felt bored or restless.** If you're an active person, you may find the body scan boring and begin to feel restless. Just notice the feeling of boredom or restlessness within your body. Become interested in the boredom or restlessness instead of trying to push it away. Watching the feelings of boredom, restlessness and difficulty in concentration is part and parcel of mindfulness. The experiences will pass with time.

✔ **You felt strong emotions.** Sometimes emotions that have been suppressed can become released during the body scan meditation. Your body can unconsciously hold unresolved issues as tension. As you relax into the body scan, the thoughts and emotions can arise into your conscious awareness and then be released. (See the sidebar 'Unlocking emotions from your body' for more information on this.)

✔ **You felt dizzy.** Feeling dizzy during the body scan isn't common, but can happen. If you feel dizzy as you practise, simply open your eyes and come out of the meditation for a few moments until your mind settles down. Then begin again, perhaps keeping your eyes open to steady yourself.

✔ **You felt physically uncomfortable.** Lying down still in one position can feel uncomfortable after some time, especially if you aren't used to it. Slowly and mindfully move your position. Try lying on top of your bed or use pillows under your knees or elsewhere to ensure you're more cosy and comfortable.

In Worksheet 5-4, record what sort of difficulties you encountered in the body scan meditation. Remember that these are quite common experiences, so don't judge the meditation as bad or feel that you did it wrong. Just gently persevere, whatever your inner critic seems to say. Then complete Worksheet 5-5.

Worksheet 5-4	**Monitoring My Body Scan Experiences**	
Difficulty	*Yes/No/A Little*	*How I Overcame the Difficulty*
I felt more pain in my body than I normally do.		
I wanted to stop the body scan.		
I couldn't concentrate.		
I fell asleep.		
I became more anxious, depressed or frustrated than when I started.		
I couldn't do the body scan.		
I didn't like the body scan.		
I cried.		
I couldn't see the point of the body scan.		

Worksheet 5-5	My Thoughts After the Body Scan

What did you find most difficult about the body scan?

_____

_____

What action can you take to help manage your difficulty?

_____

_____

Practising Sitting Meditation

Sitting meditation, also called expanding awareness meditation, lies at the heart of mindfulness meditation practice. The sitting position has been used for meditation for thousands of years and for good reason. Learn how to practise formal mindful sitting meditation in this section and discover ways of overcoming common challenges that may arise.

Listen to Track 3 on the audio (www.dummies.com/go/mindfulnessworkbookuk) for a wonderful 12-minute sitting meditation.

Exploring different sitting positions

How do you normally sit? If you're like most people, probably leaning against the back of a chair or sofa. While fine if you're relaxing, this position doesn't work so well with mindfulness meditation.

With sitting mindfulness meditation, you need to sit with a relatively straight back, not stiff or forced, but dignified, balanced and upright. This posture is an external representation of the kind of inner attitudes that you're aiming to adopt – open and awake to your moment-to-moment experience.

You can do sitting meditation on a chair or seated on the floor.

Sitting on a chair

Follow these tips so that it's easy to be upright and balanced and see Figure 5-3. If you find the instructions too prescriptive, just sit naturally upright. The inner attitudes of mindfulness are more important than your posture.

1. **Find a chair that's the right height for you.** When you sit, your knees should be lower than your hips by a few inches. Your feet should be flat on the ground or rest on a small stool.

2. **Tilt your chair slightly forwards.** Place a few magazines under the back legs. By tilting the chair forwards, your pelvis is rotated in such a way that your back adopts an upright posture quite naturally. Try it out!

3. **Place your hands wherever feels comfortable for you.** You could place a cushion on your lap and rest your hands there. Avoid placing your hands too far forwards as they drag your shoulders down.

4. **Allow your head to balance on your neck and shoulders.** Imagine your head is gently floating upwards, straightening your spine.

5. **Tilt your body forwards and backwards, left and right to find a central balanced place.** Then just be still at that point.

6. **You're ready to meditate!**

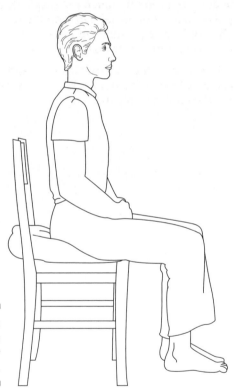

Figure 5-3:
Sitting on
a chair for
meditation.

Sitting on the floor

Many people practise meditation sitting cross-legged on the floor. The position is grounding, and many people prefer it to sitting on a chair.

The two main options are:

Burmese position

The Burmese position is a fairly comfortable cross-legged sitting position (as shown in Figure 5-4). Place a mat or a soft blanket on the floor. On top of that, place a firm meditation cushion or several soft cushions on top of each other.

1. **Have a stretch (especially your legs and back) to prepare yourself to sit.**

2. **Sit cross-legged on the cushion.** Allow the sides of your knees to touch the ground. If your knees don't touch the ground, use more cushions to support your knees or try one of the other positions suggested in this section.

3. **Allow the heel of your left foot to be close to or gently touch the inside thigh of your right leg.** Allow the right leg to be in front of the left leg, with the heel pointing towards your lower left leg. If your legs aren't that supple, adjust as necessary, always ensuring that you're as comfortable as possible.

4. **Invite your back to be quite straight but relaxed too.** Gently rock back and forth to find the point where your head is balanced on your neck and shoulders. Tuck your chin in slightly, so the back of your neck isn't straining.

Figure 5-4:
The
Burmese
position.

Kneeling position

If you choose to try the kneeling position, you need a meditation kneeling stool. You can purchase one online. See Figure 5-5 for how to use a meditation stool.

1. **Stretch your legs to prepare to sit.**

2. **Kneel on a carpet, blanket or mat on the floor.**

3. **Raise your bottom up and place the kneeling stool between your lower legs and bottom.**

4. **Gently sit back down on the kneeling stool.** Ensure that you're in a position that feels balanced and stable for you.

Figure 5-5:
The kneel-
ing position,
using a
meditation
stool.

Answer the quick questions in Worksheet 5-6 to reflect on your choice of posture for this sitting meditation.

Worksheet 5-6 **Thinking About My Choice of Position
for the Sitting Meditation**

Which position did you choose to use?

_____

What did you like or dislike about it?

_____

Did you sit upright? How did you check? (For example, use a mirror or ask a family member or housemate.)

_____

Exploring the stages of sitting meditation

Mindful sitting meditation is made up of five distinct stages. You may like to begin with practising one stage and move on to add an additional stage when you feel you've understood it. Alternatively, if you're feeling adventurous, dive in with the full sitting meditation and see how you go. Here are the five stages and how to practise them:

- **Mindfulness of breath**

  - Sit in an upright, dignified position if you can (described in the previous section).

  - Become aware of the physical sensation of your natural breathing wherever it's most predominant for you (for example, the chest or belly).

  - When your mind wanders off to other thoughts, as it naturally will, smile and gently bring your attention back to your breathing.

  - Allow your breathing to be natural. You breathe all night without any effort. So just be aware of the process.

- **Mindfulness of body**

  - Have a wider awareness of your body as a whole.

  - Notice all the sensations in your physical body as they fluctuate and change from moment to moment.

  - Gently bring your attention back to your body when it wanders.

  - If a certain part of your body causes discomfort, turn your attention towards that area and imagine your breathing going into and out of that part of your body. See if you can allow that sensation to simply be. Have an attitude of acceptance as best you can.

  - Remember, the sensation of your own natural breathing is also a bodily sensation that you can focus on.

- **Mindfulness of sounds**

  - Open your awareness to sounds.

  - Notice how your mind labels and judges sound. Be aware of that and go back to listening to the sound itself.

  - Be aware of the volume, pitch and quality of the sounds as they change from moment to moment.

  - Notice the silence, which is between and underneath all sounds. The sounds arise from a background of silence.

  - Let the sounds come to you instead of reaching out for the sounds.

  - Rest your attention on sounds.

- **Mindfulness of thoughts**

  - Now turn your attention inwards to thoughts.

  - Be aware of your thoughts in an impersonal way.

  - Remember that thoughts are just thoughts, not facts.

  - Watch thoughts arise and pass away, just like the sounds.

  - If you find it helpful, imagine clouds passing through the sky. Place your thoughts on the clouds and watch them come and go. You're taking a step back from your own thoughts.

✔ **Open awareness**

- In this final stage of the sitting meditation, allow your attention to be open.

- Notice whatever is most predominant in your awareness. It can be your breath, body, sounds, thoughts, emotions – it doesn't matter.

- If you find your mind gets caught in a train of thought, come back to an awareness of your breathing for a few moments and then go back to an open awareness.

- This practice can be tricky, so just have a go and try to be patient with yourself.

Practise the sitting meditation once a day for at least a week and record your experiences in Worksheet 5-7.

Worksheet 5-7		Sitting Meditation Log			
Day	*Time and Length of Practice*	*Stages of the Meditation I Did*	*How I Felt Before the Practice*	*Thoughts, Feelings and Bodily Sensations I Noticed*	*How I Felt After the Sitting Meditation*
Monday					
Tuesday					
Wednesday					
Thursday					
Friday					
Saturday					
Sunday					

Overcoming common issues

Many of the difficulties you may experience in the sitting meditation are similar to those you'd experience in the body scan. So begin by checking that section on overcoming issues. In addition, you may face:

✔ **You find it painful to sit for so long.** This problem is common for beginners if their back muscles aren't accustomed to holding them upright and still for long periods of time. If sitting is too uncomfortable for you, try slowly standing up, stretching mindfully with full awareness and then going back to sitting.

✔ **You feel a discomfort in your body that won't go away.** Try moving your attention toward the difficulty. If you feel okay, move your attention right into the centre of the difficult sensation and allow it to be there, together with an awareness of your breathing. Although it sounds counterintuitive, try to relax into the discomfort.

Explore the questions in Worksheet 5-8.

Worksheet 5-8   **Exploring Ways of Overcoming Difficulties**

If you felt a lot of discomfort or pain, what can you do to manage the discomfort?

_____

If you kept falling asleep, what changes can you make?

_____

If you experienced strong emotions, how can you manage them?

_____

If your mind wandered a lot, what attitudes can you try to develop to accept this for now?

_____

Trying Loving Kindness Meditation

This mindful exercise is called loving kindness, compassion or metta meditation. We recommend trying loving kindness meditation after you've had some experience with the body scan and sitting meditation.

This meditation is quite different compared to the other mindfulness exercises because it's about deliberately bringing images to mind and cultivating the positive emotion of well-wishing or compassion, both to yourself and others.

Some people love this meditation while others find it too challenging. Give it a go and if you find it difficult, stick with the sitting and body scan practices and come back to this one in a few months or so.

Preparing for loving kindness meditation

You can get cosy for this meditation! Find a nice, warm, comfortable place to sit. Wrap yourself in a blanket. As with the other meditations, switch off your gadgets to ensure that you won't be disturbed for 20 minutes or so. You don't have to sit in an upright position for this one if you don't want to.

You could prepare for this meditation by doing something kind and relaxing for yourself, like having a bath or getting a massage. Alternatively, you could go for a casual, mindful walk around the block to get you into a focused state of mind.

Fill in Worksheet 5-9.

Worksheet 5-9   Preparing for Loving Kindness Meditation

Where do you hope to practise this meditation that is sufficiently warm and comfortable?

When do you hope to practise this meditation?

Would you like to practise it on your own, or with a friend or family member?

Practising loving kindness meditation

Loving kindness meditation is made up of seven stages:

1. **Mindful breathing with gratitude.** Begin by feeling your natural breathing with a sense of affection. Feel thankful that you're breathing, nourishing your body with lovely oxygen!

2. **Well-wishing towards someone you find it easy to show affection to.**

   Choose someone with whom you have a simple, unconditionally loving relationship. Perhaps an aunt or uncle, your son or daughter, a spiritual or wise person that you respect or even your pet. (We suggest you don't choose your partner because that can be quite a complex relationship.)

   Visualise the person and, in your mind, say to yourself several times, slowly and thoughtfully: *'May you be well, may you be happy, may you be healthy, may you be free from suffering.'*

   Say it with kindness and affection.

3. **Well-wishing towards yourself.**

   Now transfer that same sense of well-wishing to yourself. Some people find this challenging, with difficult emotions arising. If you experience this, continue to explore the effect or leave this step out for now. You don't need to fight or struggle.

   Visualise yourself and wish yourself a sense of wellbeing. Say to yourself, several times: *'May I be well, may I be happy, may I be healthy, may I be free from suffering.'*

   Feel the words coming out of your heart area if you can. Feel as if you're absorbing any pleasant feelings that arise.

4. **Well-wishing towards someone neutral.**

   Now think of someone to whom you have neither particularly positive nor negative feelings. Perhaps a ticket seller at the railway station, the assistant at your local shop or someone you often see on the bus. As before, say *'May he/she be well, may he/she be happy, may he/she be healthy, may he/she be free from suffering.'*

   Visualise the person and wish them well, as best you can.

5. **Well-wishing towards someone difficult.**

   Uh oh. This step is often tricky. Think of someone who you don't particularly like; perhaps someone who irritates or annoys you. Essentially someone with whom you have a difficult relationship but who you're willing to work with today.

   Say 'May he/she be well, may he/she be happy, may he/she be healthy, may he/she be free from suffering.'

   Notice what emotions arise for you as you do this. Remember, you're not condoning any inconsiderate behaviour, you're just wishing them a sense of wellbeing rather than holding a grudge against them. The meditation makes no difference to the difficult person, but you may feel a weight coming off your shoulders as you let go of a sense of frustration with them.

6. **Well-wishing for all four of you together.**

   Imagine yourself, your loved one, your neutral person and your difficult person all together. See if you can wish everyone a sense of wellbeing together, in equal measure. After all, you're all living beings, seeking happiness in your own different ways.

7. **Well-wishing to everyone on the planet.**

   In this final stage, zoom out to the planet as a whole. Think about all the human beings in all the different countries around the world. All the families and friends. All the children and elderly people. Think of all the animals. All the creatures in the oceans, lakes and rivers. Wish them all wellness. Use the words: *'May we all be well, may we all be happy, may we all be healthy. May we all be free from suffering.'*

If the sentences that we've offered here don't resonate with you, choose your own words. The words aren't that important. What's important is your intention of well-wishing in each stage.

You don't have to do all the stages in this meditation. Pick and choose whichever stages you feel comfortable with – you're in control and can decide.

Practise this meditation every day for a week. Record your experience of the loving kindness meditation in Worksheet 5-10.

Worksheet 5-10	My Loving Kindness Meditation Log				
Day	*Time and Length of Practice*	*Who I Meditated on*	*How I Felt Before the Practice*	*Thoughts, Feelings and Bodily Sensations I Noticed*	*How I Felt After the Loving Kindness Meditation*
Monday					
Tuesday					
Wednesday					
Thursday					
Friday					
Saturday					
Sunday					

Overcoming possible issues

As well as the issues that may arise in the meditations that we cover in the previous sections, here are a few unique additional challenges in the loving kindness meditation and how to overcome them:

- ✔ **You didn't feel any compassion or affectionate feelings.** That's totally okay. All you need to do is wish a sense of wellbeing in each stage. You can't force emotions to arise. Whether the emotion arises or not doesn't really matter. What matters is your *intention* to wish that person or yourself a sense of wellness.

- ✔ **You felt worse after the meditation.** Sometimes because you're not used to evoking such emotions, this can happen. Feeling worse could actually be a good thing, as you're detoxing suppressed emotions and are now letting them go. If the emotions are overwhelming, have a break from the meditation and come back to it when you feel more grounded.

- ✔ **You couldn't feel any affection towards yourself.** Sadly, this problem is quite common. We live in such a strange society that says it's selfish to think about ourselves. If you always think about others and never about your own wellbeing, be gentle with yourself. Take your time. Come back to this practice in the future or go into it after doing some sitting meditation or a body scan practice.

- ✔ **You couldn't feel any compassion towards your difficult person.** This issue is also very common! Again, it's fine. If you can send any sort of positive well-wishing to that person, you're doing well. The process may even improve your relationship with that person.

Consider the questions in Worksheet 5-11 after trying the loving kindness meditation to reflect on your own experience.

Worksheet 5-11   Reflecting on the Loving Kindness Meditation

---

What did you enjoy about the practice?

What sort of difficulties arose for you, if any?

What did you notice when you sent well-wishing to yourself?

What did you notice when you sent well-wishing to a loved one?

Are there any other observations or experiences that you noticed?

Chapter 6

Living Mindfully Day to Day

Mindfulness is more than formal sitting meditation. You can practise it in your everyday life. In fact, the great thing about mindfulness is that it can permeate your relationships, work and home life and improve them by helping you fully pay attention and respond to life's challenges consciously, creatively and with wisdom.

In this chapter you discover how to do handy, short meditations. You can then use those mindful exercises whenever you have a bit of time, or if you're feeling stressed. This chapter also has lots of suggestions for integrating mindfulness into your relationships and physical activities. Finally, you'll find some suggestions for ways of getting a good night's sleep.

Remembering to be mindful is a big challenge. You can set a timer with a gentle bell noise every few hours if that's practical to remind you to be aware of what you're doing instead of acting automatically.

Short and Sweet: Using Mini Meditations

You don't need to set aside hours in your day to practise mindfulness like a Zen Buddhist monk – you can use short meditations in your everyday life. When I (Shamash) teach my online mindfulness course, most people are relieved to discover the benefits to be gained from these bite-sized three-minute meditations.

Short mindfulness meditations are portable, accessible and simple to do – ideal for most people's busy lives. They help to make your next activity more mindful and therefore more focused, productive and enjoyable.

Practising the breathing space meditation

The breathing space meditation is a short three-stage meditation that's often taught in mindfulness courses all over the world (listen to Track 6 on the audio at www.dummies.com/go/mindfulnessworkbookuk). The meditation is supposed to be about three minutes long, but that's just a guideline. You can practise for just a minute if you want, or for as long as ten minutes or more. The length of time you choose depends on how much time you have available and how you're feeling at the time. If you're feeling very stressed, you may want to do it for longer.

For the breathing space meditation, sit upright on a chair with a dignified posture. Not stiff, but away from the back of the chair with your back relatively straight and your head balanced centrally on your neck and shoulders (See Figure 5-3 in Chapter 5). Your posture impacts on the quality of the experience because your body and mind are intimately connected. Sitting up straight signals to your mind that you're doing something different and a more mindful mind-set is easier to create.

If you feel overwhelmed with emotion, try just sitting up straight, closing your eyes and being still. See if you can keep your eyes still too, behind your eyelids. Just doing this for a few minutes, together with some deep breathing, can help you to find some respite.

The breathing space meditation is made up of three stages: A for awareness, B for breath and C for consciously expanding.

- ✔ **Step A – Awareness inwards.** In this stage, become aware of three aspects of yourself: your physical sensations, your emotions and your thoughts. This part only takes about a minute or two. Here's how to do this in a little more detail:

  - **Physical sensations.** Get a sense of your physical bodily sensations. You may notice some parts of your body feeling tense or uncomfortable, and other parts warm or relaxed. Notice all sensations if you can to bring yourself into the present moment.

  - **Emotions.** Ask yourself, 'How am I feeling at the moment?' Notice your current emotional state. If you know what the emotion is, label it gently in your mind. If you're not sure what the emotion is, that's okay too – just feel it. In particular, notice where you feel your current emotion within your body.

  - **Thoughts.** Now turn your attention to your thoughts. Simply watch these thoughts without getting too drawn in, judgemental or caught up if you can. Watch the thoughts as if they aren't yours, but just neutral experiences arising in awareness.

- ✔ **Step B – Breath.** Now, bring your attention to your breathing. Feel the whole of your in- and out-breath for about one minute. If you can, feel your breathing down in your belly (your lower abdomen). You're gathering your attention into your breath, using your breath as a stable place to rest your focus.

- ✔ **Step C – Consciously expanding.** Open up your awareness from your breathing to your whole body. Step B was a focused attention. In this stage, your attention is more wide and spacious, feeling all the sensations in your complete body, with a sense of kindness and curiosity if you can. Allow space for all sensations to just be there, including the sensation of your breathing. Do this for about a minute too.

If you want to lengthen this meditation to ten minutes or so, just lengthen the amount of time you spend on each stage of the process.

Try the breathing space meditation three times a day for the next week, using the audio (Track 6) or the guidance above, and write down your experiences in Worksheet 6-1.

Worksheet 6-1	The Breathing Space Meditation			
Day	**Time I Practised**	**Thoughts I Noticed**	**Feelings I Noticed**	**Physical Sensations I Noticed**	**How I Felt Afterwards**
Monday				
Tuesday				
Wednesday				
Thursday				
Friday				
Saturday				
Sunday				

Answering the questions in Worksheet 6-1 is useful because doing so makes you more curious about your own experiences. Curiosity is a good friend of mindfulness! When you're curious about your experiences, you're less likely to be critical or judgemental. And if you do find yourself being judgemental, remember, you can be curious about that – notice where you feel it in your body, how long it lasts and how you let it go.

Discovering the mini breath meditation

The mini breath meditation is one of the simplest and yet most powerful meditations that we've ever learnt. Here's how it goes:

1. **Sit on a chair in a comfortable yet upright balanced position, away from the back of the chair so that you're self-supporting your body if you can.** Close your eyes if that feels okay with you.

2. **Become aware of your breath around the area of your belly.** If you can't feel it there, just feel your breathing wherever you can – around your nose or chest for example. Focus on your breath.

3. **When your mind wanders off to other thoughts, notice what you were thinking about and gently guide your attention back to your breath.**

4. **After a few minutes, gently open your eyes and be mindful of whatever you do next.**

You can do this mini breath meditation at any time of day – not necessarily in a sitting posture. You can feel your breathing when you're in a traffic jam, waiting in a queue in a coffee shop or while listening to a customer who's complaining about something. You can feel your breathing anywhere. The nice thing is, no matter how forgetful you might be, you'll never forget to take your breathing with you wherever you go.

Practise the mini breath meditation every day for a week. If you're focusing on the breathing space meditation (described in the preceding section) this week, you can do this one the following week. Note down your experience in Worksheet 6-2.

Worksheet 6-2		Mini Breath Meditation		
Day	*What Time Did I Do It?*	*How Did I Feel Before The Meditation?*	*How Did I Feel After the Meditation?*	*Any Other Observations?*
Monday				
Tuesday				

Day	What Time Did I Do It?	How Did I Feel Before The Meditation?	How Did I Feel After the Meditation?	Any Other Observations?
Wednesday				
Thursday				
Friday				
Saturday				
Sunday				

In mindfulness, awareness of breath is the cornerstone of the practice. Because focusing on your breath brings you straight back into the present moment, it's often calming and feels like coming home – it has a sense of comfort and stability about it. Think of breath awareness like an anchor that grounds you in the here and now and protects you from the winds of change that try to blow you off balance.

Centring yourself with the mini grounding meditation

This meditation is about helping you to feel centred and grounded. The short exercise is particularly helpful when you feel flustered, frantic or just fed up with the world.

In this meditation, your feet need to be firmly on the ground.

1. **Sit in a chair in a dignified, upright position. Gently close your eyes, if you like.**

2. **Feel the physical sensation of your feet on the floor and the weight of your body on the chair.**

3. **Each time you breathe out, allow your body to sink a little deeper into the chair and let your feet feel more rooted to the earth.**

4. **If you like visualising, imagine your body rooted to the earth, flexible but unshaken by the changing thoughts and emotions that you may be experiencing.**

5. **After a few minutes, gently bring the exercise to a close and continue whatever you were doing with a focused, mindful attention.**

Being Mindful in Everyday and Intimate Relationships

Mindfulness lies at the heart of relationships. Through cultivating a greater awareness of both your own internal state and that of the other person, you're far better able to connect in a deep, authentic and satisfying way.

In this section we focus first on your key relationships with the most significant people in your life, then move on to considering relationships in general with the people you interact with every day.

Discovering how well your relationships are going

The deeper the mindful awareness between you and your partner, the deeper the quality of your relationship.

Assess how well your most significant relationships are going in Worksheet 6-3. Examples of key relationships may be your partner, parents, children, close friends and perhaps work colleagues or managers.

Worksheet 6-3		Assessing My Key Relationships			
Relationship	How Well is the Relationship Going? (/10)	What do I Like About the Person?	What do I Find Difficult about the Person?	How Does My Body Feel when I Imagine the Person?	Would I like to Work on Improving this Relationship?
Boyfriend	Quite well. (7/10)	He's funny, thoughtful, spontaneous.	He often complains about trivial things.	Tense shoulders, jaw a bit clenched.	Yes, definitely.

By completing this worksheet, you now have a better idea of the relationships in your life you want to work on. Use this knowledge as you read on about ways of applying mindfulness with those relationships.

Be mindful of any self-critical thoughts popping up in your head as you fill in the worksheet. Try not to use the results to judge yourself or others in your life. If you didn't discover many positive relationships, at least you have the courage to take a look. You can now begin to discover mindful ways of building or improving your relationships.

Finding out how mindfulness helps relationships

Mindfulness helps improve the quality (and perhaps quantity!) of your relationships in three different ways.

Dr Marsha Lucas, the author of *Rewire Your Brain for Love* (Hay House) explains the following ways in which mindfulness improves relationships:

- ✔ **Mindfulness reduces stress.** If you and your partner are feeling stressed out, you're more likely to be reactive to small problems. Tiny issues can get blown out of proportion, and before you know it, you're both in the midst of a full-blown argument and saying horrible things to each other, which you don't really mean to do. Regular practice of mindfulness meditation reduces your stress levels so unnecessary arguing is less likely to take place.

- ✔ **Mindfulness integrates your emotions with your intellect.** Researchers are discovering that the regular practice of mindfulness activates and strengthens the connections between your prefrontal cortex (your intellectual brain) with areas like the amygdala (your more emotional brain). You can therefore deal with your emotions in a more integrated way.

  For example, imagine your partner calls, sounding cold and controlling, and asks you to go to the shops to get some food and start cooking dinner. Two different scenarios can occur:

  You react emotionally. Without thinking, you shout back on the phone explaining how many times you've had to do the shopping and cooking this week and how tired you feel. Your emotional brain immediately reacts out of anger.

  You feel the sensation of anger rising in your chest but think, 'This is just a feeling that's arising'. You take a few mindful breaths and feel back in control. You ask your partner about her day, and she explains that her boss has been putting too much pressure on her and apologises for all the late nights she's been coming home. You both agree to have a light meal tonight and make sure that you relax and eat well at the weekend.

  Mindfulness is the difference!

- ✔ **Mindfulness builds your empathy.** As you become more mindful, you spend less time on automatic pilot and more time being conscious and aware of your own state of mind (head to Chapter 4 for more about doing and being modes of mind). This enables you to attune to your feelings and feel a sense of empathy for yourself when things aren't going so well. And more empathy for yourself has a great side effect – it generates more empathy for your partner too. Empathy is all about a sense of caring, kindness and understanding – the heart of relationships.

Cast your mind back to the last time you reacted towards someone in a negative way, with an emotion like anger or fear. Then, answer the questions in Worksheet 6-4.

Worksheet 6-4   **Assessing Negative Emotions**

What was the emotion you felt?

_____

Was there space between your emotion and your reaction, or was it automatic?

_____

Where did you feel the emotion in your body?

_____

How did you feel just before your emotional reaction? (For example, tired? Hungry? Frustrated? Happy?)

_____

How did you deal with the situation in the end?

_____

What will you try next time? (For example, mini meditation, go for a walk, mindful breathing as you're listening to the other person.)

_____

Seeing relationships as a mindful practice

Relationships can be a challenging yet fulfilling mindfulness practice. Mindful relationships are an oasis of sanity in a world of high-speed communication but less real connection. Making a relationship more mindful involves a two-pronged approach. Firstly, you need to practise some mindfulness meditation daily to help retrain your brain to be less reactive and more focused. Secondly, follow the steps below, moment by moment, to have a mindful conversation with your chosen person.

✔ **Stop.** Try doing a mini mindful meditation before you see the person. This could be as simple as feeling a few mindful breaths.

✔ **Look.** Be aware of the other person's posture and facial expression. Is she looking sad, happy or some other emotion?

✔ **Listen.** Be aware of her tone of voice as well as what she is actually saying. Quite often people's tone of voice determines what they're trying to communicate to you.

✔ **Inner awareness.** Notice your own thoughts. Are you judging, criticising or thinking about what you're going to say next? Take a step back from your thoughts if you can, as you listen. Be mindful of your emotions as the other person speaks. Honour your own feelings without allowing them to overwhelm you. Feel your breathing or the sensation of your feet on the floor to help ground you.

✔ **Pause.** Reflect for a few moments before you respond. This pause gives the wise part of your brain time to reflect and ponder on the best response.

✔ **Speak.** When you speak, listen to the sound of your own voice. Notice if your voice is calm and resonant, or harsh and cutting.

Try the tips above and then answer the questions in Worksheet 6-5.

Worksheet 6-5   Reviewing the Mindful Conversation Exercise

Who did you try the mindful conversation exercise with?

_____

What did you notice about the person?

_____

What did you notice about your own thoughts, feelings and bodily sensations?

_____

What could you do next time to be even more mindful? (For example, do a mini meditation before the conversation, focus on your breathing a bit more, pay more attention to the other person's posture as she speaks?)

_____

One way of improving the quality of your communication is through mindfulness. The next time you talk to someone you know, be mindful and record what you noticed in Worksheet 6-6. You'll respond to the person with a greater understanding. This ability to listen is the most powerful way of improving relationships – everyone likes to be heard and understood.

Worksheet 6-6		Applying Mindfulness to My Relationships			
Relationship	*Their Tone of Voice*	*Their Possible Emotional State*	*Their Body Language*	*My Attitude Towards Them*	*What I Learned About Myself*
Best friend.	Soft, slow.	Calm.	Relaxed, open.	Affectionate, loving.	I'm comfortable with her.

Exploring the mirror of relationships

All relationships, whether with a partner or work colleague, are like a mirror. Relationships can help you see your own desires, judgements and expectations. Seeing relationships as a mirror can be hugely transformative.

What does it mean to see relationships as a mirror? When communicating to someone, the way you feel, think and act indicates something about your own nature. The relationship not only shows you what the other person is like, but also it shows what you're like. To discover this, you need to be mindful of the way you think and react to others.

For example, maybe you don't like your colleague because she gets angry so easily. She snaps at the smallest problem. But what about you? Maybe you get angry quite easily too? Or perhaps you turn your anger inwards and are quite self-critical when things don't go your way.

Finding out about yourself helps. By being mindful, you learn about your typical, habitual ways of reacting to others and begin exploring ways to let them go. You can then be less judgemental of both others and yourself. After all, they're not perfect, just like you. Everyone is different, and although you won't become close to everyone you meet, at least you understand them and see a bit of them in yourself too. Try filling in Worksheet 6-7.

Worksheet 6-7   **Discovering Yourself through Relationships**

Think about someone you have a relationship with (for example, a colleague, friend, partner). Write the person's name here.

_____

_____

What do you like about the person? Do you like that same quality in yourself?

_____

_____

_____

What do you dislike about the person? Is there any aspect of that quality within yourself too?

_____

_____

_____

Dealing with difficult relationships

Most people experience at least one difficult relationship. Perhaps many of your relationships are difficult – that's not something to be ashamed of. Relationships can stir up all sort of challenging emotions. In this section you discover how to manage tricky relationships more mindfully.

Follow these tips to handle difficult relationships:

- **Regular meditation practice.** Meditating regularly is the best way to turn down your stress response when you next encounter the difficult person. You'll be more mindful of the situation and will respond wisely instead of reacting by withdrawing or attacking.

- **Move toward your difficult emotions if you can.** An absolutely key aspect of mindfulness is to learn to move towards difficult thoughts, feelings and bodily sensations. Avoiding difficulties creates an unhelpful, negative state of mind. By approaching difficulties, you feel more empowered and in control, and quite often the difficulties don't seem as bad as you thought, or may even dissipate altogether. Chapter 9 has more about dealing with difficult emotions.

✔ **Be aware of the person's positive qualities.** Nobody is all bad. Everyone has good qualities. Your boss always makes sure that you're paid on time. Your aunt cooks delicious food. Your friend's partner always pays for dinner. Be mindful of people's positive qualities, not just the negative ones.

✔ **Anchor yourself with your breath.** While you're in the company of someone difficult, feel the sensation of your breathing. You could even do a mini meditation just before the meeting, focusing fully on your breath. This meditation helps to get your head out of the 'story' of your relationship with this person and focuses on the now.

✔ **See the person as separate from their behaviour.** If you behave badly for an evening or in a situation, that doesn't mean *you're* a bad person – you just made a mistake. In the same way, consider a person's behaviour as separate from that person. You are not your behaviour, and they are not their behaviour. You can disagree with the behaviour rather than the whole person. You can then say, for example: 'I love you, but felt disappointed with the way you behaved yesterday.'

✔ **Think why.** Whatever the person has done to hurt or annoy you was done for a reason. Perhaps he's had a tough childhood, a bad set of genes or just a rough day. Think about why he behaves the way he does, and you won't feel so threatened by him. You'll understand the underlying reason for his actions and therefore you may be a bit more forgiving. For example, if your colleague always ignores you in conversations, maybe it's because you remind her of her sister who was really nasty to her when she was growing up, or maybe her mother always ignored her, or perhaps the part of her brain that deals with empathy or attention just isn't working that well. Considering these possibilities may foster compassion in you towards that person.

Think of a difficult person and complete the questions in Worksheet 6-8.

Worksheet 6-8   Mindfully Re-evaluating a Difficult Relationship

---

What meditation or mini meditation can you do before you next meet this person?

Try moving towards the difficult emotions that arise while you're in conversation with the person. Feel it in your body. Try to feel the sensations rather than react to the sensations. What effect does this have? What emotions did you notice? Be curious and inquisitive about your experience.

Note down some positive qualities about this person.

Feel your breathing as you listen to this person. Again, be curious. What effect does this have?

Think of a few reasons why this person may be behaving in a difficult way.

Notice what effect answering these questions has on the quality of your relationship. Does the relationship feel just as difficult, or less so? If you found the process worked, try the questions again next time you meet the person, or with a different relationship.

Exercising Mindfully

When you're stressed and exhausted, your mind and body are obviously not in ship-shape condition. Exercising regularly, eating well and having a daily routine of meditation to keep your mind calm are important, especially if you give a lot of your energy to others. If you look after yourself first, you can better help others because you're less likely to be drained mentally and physically.

Exercise is a great way to boost endorphins (hormones associated with happiness and reduced pain) and be mindful at the same time. If you're able to exercise, you can always start with some mindful walking and build up to more demanding exercise. (Check with your doctor first if you have health problems.)

Clarifying the elements of mindful physical activity

Much of this book explains how to be mindful while still, whether in seated meditation or lying down for the body scan. Practising mindfulness while your body is moving is an important step in your journey to mindful living because you probably spend a fair amount of your day moving about engaging in all sorts of physical activities rather than just exercise itself. Life feels better in a mindful mode!

Here are the key principles of mindful physical activity:

- ✔ You're fully aware instead of doing the activity automatically.
- ✔ You change your routine every now and then to break any habits and try something new.
- ✔ You avoid being too competitive or judgemental. Instead you enjoy the activity for what it is.
- ✔ You focus on the experience of the present moment rather than how things were last time, or on how you want to be super-fit in the future.
- ✔ When your mind gets caught up in other thoughts, you bring your attention back to the activity.
- ✔ As far as you can, you enjoy the activity!

If you always go running with your headphones on full blast, or daydream when doing the housework, try answering the questions in Worksheet 6-9. They may inspire you to have a go at being mindful in your activities.

Worksheet 6-9   **Considering Mindful Exercise**

List the benefits of being **unmindful** when you do your activities.

List the benefits of being **mindful** when doing activities.

List the most enjoyable moments while doing a physical activity. Were they mindful or automatic?

Discovering examples of mindful physical exercise

In this section, you discover some ways of being mindful in various physical activities. Remember, these are just examples – every activity can be done mindfully!

Slow mindful walking

Mindful walking is actually a core mindfulness practice. When you feel restless, it's a great way to be fully mindful. You can do this at home or perhaps outside in a garden or even in a park if you don't mind other people watching! Try to practise for ten minutes or so.

1. **Stand upright in a stable position.** Gently lean to the left and right, forwards and backwards, to find a central balanced standing posture. Let your knees unlock slightly and soften any unnecessary tension in your face. Allow your arms to hang naturally by your sides. Ensure your body is grounded like a tree, firmly rooted to the ground with dignity and poise.

2. **Become aware of your breath.** Come into contact with the flow of each inhalation and exhalation. Enjoy breathing.

3. **Now slowly lean onto your left foot and notice how sensations in your feet change.** Then slowly shift your weight onto your right foot. Again perceive how the sensations fluctuate from moment to moment.

4. **When you're ready, gradually shift most of your weight onto your left foot, so almost no weight is on the right foot.** Slowly take your right heel off the ground. Pause for a moment here. Notice the sense of anticipation about something as basic as taking a step. Now lift your right foot off the ground and place it heel first in front of you. Become aware of the weight of your body shifting from the left to the right foot. Continue gradually to place the rest of the right foot flat and firmly on the ground. Notice the weight continue to shift from left to right.

5. **Continue to walk in this very slow, mindful way for as long as you want.** Be aware of the different stages of the movement in your legs – lifting, moving, placing, shifting your weight, lifting, moving, placing and so on.

Does slow mean boring?

Earlier this year, I (Shamash) attended a week-long mindfulness retreat with Zen Master Thich Nhat Hanh in Nottingham. Thich Nhat Hanh, considered one of the greatest mindfulness teachers alive today, began slow, mindful walking with about 500 people walking behind him. The experience was very calming and the walking was extremely slow. Everyone was walking in silence. I noticed a young child, about seven years old, dressed up in a Spiderman outfit, approaching the crowd. He was jumping around as his mother guided him towards the group. He looked at everyone, turned to his mother and said 'Oh no mum, I don't have to do that slow mo walking again, do I? It's boring!' The sight of Spiderman calling it slow mo walking was very funny.

Remember not to take mindfulness too seriously – have fun with it too.

After having a go at the slow mindful walk above, make some notes in Worksheet 6-10.

Worksheet 6-10   Evaluating the Mindful Walking

How did you feel physically and emotionally before doing the mindful walking?

_____

What did you discover about your body, thoughts or emotions when walking mindfully?

_____

How do you feel at the end of the mindful walking?

_____

Mindfulness doesn't always lead to pleasant experiences. After doing some mindful walking, you may feel frustrated, angry, tired or sad. That's not a bad thing. These feelings are just emotions arising from the experience. Who knows, maybe the emotions are being released from your body and you'll feel much better later on. Mindfulness is about simply accepting your experience and learning from it.

Mindful tennis

Here's a suggestion for a way of being mindful while playing tennis.

1. **Begin with a few mindful breaths.** Feel the sensation of your breath as you're standing or sitting in preparation for the game.

2. **Become aware of your surroundings.** Notice the weather, the court, what your opponent looks like.

3. **Allow yourself to notice what your own body feels like.** Are there any areas of tension? What thoughts are going through your mind? How are you feeling?

4. **As you serve your shot, begin by actually feeling the tennis ball in your hand.** Allow your body to relax as much as you can before you throw the ball up and hit it.

5. **Be mindful as you play.** Watch the ball. Feel the physical sensations as you hit each shot. Feel the wind as you wait. Keep your attention on the game.

6. **Let go of the outcome.** Just play your best and don't worry too much about the score. You'll play better if you focus in the moment rather than on the result.

Have a go at doing a mindful physical activity. It could be anything: football, tennis, badminton, darts, cycling, swimming, rugby, walking, running, skiing, table tennis, squash. You can even do activities like ironing, cooking, cleaning, washing the dishes or vacuuming mindfully. Practise the activity with beginner's mind (as if you're doing it for the first time – refer to Chapter 3 for more on beginner's mind).

Worksheet 6-11	**Assessing My Mindful Exercising**

Which activity did you do?

_____

How long did you practise for?

_____

How was the experience different compared to normal? What did you notice?

_____

What other activities can you practise mindfully, and when?

_____

Mindful sports coaching

Mindfulness training is a great way of boosting sports performance because most sports are about maintaining a calm, focused attention. If you're too tense, your mind drains your energy too fast. If your attention is too relaxed, your mind drifts off. If you get too stressed, angry or frustrated, you're channelling your energy in the wrong direction. If you focus on winning, then your attention is on the result, not on the game. The finest sports people know how to manage their minds when playing the game.

I (Shamash) have coached sportsmen and women in mindfulness, and they say it improves their game and helps them to enjoy their sport more. Regular mindfulness makes it easier to focus and stay centred. The mindful coaching also helps to improve their personal relationships as they start to live mindfully – a lovely side effect!

Overcoming Insomnia

Sleep. If it comes naturally to you, you're a lucky person. A good night's sleep is so easy to take for granted. For many people, insomnia is something they battle with every night.

If you suffer from insomnia, begin by trying the following:

- ✔ Avoid watching television or being on the computer late into the evening.
- ✔ Cut out stimulants like coffee or cigarettes.
- ✔ Avoid aerobic exercise in the evening.
- ✔ Have a relatively cool, dark and quiet bedroom.
- ✔ Have a sleep routine – try to go to bed at the same time every day.

In this section, try our suggestions to overcome your sleep problems using mindfulness.

Mindfulness helps to reduce your stress and cut down on rumination (worrying), and can have a side effect of greater relaxation. For these reasons, mindfulness is a powerful tool for managing insomnia.

- ✔ Do some meditation, mindful walking, mindful yoga or other mindfulness exercise before going to bed. Some people find it more effective than others, so give it a try to see if it works for you. The meditation needs to be a relaxing rather than energising one.

- ✔ If you wake up at night and can't get back to sleep, try doing the body scan meditation as you lie in bed, on your own or using the audio that accompanies the book. (Track 2 on the accompanying audio.)

- ✔ If you find your mind racing at night, turn your attention to your breathing. Place one hand on your belly and feel your breathing until you drift off to sleep.

- ✔ Here's a mindful technique a friend swears by. Count as many different sounds as you can hear. For example, your breathing, the noise of traffic in the distance, a plane passing over, your partner shuffling around (hopefully not snoring too loudly!). By the time you get to six or seven sounds, you may be asleep. If not, just keep going.

- ✔ Count your exhalations. Each time you breathe out, say to yourself 'one', then on the next outbreath 'two' and so on. Every time you get to ten, start again from one. It's a more relaxing version of counting sheep!

- ✔ If you really can't sleep, don't fight with it. Try sitting up and doing some mindfulness of breath meditation or some slow mindful walking, as described earlier in this chapter. Even some gentle mindful yoga may help to relax you.

A lot of these techniques work because you shift your mind away from your worries and on to something else. Even worrying about the fact that you're not sleeping can often prevent you from falling asleep. So, as best you can, let go of your worries and try the above approaches. Even if you don't fall asleep, at least you get to do lots of mindfulness, which in *some* ways is even more healthy than sleep!

Keep a sleep diary for a week in Worksheet 6-12. Note down what mindfulness meditations or mindful exercises you did every day and what effect they had. Did you sleep well?

Worksheet 6-12	My Sleep Diary			
Day	*Mindfulness Practices I Used During the Day*	*Mindfulness Practices I Used at Night*	*Number of Hours I Slept*	*Quality of My Sleep*
Monday				
Tuesday				
Wednesday				
Thursday				
Friday				
Saturday				
Sunday				

Chapter 7

Getting Started on an Eight-week Mindfulness Course

· ·

In This Chapter

▶ Preparing yourself for the course

▶ Engaging in the first half of the course

▶ Discovering the basics of mindful practice

· ·

Mindfulness has become so popular in the West because of the research carried out by Dr Jon Kabat-Zinn and colleagues at the University of Massachusetts Medical School back in 1979. Kabat-Zinn developed a course called Mindfulness-based Stress Reduction or MBSR. It's an eight-week secular course in mindfulness for people who want to reduce their stress levels.

The course has now been running for over 30 years and in that time probably hundreds of thousands of people have completed it. Adaptations of the course are now used in schools, universities, prisons and workplace settings. In this and Chapter 8, we outline an eight-week mindfulness course based on the meditations used in MBSR.

If you prefer to learn this mindfulness course online, with audio downloads, weekly emails and online group support, visit www.livemindfulonline.com.

This mindfulness course is *not* the best thing to do if you're in the midst of an episode of depression. If you're not sure what to do, talk to your doctor or a suitably trained and experienced mindfulness-based therapist. Practising this mindfulness course on your own may also not be suitable if you suffer from psychosis or bipolar disorder. Check with a health professional first if you have any concerns.

Preparing for an Eight-week Course in Mindfulness

You need to prepare yourself before starting an eight-week mindfulness course so that you know what to expect and what sort of commitment to give. You may be tempted to just dive in, and nothing's stopping you. But if you prepare yourself for what lies ahead, you're in the best possible position to complete the course and be able to navigate any potential obstacles.

Discovering the evidence

If you like to know the scientific basis for doing things, read on! If not, you can skip this section, knowing that the course you're about to embark upon has been found to have a range of benefits for most people.

Here are just some of the benefits noted in the research into the effectiveness of an eight-week mindfulness course:

✔ 70 per cent reduction in anxiety.

✔ Improvements to immune system.

✔ Fewer visits to the doctor.

✔ Longer and better sleep, with less sleep disturbance.

✔ Continued reduction in anxiety, at least three years after course is completed.

✔ Reduction in anger, tension and depression.

✔ Improvement in many physical conditions like psoriasis, chronic fatigue and fibromyalgia.

The evidence is so good that three-quarters of doctors in the UK have said that all their patients would benefit from learning mindfulness.

Working by yourself or with a therapist

If you want to use this book to do the eight-week course yourself, you need to make time for it:

✔ Set aside one or two hours every week to read the content for that week and do the mindfulness exercises.

✔ Set aside at least half an hour daily to do the recommended mindfulness meditations.

You need to actually *make* the time rather than *find* the time because your day is probably already pretty full with other activities. See Chapter 9 for ideas on ways of making time to practise the formal mindfulness meditations.

You may not be ready to commit to a full mindfulness course with the time and effort that it takes. Perhaps you're just curious to get a taste of what MBSR is about. In this case, you could commit to do the following for four to eight weeks – effectively a light version of the course. Choose from one of the following:

✔ Do the recommended mindfulness meditations every other day rather than daily.

✔ Choose shorter ten- to fifteen-minute meditations every day rather than the 30-minute practices recommended.

✔ Just practise being more mindful in your everyday activities and do the breathing space meditation everyday (Chapter 6 describes the breathing space meditation).

If you're learning mindfulness with a teacher or therapist, you may have bought this book to complement those sessions. If this is the case, follow your teacher's advice regarding working through the book.

Making the commitment and preparing yourself

In some ways, doing the MBSR course is like learning any other skill. You need to make sure that you put the time in to learn the concepts and practise your new skill regularly. But in other ways, it's very different. Here are the main ways mindfulness is different to, say, learning a new language:

- ✔ If you get bored of learning a new language, you can just give up. With mindfulness, you can expect feelings of boredom sometimes and work with them, rather than act on them.

- ✔ With learning a language, you learn words and concepts. With mindfulness, you go beyond words and just watch, observe and notice what arises.

- ✔ In language learning, you learn a certain set of things. With mindfulness, you learn in an on-going way about yourself, how your mind works and its patterns, and your relationship to the world and other people.

- ✔ With a language, you eventually become an expert. With mindfulness, the less you feel like an expert and the more you feel like a beginner, the better!

Engaging in the eight-week course

We've broken down this eight-week course into two distinct halves. This first half of the course is about introducing you to mindfulness, turning your attention to your inner experiences and noticing what happens. In a nutshell, weeks one to four are about honing your attention. You'll learn about the nature of your own mind, how your focus naturally drifts off and how to gently keep shifting your attention back with a mindful attitude. The second half (explored in Chapter 8) is about responding to difficulties in a more mindful way that's helpful and soothing instead of making things worse for yourself. You also begin to explore more ways of living mindfully.

So, here you are – at the start of the eight-week course. How do you feel about it? Are you looking forward to it, or a bit apprehensive? Record your thoughts and feelings in Worksheet 7-1.

Worksheet 7-1   My Feelings About the Mindfulness Course

What do you hope to achieve from doing the eight-week mindfulness course?

What obstacles do you foresee in completing the course?

How could you overcome them?

What first small step could you take today, to begin preparing yourself for the mindfulness course?

Week One: Automatic Pilot

The intention for this week is to understand the automatic pilot mode of mind and explore mindfulness as a different mode of mind.

Have you ever had the experience of walking along, totally lost in thought? You were walking, but weren't conscious of the process. You were walking on automatic pilot. You may have also experienced this when driving a car and arriving at your destination with no concept of how you got there, or perhaps doing your work and yet thinking about something else.

To be on automatic pilot from time to time is fine. However, if you're on automatic pilot most of the day, some key problems arise:

✔ You miss out on really experiencing and enjoying your life.

✔ You could be having negative or unhelpful automatic thoughts that you're not really aware of, and so are not able to change or even question them. (Head to Chapter 4 for a more detailed explanation of automatic thoughts and how to deal with them.)

✔ You relate to your emotions as problems to be solved rather than messengers to be accepted and experienced.

✔ It's harder to be creative or change the way you live your life.

✔ You can end up behaving in situations or in relationships in the same habitual way.

So in this mindfulness course, the first step is just to become more aware of your habitual, automatic tendencies and begin to start doing small things more mindfully.

Mindful eating

To explore automatic pilot, begin with a simple exercise of mindful eating. If you like, read through the instructions and write down your experience after each stage. Take at least ten minutes to do the mindful eating. The longer it takes, the better!

The purpose of starting this course with mindful eating is also to show you that mindfulness isn't just about meditation. You can achieve a mindful state through any activity if you give that activity your full attention. Well, apart from sleeping perhaps!

Place a small piece of food, like a cranberry, sultana or raisin in your hand. Think of the way a baby picks up something new and looks, explores and enjoys it. Spend a few minutes looking at the colour and texture of the food. Feel it in your fingers and observe your fingers holding it. Hold it up to the light. Is it translucent? What colour is it exactly? Record your observations from the exercise in Worksheet 7-2.

Worksheet 7-2   **Mindful Eating Exercise**

What do you notice about your food's appearance? Record colour, reflection, shape. Be as specific as you can.

Rotate the food between your fingers and thumb. Notice the texture of the food. Close your eyes to tune into the sense of touch more deeply. Feel the shape of the object and its weight. Gently squeeze the food and see if you can get a sense of the texture of its inner contents. Take your time.

What does the food feel like? Try to describe it as best you can.

Hold the food to your ear. Rotate it gently between your thumb and finger and listen to it. When you've done this, bring your arm back down mindfully.

Did you hear any sound? If not, what was it like to not be able to hear anything?

Bring the food towards your nose. Feel the sensations in your arm as you bring the food towards your nose. Notice at what point you're able to pick up some scent. What does it smell like? Did the experience evoke any memories?

Bring the food towards your mouth. Are you salivating? If so, your body has already begun the first stage of digestion. Touch the food gently to your lips to see what sensations you can detect. Place the food on your tongue and feel its weight. Move the food around your mouth, noticing how skilled your tongue is at doing this. Place the food between two teeth and slowly bring your teeth together. Observe the phenomenon of tasting and eating. Spot the range of experiences.

Describe in as much detail as you can what your experience was like, of eating the food. The taste, scent and texture as you chewed it. The way it broke down in your mouth. The way the taste spread. At what point you swallowed it. Whether or not your attention drifted to other thoughts.

How do you feel about the experience?

How does it compare to your usual experience of eating?

You don't have to enjoy this experience. If you don't like the food you chose, it's interesting and insightful to notice how your mind and emotions react as you go through your senses and eat it. Any piece of food is fine, including chocolate, marshmallows or a crisp!

Perhaps you felt like you couldn't do the mindful exercise because you were aware of how much you were thinking. Maybe you just couldn't focus. That's okay. In mindfulness, you don't need to stop your thinking. You just need to be aware of how easily your mind gets caught up in thoughts. To notice that is great!

The chances are, this wasn't your normal experience of eating. Consider why this may be so. You probably eat more than one piece of food at a time, you may usually multitask with other activities like working or watching TV, and you may not give the food your full attention and eat quite so slowly.

Try this exercise again, but this time, just eat the food mindfully, without stopping at each stage to write down your experience. Take your time and then, at the end, jot down your overall experience in Worksheet 7-3.

Worksheet 7-3	Observations

Body scan meditation

Now, try out the body scan meditation. Read the detailed advice on the body scan in Chapter 5 and play the body scan audio (Track 2 at www.dummies.com/go/mindfulnessworkbookuk). Now answer the questions in Worksheet 7-4.

Worksheet 7-4	My Observations of the Body Scan Meditation

How did I find the experience of the body scan?

What did I like about it?

What did I find difficult or challenging?

_____

What emotions did I experience?

_____

What parts of my body did I feel? What parts had seemingly no sensation in them?

_____

The body scan meditation isn't a relaxation exercise; it's an awareness exercise. Relaxation or anxiety could be side-effects of the practice. The key is to simply keep noticing what's happening with curiosity. The benefits of mindfulness meditation are long-term outcomes, not short-term moment-by-moment experiences.

Home practice for week one

Your home practice for week one is:

- ✔ **Daily body scan.** Use the audio (Track 2) to practice the body scan. Remember, it doesn't really matter how relaxing or even anxious you feel as you do the practice. Just keep engaging in the body scan and see what happens in the long term.

- ✔ **Do one daily activity in a mindful way.** Choose something that you do habitually every day, like having a shower or brushing your teeth, and do the activity mindfully. You do the same activity as usual, but more consciously. If you're having a shower, listen to the sounds, smell the scent of the soap, feel the heat of the water against your skin. You could slow down the activity a little bit, but you don't have to. The key bit is the awareness, not the speed.

- ✔ **Eat one meal this week in a mindful way.** Stop multitasking for this meal and eat it consciously. Turn off the TV, avoiding reading while eating and switch off your phone for now. Look at your food, notice the flavour as you chew and become aware of how easily your mind wanders into other thoughts. Because eating is so habitual for most people, this practice isn't easy.

- ✔ **Do something different this week.** When you do something different to your normal habits, you're more likely to become mindful because that's the way your brain works. Mindful awareness automatically arises with new experiences. Take a different route to work, sit in a different seat at home or buy a different book or magazine than usual.

Put the different home practices in your diary or calendar to remind you when to do each particular activity and fill in Worksheet 7-5.

Worksheet 7-5		Week One Experiences		
Day	Experience of the Body Scan	Experience of Daily Mindful Activity	Experience of Doing Something Different	Experience of Eating Meal in a Mindful Way
Monday				
Tuesday				
Wednesday				
Thursday				
Friday				
Saturday				
Sunday				

Week Two: Dealing with Difficulties

Now that you've started practising mindfulness, this week is all about considering the various challenges of the practice and how to overcome them. You'll also begin to discover how your interpretation of events shapes how you feel, rather than the event itself. Your first challenges may have been to make the time to practice and then to actually do the mindfulness practice. Quite often, you may have found the time but still couldn't make yourself actually do the practice itself. Maybe you didn't feel like it, or just couldn't find the motivation early in the morning, or after a hard day at work. See Chapter 11 for advice on overcoming tiredness.

The next challenge is within the practice itself. You may have experienced sleepiness, boredom, frustration, confusion, sadness or anger with your practice in week one. Don't feel disheartened about this – all experiences are welcome visitors. For specific advice on coping with challenging experiences within the body scan, see Chapter 5.

The idea of mindfulness is not to try to create a special, mindful state of mind all the time. The point is to be aware of whatever happens with a sense of openness and warmth as best you can. And if you can't be open to the experience, noticing that you can't be open is also mindfulness! If you find you're struggling to actually lie down and do the body scan, even though you have the time, try just being mindful of the resistance. Sit down and feel the sense of resistance and notice what happens.

How you react to pleasant events

Think about the nice little things you encounter every day. These events don't have to be life-changing moments, they can be as simple as someone showing kindness by smiling at you or holding a door open. Fill in the pleasant events diary in Worksheet 7-6 every day for a week. Use this exercise to become aware of your thoughts, feelings and bodily sensations when you experience something pleasant, in as much detail as you can.

Worksheet 7-6	Pleasant Events Diary			
Pleasant Occurrence	*How Did I Know this Was Pleasant?*	*What Did I Feel in My Body at the Time?*	*What Emotions Did I Feel?*	*What Thoughts Popped into My Head?*
Monday				
Tuesday				
Wednesday				
Thursday				
Friday				
Saturday				
Sunday				

Mindfulness of breath

In addition to the body scan meditation, every day this week, try a ten-minute mindfulness exercise called mindfulness of breath or mindful breathing meditation. Have a go at this exercise right now, if you have time. The guidance for the practice is in Chapter 5. Make a note of your experience in Worksheet 7-7.

Worksheet 7-7   **My Observations of the Mindfulness of Breath**

Thoughts and feelings exercise

This next exercise isn't a meditation but a thought experiment. Imagine the following scenario:

> *You plan to go for a bike ride in a new area for about an hour. You get your bike and set off. After 20 minutes or so, you lose your way. You're not too sure how to get back and there's no one around you can ask. Consider what thoughts pop into your head and how you feel. You keep going into this unexplored part of town, getting even more lost. You have no idea how to get back. What thoughts and feelings arise for you now? Eventually you manage to find your way back, after about 2 hours.*

That's the end of this little exercise. Have a go at answering the questions in Worksheet 7-8.

Worksheet 7-8   My Reflections on the Thoughts and Feelings Exercise

---

What thoughts popped into your mind as the time passed?

What emotions did you feel as the time passed?

Different people usually have different thoughts about the situation, and therefore different emotions. The emotions they feel are directly related to the thoughts that popped into their head.

Take a look at Worksheet 7-9 and consider how you'd feel if you had the following thoughts.

Worksheet 7-9   **Considering Feelings Associated
with the Following Thoughts**

'Oh, this is an interesting challenge!'

'Oh my goodness, what if I never find my way back home?'

'That's typical. I always get lost. I'm useless.'

'What's wrong with this town? No maps anywhere. The local government need to sort themselves out.'

'Finally, a bit of time to explore this new part of town. Let me keep going and see what turns up.'

'I must have gone the wrong way. I can't get anything right.'

'What if it gets dark and I can't find my way home? What if someone tries to mug me?'

The situation is *exactly the same,* but the thoughts are different, and so the emotions are different. It's amazing – the fact that the same description can cause anything from anger to no feeling at all, depending on the thought that happens to pop into your head.

So, this week, look out for how your thoughts automatically interpret situations in your life. If you interpret a situation in a negative way, see if you can just be aware of this. At this stage, just notice as much as you can.

Your emotions are a consequence of an event together with your interpretation of the event.

Home practice for week two

Here's your homework. Keep track of everything in Worksheet 7-10.

✔ Practise the body scan meditation every day, using the accompanying audio track.

✔ At another time of day, practise ten minutes of mindfulness of breath meditation (refer to Chapter 5 for how to do this meditation).

✔ Complete the pleasant events diary.

✔ Be mindful of a different daily activity everyday – for example, getting dressed, talking to your partner or drinking your tea.

✔ Do something different – for example, visit your local library, call up a friend you haven't spoken to for ages or shop in a different store to your usual choice.

Worksheet 7-10	Week Two Diary			
Day	**Experience of the Body Scan Meditation**	**Experience of Daily Mindful Activity**	**Experience of Mindfulness of Breath Meditation**	**Experience of Doing Something Different This Week**
Monday				
Tuesday				
Wednesday				
Thursday				
Friday				
Saturday				
Sunday				

Week Three: Mindfulness and Your Breath

The main intention for this week is to discover how to use your breath to bring yourself back into the present moment. You're introduced to the sitting meditation too.

Sitting meditation – mindfulness of breath and body

You begin this week with a new practice. You've been practising the body scan meditation for the last two weeks. Now you can leave that practice for now and try the sitting meditation. You can find out how to do the sitting meditation in Chapter 5 and by listening to Track 3 on the audio (at www.dummies.com/go/mindfulnessworkbookuk). Sitting meditation has several stages. For now, just do the first two stages – mindfulness of breath and mindfulness of body.

If, for medical reasons, you're unable to sit for an extended period of time, you can do this in whatever position suits you.

Breathing space meditation

This week you also get to learn another new mindfulness practice. This is a very short meditation called the breathing space meditation (different to the mindfulness of breath exercise you did in Week 2). To practise this meditation, go to Chapter 6. Try the practice now, see what effect the practice has and note it down in Worksheet 7-11.

Worksheet 7-11	Exploring the Breathing Space Meditation

What did you notice when you did the breathing space meditation?

Many people like the breathing space meditation because it's so short. After the long practices of the body scan, you may find the practice to be a nice relief.

Your home practice from now on is to practise the breathing space for roughly three minutes, three times a day. You may like to put the times you plan to do the practice in your diary to remind you.

The purpose of the breathing space is not relaxation, a break or an escape from anything. The point is to be more fully aware and conscious within yourself. Calmness and relaxation may come as a welcome side effect or may not.

Mindful stretching

This week, you learn to practise mindful stretching. The purpose of this is mindfulness rather than physical exercise, so do the movements slowly and really feel each sensation as you make the stretch, as best you can. Then fill in your observations in Worksheet 7-12.

1. **Stand in a balanced, upright position with your weight balanced equally on your feet and with your chest feeling wide and open.**

2. **Allow your eyes to close and feel your breathing. Take a few deep, mindful breaths.**

3. **Slowly raise your arms towards the sky.** Feel the stretch in the muscles of your arm and back. Continue to feel your breathing together with your bodily sensations if you can.

4. **After a few moments, slowly bring your arms down to your sides and notice how it feels to do this in your body.**

5. **Repeat this stretching process three times.**

6. **Now raise your arms so your body creates a T-shape, with your arms in line with your shoulders.** Again, feel the stretch in your arms and continue to feel your breathing. Be gentle with your body.

7. **Slowly bring your arms back down again slowly after a few moments. Repeat three times.**

8. **Now, attempt to touch your toes.** Notice any negative thoughts that pop up as we make this suggestion and take a step back from those thoughts. Stretch down and see how far you can go. Feel the stretch in the back of your legs. Don't force yourself to do down any deeper. Just gently feel your breathing and notice what happens as you stretch. Relax into the stretch if you can. Then, when you're ready, move back up again into a standing position. Allow all movements to be slow and mindful and bring your attention back kindly when your mind wanders off. Repeat this process three times.

9. **Stand upright with your knees slightly bent and your feet hip-width apart.** Rotate your hips and pelvis so your lower back isn't strained and swing your arms around your body, gently tapping your back with your fingers as they swoosh round. Swing one way and then the other. Feel your breathing at the same time. Let your arms be loose. Notice how your breathing rate and heart rate change as you do this movement. Stop after a couple of minutes or so.

10. **Come back to your original standing position and scan through your body, noticing what your body feels like now that you've done these stretches.**

For more on mindful stretching and mindful movement, see Chapter 5.

Worksheet 7-12	**My Experience of Mindful Stretching**

How did you find the mindful stretching? What did you notice? Be curious about your own experience as far as you can.

If you suffer from a health condition such as high blood pressure, check with your doctor before doing these exercises. Some of them may not be appropriate for you.

Mindful walking

You may like to try some mindful walking this week too. Mindful walking is a great way to integrate mindfulness into your life. Most people walk every day – now you can be mindful as you walk.

Practise some mindful walking (also called walking meditation) this week. To learn how, see Chapter 6.

Unpleasant events diary

Last week we invited you to complete a pleasant events diary. This week you may be surprised to see an unpleasant events diary for you to fill in. The purpose of this diary is to discover how you automatically react to an unpleasant event. What you think and feel, and where that feeling manifests in your body – that's what this diary is about. You can also discover patterns – are the same situations particularly unpleasant for you? Or is it the same pattern of thought that makes an event unpleasant?

For example, if you always find yourself feeling impatient when waiting in a traffic jam or on hold when making a phone call, you can identify what your underlying thoughts are. You may always be having the thought 'I've got so much to do'. So, next time, when you notice that thought popping into your head, you can step back from it.

So, fill in Worksheet 7-13 this week and see what you discover.

Worksheet 7-13		Unpleasant Events Diary			
Day	*Unpleasant Occurrence*	*How Did I Know This Was Unpleasant for Me?*	*What Did I Feel in My Body at the Time?*	*What Emotions Did I Feel?*	*What Thoughts Popped into My Mind?*
Monday					
Tuesday					
Wednesday					
Thursday					
Friday					
Saturday					
Sunday					

Home practice for week three

Keep track of your progress in Worksheet 7-14.

- ✔ On Monday, Wednesday, Friday and Sunday, practise some mindful stretching (about 15 minutes) followed by mindful sitting (mindful breathing and body).

- ✔ On Tuesday, Thursday and Saturday, practise mindful stretching for about half an hour or do some mindful walking for half an hour.

- ✔ Complete the unpleasant events diary every day.

- ✔ Practise the breathing space meditation for about three minutes, three times every day.

- ✔ Be mindful of a different daily activity every day. For example, walking to work, preparing breakfast or getting ready for bed.

- ✔ Try something different as you did last week. For example, eat something you've never tried, try a new hobby or read a book, blog or website that you normally wouldn't.

Worksheet 7-14	Week Three Diary			
Day	**Experience of Mindful Sitting Followed by Mindful Stretching**	**Experience of Mindful Activity**	**Experience of Breathing Space Meditation**	**Experience of Doing Something Different This Week**
Monday				
Tuesday				
Wednesday				
Thursday				
Friday				
Saturday				
Sunday				

Week Four: Staying Present

The intention for this week is to deepen your experience of the sitting meditation and practise being present during the breathing space meditation. Feel your breathing whenever it comes to mind to help you come into the here and now.

Being mindful means going from living in a reactive, habitual way to being in a more conscious and open state. You can cultivate this mind-set (and heart-set) by simply being present in your body whenever it comes to mind. Feel the sensation of your body as you're sitting on an office chair. Feel your feet as you walk down the stairs. Feel your breathing as you're waiting in a queue at the bank, shops or on the phone.

Mindfulness is particularly helpful in more challenging moments, when difficulties arise. The unpleasant events diary may have shown up some personal patterns that you can look out for. Notice what happens to your body when a difficulty arises. Does your chest tighten, your eye twitch or your shoulders tense? See if you can open yourself up to these sensations with a mindful curiosity and notice what happens. In Chapter 9, we explore some more helpful attitudes for meeting these difficulties, instead of the automatic aversion that usually arises.

Sitting meditation

This week, lengthen your sitting meditation practice to doing all five stages every day. Use the accompanying audio track to practise mindfulness of breath, body, sounds, thoughts and open awareness. For more advice and ways of overcoming difficulties with the sitting meditation, see Chapter 5. Record your observations of the sitting meditation in Worksheet 7-15.

Worksheet 7-15	Sitting Meditation Observations

What did you notice when you practised the sitting meditation today?

Coping breathing space

Now that you've been practising the breathing space for a couple of weeks, you're ready to have a go at the coping breathing space. You can use the coping breathing space exercise, about three minutes long, when a difficulty arises for you, such as your child having a tantrum or when you recall a bereavement. You can use the meditation for handling any difficult situation. During a difficult time, you do the breathing space meditation (fully described in Chapter 6) and notice what happens. Record your experiences in Worksheet 7-16.

The coping breathing space doesn't enable you to escape from the difficult feelings within your body. In fact, it's the opposite. Tune in to the difficult sensations just as they are and simply notice what is going on within you, with a sense of curiosity and warmth, as far as you can. Watch and learn about difficult sensations rather than run away from them. Much easier said than done, we know, but try to take a tiny step in this direction. Any step towards doing something difficult, no matter how small, is hugely significant. As the old saying goes, 'a journey of a thousand miles begins with a single step'.

Home practice for week four

Mark your progress in Worksheet 7-16.

- ✔ Practise the sitting meditation every day – mindfulness of breath, body, sounds, thoughts and open awareness.

- ✔ Practise the breathing space meditation for about three minutes, three times a day.

- ✔ Practise the coping breathing space meditation whenever difficulties arise for you.

- ✔ Be mindful of a different daily activity every day. For example, listen to some different music or experiment with a new piece of technology.

- ✔ Do something different. For example, talk to someone new, spend time looking at nature if you don't normally do that or watch a different genre of film to your favourite.

Worksheet 7-16		Week Four Diary		
Day	*Experience of Sitting Meditation*	*Experience of Different Mindful Activity*	*Experience of Breathing Space and/or Coping Breathing Space Meditation*	*Experience of Doing Something Different This Week*
Monday				
Tuesday				
Wednesday				
Thursday				
Friday				
Saturday				
Sunday				

Chapter 8

Completing the Eight-week Mindfulness Course . . . and Beyond

In This Chapter
▶ Discovering the key learning points for the second half of the course
▶ Completing the second half of the mindfulness course
▶ Taking the next step

*I*n Chapter 8, we introduce you to the second part of an eight-week mindfulness course. In this half of the course, the emphasis is on learning how to relate to your experiences, particularly challenging, difficult or uncomfortable experiences, with acceptance. We end the chapter with practical tips for ways you can maintain your mindful awareness.

If you managed to complete most of the mindful exercises in the first four weeks of the mindfulness course, congratulations! The course is challenging, so don't worry if you found the process difficult. If you didn't manage to do most of the practices, you can always go back and have another go before moving on to the second half at another time.

To help you assess how the eight-week course is going for you, try answering the questions in Worksheet 8-1:

Worksheet 8-1   Assessing How the Course is Going So Far

How am I doing on the mindfulness course?

What am I doing well?

(continued)

What do I need to focus on improving?

_____

What can I do, or who can I ask, to help support me through this course?

_____

Week Five: Discovering the Power of Acceptance

The intention for this week is to discover a different and healthy way of relating to experience that is acceptance, allowing, acknowledging or letting be.

When you have a difficult feeling like sadness or anxiety, or even physical discomfort, the temptation is to run away from the feeling. However, the desire to run or push away feelings can strengthen them. So, this week, you experiment with moving in close to your difficulty within your physical body and notice what effect that has.

Acceptance is about letting go of the fight with your difficulty. Acceptance doesn't mean resignation, nor does it mean clinging on. Acceptance is a radical first step of acknowledging your present moment experience, just as it is. Discover more about acceptance in Chapter 3.

Mindful sitting meditation – exploring a difficulty and associated body sensations

Have a go at doing a slightly different sitting meditation. Begin with the normal sitting meditation (described in Chapter 5), which involves mindfulness of breath, body, sounds, thoughts and open awareness. Then do the following steps, as part of the meditation. Afterwards, complete Worksheet 8-2.

1. **Bring to mind a difficulty that you're going through in your life.** Something that you're willing to work with in this meditation. Perhaps you're having trouble with a colleague at work, or your parent is ill and you're concerned. Bring the situation to mind – visualise the situation if you wish. Immerse yourself for a minute or so.

2. **Notice where you feel that difficulty within your body.** Is it in your neck, shoulders, stomach, chest or somewhere else?

3. **Focus your attention on the difficulty in your physical body.** What shape is it? What size is it? Does the difficulty have a colour or texture?

4. **Imagine or feel your breathing going into and out of the difficulty in your body.** Bring a sense of acceptance of the sensation, just as it is. Say to yourself 'It's okay . . . this sensation is already here . . . let me gently feel it, as best I can.' Bring a sense of openness to the experience. You may not find it easy, but just try your best and see what happens.

5. **Remember not to have the aim of getting rid of the feeling.** You're simply accepting and allowing the feeling to be there. Whether the difficulty stays or goes isn't the aim of this exercise. Have an attitude of 'whatever happens, happens'.

Worksheet 8-2	**Reflections on Sitting Meditation and Introducing a Difficulty**

Write down what happened when you tried the sitting meditation, focusing on a difficulty:

_____

_____

The purpose of this meditation is to practise bringing an attitude of acceptance in a relatively controlled environment. So when a difficulty arises again, you have had some practice of meeting difficulty with an attitude of acceptance.

Home practice for week five

Here's your homework for this week. Keep track in Worksheet 8-3:

- ✔ Practise the sitting meditation every day. Mindfulness of breath, body, sounds, thoughts and open awareness. Alternate days between using the audio and just sitting in silence without the audio and practising from memory as best you can.

- ✔ Do the breathing space meditation for about three minutes, three times a day (see Chapter 6).

- ✔ Practise the coping breathing space when difficulties arise for you (explained in Chapter 7). Do the normal short breathing space meditation and make space for difficult emotions to be present for you, with a sense of curiosity, and record what happens.

- ✔ Be mindful of a different everyday activity, such as washing, walking or preparing food.

- ✔ Do something unusual or different this week and be mindful about it.

Worksheet 8-3		Week Five Diary		
Day	**Experience of Sitting Meditation**	**Mindful Experience of Everyday Activity**	**Experience of Breathing Space Meditation (Exploring a Difficulty)**	**Experience of Doing Something Different This Week**
Monday				
Tuesday				
Wednesday				
Thursday				
Friday				
Saturday				
Sunday				

Week Six: Realising that Thoughts Aren't Facts

The intention for this week is to explore a new way of relating to your thoughts. You experiment with seeing thoughts as just sounds and images in your mind and understand that your thoughts aren't necessarily hard and fast facts.

Thoughts and images pop into your mind all day long. Due to your past experiences, thoughts can have certain habitual patterns. You may often have worrying thoughts about the future or regrets about the past, or you may be constantly planning what you'll do next without ever connecting with the moment. You may have strict thoughts like 'I should be more ambitious' or 'I must keep the house spotless' or negative thoughts about yourself like, 'I'm useless', 'I can't do it', 'I can't stand this anymore' or 'I'm too tired'. You may think, 'I'm ugly', 'I can't do anything right' or 'I can't deal with technology'.

Whatever thoughts pop into your head, remember that thoughts are just thoughts, not necessarily facts. For example, perhaps you think 'I'm so stressed; I can't cope'. Well, first of all, do you believe this to be true? If you really think the thought is true and you are stressed, is holding that thought helping you to achieve your aims in life? Perhaps not. In fact, the thought itself may be causing you *more* stress. So, rather than fighting the thought, which ends up making it more powerful, we recommend stepping back from the thought. All the mindfulness exercises and meditations help you do this by encouraging you to see that you're separate from your thoughts and don't have to believe them or do what they say, if you don't want to.

If you want to take a different approach to challenge negative thinking, take a look at *Cognitive Behavioural Therapy For Dummies* by Rhena Branch and Rob Willson (Wiley), or the series of *For Dummies* books tackling depression, anxiety and anger with CBT.

This week isn't about positive thinking, ignoring or controlling thoughts or emptying your mind. This week you cultivate a new relationship with your thoughts. You become more in control of your mind by acknowledging that your thoughts are just thoughts and you don't need to believe them.

Stepping back from thoughts

Freedom from being controlled by your thoughts lies in the possibility that, from time to time, you step back and create a space between you and your thoughts.

In Worksheet 8-4, try the ways of stepping back from your thoughts and note down what effect they have. This stepping back is called *decentring* and can help to ease the emotional connection from the thought so that you can see the thought from a wise and considered perspective.

Worksheet 8-4	Trying Different Decentring Practices
Decentring Practice	*Effect of the Practice*
Watch the thought come and go, without needing to follow it.	
Make the distinction between yourself and your thoughts by saying to yourself, 'I am having the thought X.'	
Visualise clouds passing through the sky and place each thought on the clouds and watch them go.	
Write down any negative thoughts to give yourself some perspective on them.	
Imagine you're watching a film of your thoughts and images while you sit back from them your seat.	
Ask yourself 'Is this thought helpful?' If not, can you take a step back from this thought and feel your breathing instead?	
Label the thought. For example, 'worrying', 'relationship story' or 'money thoughts'. Then simply say 'thanks mind!' and turn your attention back on to whatever is the need of the moment.	

Many people find these techniques helpful, so give each one a few tries and see what happens, just as an experiment. If they help, continue to use them. If not, you can cast them aside for now.

Mindful sitting meditation – exploring a difficulty and associated thoughts

This week, have a go at the sitting meditation practice using the audio track (Track 3 at www.dummies.com/go/mindfulnessworkbookuk): mindfulness of breath, body, sounds, thoughts and open awareness.

As you did last week, bring a difficulty to mind – some challenge that you're experiencing in your life at the moment.

Notice what sort of thoughts come to mind. Don't fight with them or become absorbed by them. Instead, experiment with some of the decentring practices listed in Worksheet 8-4. You can choose any that you prefer. For example, if you're having difficulties with your girlfriend at the moment, you might notice the thoughts 'What if she leaves me?' or 'She should respect me'. Then say to yourself, 'I'm having the thought *what if she leaves me*' or 'These are just thoughts, not necessarily facts' or imagine watching clouds passing through the sky and place one thought after the other on the clouds. Or you could also say, 'Thanks, mind!' and smile before stepping back from the thoughts.

Finish this meditation by feeling your breathing again for a minute or two and then gently transitioning to your everyday life. Write down your experiences in Worksheet 8-5.

Worksheet 8-5 **Discovering the Effect of Sitting Meditation with Decentring from Difficulties**

How did you find this meditation? What did you discover about the art of decentring from your thoughts?

Thoughts, mood and seeing things differently

Take your time to consider the following two scenarios and note down your answers to the questions that follow:

1. You walk down your local high street, and someone walks into you by accident. As you approach the newsagent to buy a lottery ticket, it starts raining and you get drenched. You go into the shop and the owner is rude. You buy the ticket and discover that you lost. Consider how you'd be feeling.

   You see a friend as you step out of the shop, but he says, 'Sorry, I'm really running late, I've got to go!'

Write down how you feel and what you think about your friend.

_____

_____

2. You walk down your local high street, and people are happy and smiling. As you approach the newsagent to buy a lottery ticket, you notice the sky is looking beautiful. You go into the shop and the owner is polite and helpful. You buy the ticket and discover that you won a small prize. Consider how you'd be feeling.

   You notice a friend as you step out of the shop, but he says, 'Sorry, I'm really running late, I've got to go!'

   How do you feel and what do you think about your friend this time?

_____

_____

We suspect you discovered that your opinion of your friend varied depending on what your day was like. But does that make sense? Your friend said exactly the same thing in both circumstances. Firstly, this exercise reiterates that thoughts aren't always facts. Secondly, you can see how your mood can directly affect your thoughts. By becoming more aware of your mood with mindfulness, you can be more cautious about the thoughts you have and question them or consider a different way of seeing the situation you're in.

Home practice for week six

Here's your homework:

- ✔ Practise about 30 to 40 minutes of mindfulness in chunks every day – for example, 20 minutes in the morning and 20 minutes in the evening or four lots of ten minutes throughout the day. You can choose any combination of the sitting meditation, body scan or mindful movement meditation that you prefer.

- ✔ Practise the breathing space meditation for about three minutes, three times a day.

- ✔ Practise the coping breathing space meditation any time difficulties arise for you.

- ✔ Be mindful of a different daily activity.

- ✔ Do something different this week and be mindful while you do it.

Record your home practice observations in Worksheet 8-6.

Worksheet 8-6		Week Six Diary		
Day	*Experience of My Chosen Mindfulness Meditation*	*Mindful Experience of Everyday Activity*	*Experience of Breathing Space Meditation*	*Experience of Doing Something Different This Week*
Monday				
Tuesday				
Wednesday				
Thursday				
Friday				
Saturday				
Sunday				

Week Seven: Looking After Yourself

The activities you do have a significant effect on your mood. This week you discover ways to look after yourself in a helpful and healthy way when difficulties arise in your life, causing stress.

Fill in Worksheet 8-7 with the activities that you do in a typical day. For example, watching television, travelling to work, walking the dog, washing the dishes, meditating, checking email or playing with your children. In the second column, jot down if you think the activity is nourishing (uplifting, energising, something you enjoy) or depleting (something that demoralises, tires or makes you feel bad).

Worksheet 8-7	**Considering My Nourishing and Depleting Everyday Activities**
Typical Activity	*N (Nourishing) or D (Depleting)*

Look at your list in Worksheet 8-7. What's the balance like between nourishing and depleting activities? You don't need to have all activities as nourishing, but the more uplifting activities you have in the day, the better. If you only have depleting activities, please don't despair. In the following section, you can begin trying some enjoyable activities.

Now consider the following question: accepting that you can't change some activities in your life, what can you do to increase the amount of time you spend doing nourishing activities and reduce the amount of time you spend doing depleting activities? For example, if you spend several hours a day watching television and you find it depleting, perhaps you could go for a walk every day instead? Or if checking email is depleting, maybe work out ways to be more efficient and check it twice a day rather than 10 or 20 times a day, if that's what you do. Write your answers in Worksheet 8-8.

Worksheet 8-8   Considering Ways I Can Increase Nourishing Activities

---

Enjoying pleasurable and mastery activities

In this mindfulness course, knowing your everyday *pleasurable* and *mastery* activities can help you to manage your mood when life gets difficult.

- ✔ **Pleasurable activities** are things like eating your favourite food, listening to music you like or taking a hot bath. Whatever is pleasurable for you.

- ✔ **Mastery activities** are activities that you may not enjoy at the time, but after you've done them, you feel better. Mastery activities are things you may avoid doing, like clearing out a cupboard, sorting out your email inbox or tidying up and organising your desk.

Make a list of both sets of your activities in Worksheet 8-9.

Worksheet 8-9   Listing My Pleasurable and Mastery Activities

My Pleasurable Activities	*My Mastery Activities*

When you feel stressed, you can do a pleasurable activity or an activity that gives you a sense of mastery; either can help to manage your stress levels. But remember to do the activities with mindfulness.

You can turn activities that you may normally think of as depleting into nourishing activities. For example, if you normally find it a chore to get your children ready for bed, you could try slowing it down one evening, allowing them to play with their toys in the bath and take time to read them a story, reflecting on how fortunate you are to have such beautiful children.

Acting mindfully to manage stress

Part of looking after yourself is managing your stress levels. In fact, many people turn to mindfulness to find an effective but gentle way to deal with stress. When you feel stressed, you can do a breathing space meditation and then do something pleasurable or a mastery activity. But the third option is simply to act mindfully no matter what you're doing:

1. Be focused in the present moment on whatever you're doing.

2. When your mind wanders off, just label the thought as 'worrying' or 'planning' or whatever it is and bring your mind gently back to the here and now.

Complete Worksheet 8-10.

Worksheet 8-10 **Managing Stress Mindfully**

What activity did you attempt to do mindfully? What did you notice when you acted mindfully?

Developing a stress-reduction action plan

To help look after yourself when your stress levels rise, creating a personalised stress-reduction action plan is tremendously useful. The first step of the plan helps you identify when your stress levels are getting too high. The second step is to take appropriate action to reduce that stress. The answers you write down below help you to create your own personalised stress-reduction action plan that you can turn to when you need it (Worksheets 8-12 and 8-13).

Think about when your stress levels rise too high and answer the questions in Worksheet 8-11.

Worksheet 8-11   **Reducing My Stress**

How do you behave towards others? What sort of activities do you avoid? What unhelpful things do you do?

Where do you feel the stress in your body?

What sort of thoughts pop into your head?

What sort of mood do you get into?

What activities could you do that would help you to reduce your stress?

Examples are:

Pleasurable activities done mindfully such as a hot bath, a gentle stroll around the block, calling up a friend, meeting up with a supportive colleague, eating a bit of chocolate without feeling guilty, reading your favourite book or quotes, watching a comedy, popping down to your local café or bookshop, listening to some soothing music, doing a bit of gardening, cooking your favourite meal, stroking your cat or dog, having a short nap.

Mastery activities done mindfully such as washing up the dishes, tidying the house or doing some decorating.

Worksheet 8-12   **Choosing My Pleasurable and Mastery Activities**

Choose your own from the list or something else:

Worksheet 8-13 **Summarised Stress Reduction Action Plan**

I know when I'm getting stressed because I:

_____

_____

When this next happens, I will do the breathing space meditation and then I will:

_____

_____

_____

Figure 8-1 shows the stages for managing a stressful event, from the breathing space meditation to the action step.

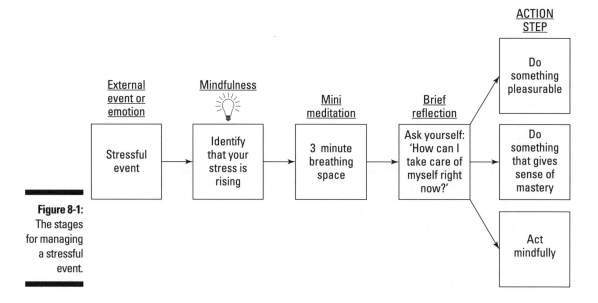

Figure 8-1:
The stages for managing a stressful event.

Home practice for week seven

Here's your plan for Week Seven; keep track with Worksheet 8-14:

✔ Out of all the mindfulness meditations, choose a pattern of mindfulness practice that you feel able to continue after the course ends.

✔ Do a routine daily activity mindfully.

✔ Continue to practise the breathing space meditation daily.

✔ Use the coping breathing space meditation for dealing with a difficulty and then carry out a mindful action as an experiment and see what happens.

✔ Do something different this week.

Worksheet 8-14	Week Seven Diary		
Day	**My Preferred Daily Meditation**	**Mindful Experience of Everyday Activity**	**Breathing Space (or Coping Breathing Space)**	**Experience of Doing Something Different This Week**
Monday				
Tuesday				
Wednesday				
Thursday				
Friday				
Saturday				
Sunday				

Week Eight: Reflection and Change

You can consider Week 8 as the beginning of the rest of your life! If you found mindfulness helpful in any way, this week think about how to continue practising after the course ends.

The core learning of this eight-week mindfulness course is to respond consciously by making choices instead of reacting automatically in potentially unhelpful habitual ways. This habit isn't always easy to develop, but it is possible; step by mindful step. Mindfulness offers the radical possibility of a more intentional, conscious and wise way of living.

Mindfulness can help ease suffering in another key way – by cultivating a different way of meeting difficulties. Instead of running away or fighting difficult feelings, you're invited to bring awareness and a mindful acceptance to them.

Finally, mindfulness can help you decide what to accept in your life and what to change. For many, this learning point is tremendously important. We've modified the serenity prayer as a mindful intention you can refer to:

'May I have the serenity to accept the things I can't change, the courage to change the things I can, and the wisdom to know the difference.'

Mindfulness is about accepting consciously what you can't change, because otherwise you're setting yourself up for suffering. The invitation is to accept your present moment thoughts and emotions so that you can see them clearly. Then, to take action based on the best option for you instead of automatically reacting the same way you've always reacted. How do you prevent yourself from reacting automatically? By practising a little bit of mindfulness every day, you gradually become less reactive and more mindfully responsive and wise.

Practice for this week

Begin this week by practising the body scan meditation using the accompanying audio (Track 5 at www.dummies.com/go/mindfulnessworkbookuk). You may have not practised this meditation since weeks 1 and 2, so you've come full circle, back to the body scan meditation. Remember, each body scan meditation is different, so practise the exercise with a sense of freshness, as if for the first time.

Bring a feeling of acceptance to the experience, which you've been learning about in the last few weeks. What does it feel like to allow your bodily sensations, emotions and thoughts to be, just as they are, instead of fighting, running away or denying them? Record your experience of the body scan meditation in Worksheet 8-15.

Worksheet 8-15   My Experience of the Body Scan Today

To finish the mindful practice this week, try the loving kindness meditation and make notes in Worksheet 8-16. You can find the details of how to practise that meditation in Chapter 5.

Worksheet 8-16 My Experience of the Loving Kindness Meditation Today

---

Home practice for week eight

Here's your plan for Week Eight; keep track with Worksheet 8-17:

- ✔ Continue to practise a daily mindfulness meditation of your choice, such as the body scan meditation, sitting meditation or mindful yoga.
- ✔ Do a routine daily activity mindfully.
- ✔ Continue to practise the breathing space meditation daily.
- ✔ Do something different this week.

Worksheet 8-17	**Week Eight Diary**			
Day	*My Mindfulness Meditation*	*Experience of Mindful Activity*	*Breathing Space Meditation*	*Experience of Doing Something Different This Week*
Monday				
Tuesday				
Wednesday				
Thursday				
Friday				
Saturday				
Sunday				

Personal reflections on the course

Take some time to reflect on what your experience of the eight-week mindfulness course was like. Ask yourself the following questions and complete Worksheet 8-18.

Worksheet 8-18 My Reflections on the Eight-week Mindfulness Course

What were your original intentions for doing the course?

_____

What benefits did you get from the course?

_____

What were the drawbacks?

_____

What are the biggest challenges preventing you from continuing to practise mindfulness?

_____

What strategies would help you to overcome those challenges?

_____

What regular mindfulness practice would you like to adopt over the coming weeks or months?

_____

By going through this series of questions and really taking your time to reflect on your answers, you may be able to come up with strategies that help you to maintain your mindfulness practice.

Exploring the Next Step

An eight-week mindfulness course isn't the end of your journey but just the beginning. Mindfulness is a life-long habit that endlessly deepens as you continue to practise. If you're interested, you can try some of these suggestions to help you to sustain and deepen your mindfulness.

Trying a silent day of mindfulness

What comes to mind when you consider being silent for a whole day? Notice how your mind responds to that prospect. Many people seem surprised or reluctant when we mention the idea of spending a whole day not talking.

Spending a day of silent mindfulness has several benefits. Your level of mindfulness rises and you're better able to notice your own inner reactions to other people, yourself or the world at large, and your mind's pattern of thinking.

People often report that the day made them feel much better than they expected. Some people describe the day as a form of mental detox.

If the prospect of a whole day of mindfulness sounds too daunting, try a half-day. That length of time may be more suitable for you.

Table 8-1 shows a sample schedule you could try, but be flexible and adjust the programme to work for you.

Table 8-1	Sample Mindfulness Day Schedule
Time	*Practice*
9 a.m.	Prepare and eat your breakfast with a mindful focus. Sit outside if the weather is nice.
10 a.m.	Mindful body scan meditation.
11 a.m.	Mindful walking and some mindful sitting.
12 p.m.	Some mindful stretching, yoga or qi gong.
1 p.m.	Prepare some lunch mindfully and eat it slowly.
2 p.m.	Mindful walking and sitting. Perhaps an afternoon nap.
3 p.m.	Mindful yoga or stretching.
4 p.m.	Prepare some herbal tea and a little snack.
5 p.m.	Mindful sitting.
6 p.m.	Take your time to prepare some delicious and healthy dinner.
7 p.m.	Eat mindfully. Perhaps go for an evening stroll.
8 p.m.	Try a loving kindness meditation or mindful breathing.
9 p.m.	Read your favourite section from a book on mindfulness and reflect on it. Perhaps treat yourself to a nice bath.
10 p.m.	Lie in bed and feel your breathing until you drift into sleep.

The purpose of the day of mindfulness isn't to try to feel better. The purpose is to treat yourself to some time for you. Some time to simply *be* rather than do, do, do all the time. You may find the day difficult and the process may release pent up emotions. However, most people feel better in the long run. Record your experiences in Worksheet 8-19.

Worksheet 8-19	Reflections on My Day of Mindfulness

Which practices did you manage to do on your day of mindfulness?

_____

Which practices did you find helpful?

_____

What did you discover about yourself, or the process of mindfulness, on this day?

_____

What will you do differently on your next day of mindfulness, if anything?

_____

Joining or starting a group

Being part of a mindfulness group is a powerful way of sustaining your practice. The discipline of a daily mindfulness practice is difficult for most people. By being part of a mindfulness group, you're more likely to stick with it.

The experience of meditating with a group has a different feel to meditating on your own. Most people find the experience is deeper when meditating with others.

If there's no mindfulness group in your local area, consider starting one up yourself. You just need to find one other person, and off you go! Here's one format you could use:

7 p.m. Arrive. Say hello and welcome any newcomers.

7.15 p.m. Some mindful stretching or mindful walking around the room, if appropriate.

7.30 p.m. Mindfulness meditation. You could play a guided mindfulness meditation audio track, or just have 30 to 40 minutes of silent time to practise.

8 p.m. Allow people to share their experiences if they wish.

8.20 p.m. Share some tea and biscuits and socialise.

8.30 p.m. Close.

Online courses and training

Ideally, you'd learn mindfulness with a fully qualified and experienced mindfulness teacher in person. However, sometimes, due to money, time or location constraints, you may need to train online. If you're comfortable with using computers, online mindfulness training may be a preferable option.

A few online mindfulness courses are available if you can't find a mindfulness course near you:

- ✔ www.livemindfulonline.com I (Shamash) offer some online mindfulness options, from an email course to more interactive sessions. Get in touch for further information about options that are right for you.

- ✔ www.bemindfulonline.com An online mindfulness course created by the Mental Health Foundation in the UK.

Attending a retreat

The word retreat originally comes from the Latin *retrahere* meaning *to draw back*. A mindfulness retreat is usually located in beautiful surrounding and offers a period of time away from your busy life to carry out some extended mindfulness practice. Retreats are a real treat for your body and mind.

The benefits of a retreat are that you can:

- ✔ Get away from your habitual patterns that may be destructive, such as excessive drinking, working too hard or reacting negatively towards your partner.

- ✔ Enjoy practising in the company of other like-minded people in an environment conducive to cultivating mindful awareness.

- ✔ Have time for yourself, away from all your usual responsibilities.

- ✔ Practise mindfulness more deeply so that you can work through and let go of any frustrations or difficult emotions.

- ✔ Learn new dimensions about mindfulness from the teacher.

- ✔ Switch on your being mode of mind for a sustained period of time (Chapter 4 is all about being mode).

Retreats are about engaging in deep mindfulness practice, so you may release deeply held emotions that you've never had the opportunity to process. People do sometimes cry in the meditations as they work through and let go of these emotions. That's fine and totally normal.

After a retreat, most people report feeling lighter and better for the practice, sometimes for several months afterwards.

Head to the extra Part of Tens chapter, available online at www.dummies.com/ extras/mindfulnessworkbookuk, for more about going on a retreat and some personal recommendations.

Chapter 9

Overcoming Difficulties in Mindfulness Practice

. . . .

In This Chapter

▶ Exploring ways of overcoming common challenges in mindfulness

▶ Discovering how to cope with a range of difficult thoughts and emotions

▶ Finding out how to manage distractions

. . . .

*L*earning isn't a quick process. When you learnt to run or ride a bike, you didn't go speeding off immediately. I (Jo) definitely fell into a few bushes when learning to ride my bike! I got up and tried again though, until I was stable enough to balance without anyone holding on to me.

In your meditation practice, try your best not to see setbacks as failures – think of them as learning opportunities as you go forward. Try to simply accept each of your experiences. In a way, expecting a few difficulties along the way helps to prepare you, and prevents you from giving up. Everyone can learn mindfulness, including you – you just need to nudge your attitude into the right direction and you'll be best positioned to move forward in the art of mindful living.

In our experience, most people experience a few key difficulties on their mindfulness journey. Read this chapter and you can prepare yourself for most of the challenges that may arise for you as you learn to practise mindfulness meditation. Time, energy and emotions seem to be key areas that challenge people. Find out how to glide your way past them, mindfully, in this chapter.

WISE WORDS

Going with the flow

Think of your meditation practice like a rubber ball floating down a very long river. Sometimes the current envelops the ball and it flows smoothly and quickly. At other times the ball becomes stuck behind a rock for a period of time before gently dislodging and moving along down the river. Whatever happens to it, the ball still carries on its journey down the river.

Finding Time for Mindfulness

'I don't have time to be mindful' is a common observation we hear. This comment is usually followed by the person saying, 'But I know I should do . . . I just don't know how. Maybe I'm just making excuses.'

Before you explore ways of finding time for mindfulness, be clear about the two distinct ways that you can be mindful:

- **Formal mindfulness meditations that you may do daily or a few times a week.** You make time to meditate, separate from your daily activities. You decide beforehand how long you're going to practise and you ensure you take time from your schedule to mindfully meditate.

- **Informal mindfulness.** You're present and as focused as you can be during your daily activities, whatever they may be. You notice when your mind wanders and bring your attention back without self-criticising. And you endeavour to do one activity at a time rather than multitasking.

So, it's the formal mindfulness meditation that really requires time to integrate into your day. Informal mindfulness is just about being more present in whatever you normally do, so actually takes up no extra time at all. In fact, informal mindfulness usually saves time, as you may be wasting time being unfocused or trying to multitask, which research suggests is actually counter-productive (see the nearby sidebar 'Multitasking is like smoking marijuana!').

Making time for formal mindfulness practice

Consider different times you could practise meditation every day. If you think you don't have time for even ten minutes of daily meditation, ask yourself the following questions:

- Do I manage to find time to eat every day?
- Do I find time to brush my teeth every day?
- Do I find time to sleep every day, no matter how busy things are?

We hope you do! Meditation is just a question of priorities. Make mindfulness really, really important to you, and you can find the time.

Multitasking is like smoking marijuana!

Research by the Institute of Psychiatry in 2005 found that multitasking led to a significant drop in mental sharpness. Workers who stopped their task to deal with new emails coming in or to answer phone calls experienced a 10-point fall in their IQ – that's twice the effective drop that you get from smoking marijuana! Surveys show that over half of employees respond to emails immediately – multitasking is a common way of working. To be more effective, avoid multitasking and switch off distractions as much as you can. Do one activity at a time with a mindful focus of your attention.

So, you need to make a clear decision in your mind to try out meditation for a few weeks and for how long each time. Just notice what excuses are popping into your head as you read these words. See if you can, just for today, let those excuses go and make a commitment. It's your choice of course – you don't have to do this. If you choose not to take time to meditate daily, that's fine. But if you do want to learn to meditate, a clear decision and commitment is required.

You need to find the best time to meditate for you. Fill in Worksheet 9-1 to experiment with times that could work particularly well for your lifestyle. The amount of time you actually meditate for is up to you, but we suggest you aim for about 20 minutes a day to start with and see how it goes. Ultimately anything is better than nothing – just like physical exercise.

Taking time out to practise mindfulness daily isn't an easy discipline. If you just can't seem to do it, don't beat yourself up. Just begin with a little of the informal mindfulness and feel your breathing every now and then as you go about your daily activities.

Set realistic expectations for yourself – you don't need to turn into a Zen Master! Start small and work your way up, gradually increasing the time you practise and how often. Stick to your discipline as best you can and observe whatever arises with curiosity.

Worksheet 9-1		Planning Your Meditation	
Suggested Time to Meditate	*Yes or No*	*What Was the Experience Like?*	*Is It a Suitable Time for Me to Meditate Regularly?*
As soon as I wake up.			
After having a wash.			
After getting dressed, just before starting my day.			
Just before lunch.			
At the end of the day's activities/end of work.			
As soon as I arrive home.			
Just before having dinner.			
Before going to bed.			
At a time of my choosing (write here):			

Fitting in informal mindfulness practice

Informal mindfulness, which is about being mindful in your daily activities, is the other key way to practise mindfulness. Look down at the list in Worksheet 9-2 for some suggested activities that you could do more mindfully.

Bear the following in mind:

- ✔ **Be aware of your intention** – briefly reflect on *why* you're doing the task in the first place, at the beginning of the activity.

- ✔ **Do that sole activity** rather than multitasking.

- ✔ **Give attention to the task in hand as best you can**, with a gentle focus, and each time your mind drifts, which it will, notice what you were thinking about and bring your attention back, without self-criticising if possible.

- ✔ **Let go of the outcome** as much as possible and let your mindful awareness be in the present moment on the task in hand.

Have a go at doing one of the activities in Worksheet 9-2 mindfully, once a day. Record your observations, being as curious and interested as you can. Don't try to do them all in one day – that's too ambitious and may make you more tired and frustrated rather than mindful! Take it easy, step-by-step – that's the mindful way!

Worksheet 9-2	Informal Mindfulness Activities	
Date and Time	**Suggested Activity to do Mindfully**	**Observations About the Experience**
	Having a shower/bath.	
	Getting dressed.	
	Brushing my teeth.	
	Drinking tea/coffee/juice.	
	Eating breakfast.	
	Washing dishes.	
	Walking to work/shops.	
	Work activities.	

Date and Time	Suggested Activity to do Mindfully	Observations About the Experience
	Using computers/Internet/email.	
	Making phone calls.	
	Driving a car.	
	Travelling on public transport.	
	Eating lunch.	
	Preparing my meals.	
	Eating dinner.	
	Doing a hobby.	
	Playing a sport or exercising.	
	Washing clothes.	
	Talking with my partner/friend/family.	
	Being with my children.	
	Getting undressed for bed.	
	Any other activity:	
	Any other activity:	

Counting Sheep: Staying Awake During Meditation

One of the challenges of mindfulness meditation is to stay awake.

If you do fall asleep, don't worry too much about it. Even the Dalai Lama falls asleep when meditating sometimes, so you're following in the footsteps of a wise teacher! He also says, 'Sleep is the best meditation,' so it can't be so bad.

Mindfulness is about being more awake and aware, rather than falling asleep. Take steps to see if you can stay awake as much as possible during meditation.

Here are five key tips to ensure that you're more likely to stay awake in your mindfulness meditation practice:

- **Try mindful movement before your sitting practice.** Or simply let your whole mindfulness practice be movement-based.

- **Experiment with meditating at different times of the day.** Some people find it easier in the morning, others in the evening. Don't meditate just after a heavy meal.

- **Adjust your posture.** Try standing up and stretching and then sit down in a more upright posture than before. Try keeping your eyes half open while you meditate.

- **Make sure that the room's not too hot and has plenty of fresh air.**

- **Have a bedtime routine and sleep at roughly the same time every day.** If you're not getting enough sleep, no matter what you do, you'll end up falling asleep in your meditation practice.

To help you find out any patterns in your sleepiness, try completing Worksheet 9-3.

Worksheet 9-3		Monitoring Your Sleepiness		
Day	*Time of Day for Meditation*	*How Sleepy Did I Feel? (0 = Not Sleepy at All, 10 = Completely Asleep for Whole Meditation)*	*My Position for Meditation (Sitting Back on Sofa/Lying Down/Sitting Upright)*	*If I Was Sleepy, What Do I Think Was a Cause? (For Example, Time, Type of Food Eaten, Amount of Physical Exercise Done)*
Monday				
Tuesday				
Wednesday				
Thursday				
Friday				
Saturday				
Sunday				

Review the worksheet at the end of the week to notice any patterns and adjust your mindfulness meditation routine so that you're most likely to stay awake in your practice. For example, you may always fall asleep if you meditate as soon as you wake up, but if you have a shower and then meditate, you never fall asleep.

Re-igniting Your Enthusiasm

If you're in a regular meditation routine, it can feel comfortable to keep practising. However, if it seems very routine, it's making you sleepy or you feel like it's always the same, you need to recharge those mindfulness batteries!

Try some of the suggestions in Worksheet 9-4 and jot down what effect they had on you.

Worksheet 9-4	Re-igniting My Enthusiasm
Suggestion	*Effect on My Mindfulness Practice*
Different meditation position (lying down, cross-legged, slow walking).	
Different time of day.	
Practise with a local mindfulness group.	
Change the time that I practise.	
Treat myself to a whole day of mindfulness. Instead of controlling it, try to let it unfold for me.	
Get in touch with a mindfulness meditation teacher or attend a course or workshop.	
Take a day off or a week off from even trying to be mindful and just be myself. Notice what happens.	
My own idea:	
My own idea:	
My own idea:	

Some days mindfulness may feel repetitive and boring and on other days you may feel a bit more connected and at ease. That's okay. What we're suggesting here is not to allow your mindfulness practice to become totally mechanical, where you're just going through the motions but not really engaging in the mindfulness practice.

Overcoming External Distractions

A distraction is something that takes your attention away from whatever you're focusing on. As a beginner, you may want to reduce external distractions as far as you can, but beyond that, distractions are useful – they're opportunities to see how your mind reacts to your attention being drawn away.

Figure 9-1 shows a simple way to manage distractions in mindfulness practice.

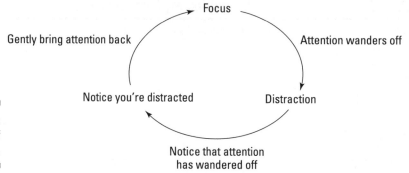

Figure 9-1:
The cycle of
attention.

Mindfulness can make good use of distraction and turn it into a learning experience. The secret is to open your attention towards the distraction with non-judgemental curiosity and acceptance.

London calling

One day I (Shamash) was in London teaching a client meditation and the window was open, allowing lots of traffic noise to come in. I asked her to close her eyes and simply open her attention and listen to the sounds of the traffic as if it were a piece of music, noticing the pitch and volume of the sounds as they rose and fell, without judging or criticising the sound. I reminded her, 'If you were deaf and hearing sounds for the first time, it would be a magical experience.' At the end of the short meditation, she told me that was the first time in her life that she hadn't felt annoyed by traffic noise and had actually enjoyed it. She also noticed the moments of silence between the sounds – a totally new experience for her. Normally the noise frustrated her, causing a constant, low-level stress as she travels around busy London.

Leave your phones on please, meditators

At a meditation retreat, a mindfulness teacher with over 100 participants asked everyone to leave their mobile phones on rather than off for the first meditation and just listen to the sounds of the phones ringing or text messages beeping from time to time. At first people felt their usual annoyance, but after a while, it was joyful and enjoyable to really listen to the range of ringtones from Bach to Michael Jackson! Some people had a huge urge to check their phones and were able to watch that urge arise and pass away.

Normally the sounds of phones ringing annoys people. Why not do something counter-intuitive and one time just listen to both the sound of your phone and the sound of your own inner thoughts, judgements and emotions as you try to meditate? To listen to the sound of the phone ringing and notice your inner reaction with acceptance is just as much a meditation as feeling your breathing or looking at a beautiful landscape. It's a question of developing the right attitude, step by step.

Here are three tips for managing distractions:

✔ Open your attention towards the distraction for a while. This helps you to stop fighting the distraction, thereby wasting less energy. Mindfulness is about awareness, not avoidance.

✔ As a beginner, you may find distractions particularly frustrating. If so, find a quiet area and practise mindfulness there for short periods of time – say ten minutes to start with.

✔ Let your whole meditation be focused on the distraction. If you can hear the noise of your children while meditating, practise mindful listening and just listen to the sounds without judging them.

Coping with Physical Discomfort

Working with physical discomfort is an important learning process in mindfulness. Usually, human beings try to avoid physical discomfort as far as possible. But discomfort can be a wonderful teacher because mindfulness is about developing acceptance and moving towards difficulties rather than running away and avoiding them. By noticing how your mind reacts to physical discomfort, you can notice the avoidant tendency of your mind and begin to develop a little more acceptance of the sensation, just as it is.

Your discomfort could be itching, stiffness, throbbing, aching, sharp, dull or some other sensation. The key is to notice both the *actual* sensation itself and your thoughts and feelings about the sensation as two distinctly different processes. Then, to go back to actually feeling the raw sensation. You may find that the actual sensation isn't as bad as you thought – the commentary in your mind can make it worse. Thoughts like 'I wish it would go away!' or 'I can't stand this' or 'Why me?' are the real culprits that make the experience one you want to avoid.

You don't need to tolerate pain – especially not to the extent that it does damage to your body! Pain is a messenger, and sometimes it's saying that something is wrong and needs fixing. So if you're experiencing an unusual pain in your body, see your doctor.

The starting point for managing discomfort in your body is to become curious and aware of the sensation itself. Identify any discomfort you have during meditation. Mark the location, size and shape of the discomfort you experienced in Figure 9-2. Be as accurate as you can.

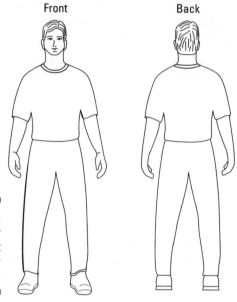

Figure 9-2:
Marking any discomfort on your body.

Now consider the following questions in Worksheet 9-5:

Worksheet 9-5 **Analysing My Discomfort**

What was the point of most discomfort (for example, ten minutes into seated meditation)?

What was the shape of the discomfort?

What was the texture of it, if any?

If it had a colour, what was it?

What size was the discomfort?

_____

_____

When I felt the discomfort with the sensation of my breath inhaling, what happened?

_____

_____

_____

When I felt it with the sensation of my breath exhaling, what happened?

_____

_____

_____

By answering these questions, you're being mindful of the sensation itself instead of getting caught up in your own inner criticisms and judgements, such as blaming yourself for not being better at meditating. You're discovering a new and mindful way of being with difficulty, which leads, in the long term, to a reduction in your suffering, despite the pain.

Pain and suffering don't have to go hand in hand. Pain is the sensation itself. Suffering is your reaction to the pain. Suffering is deepened if you believe the negative thoughts about the pain to be true, rather than seeing them simply as thoughts that pop into your mind. Suffering can deepen through avoidance strategies (such as deciding not to meditate) instead of acknowledging and accepting your present-moment experience. So, mindfulness is about learning to be with pain so the sensation causes minimal suffering. For more on pain, see Chapter 13.

Coping with Internal Distractions

Everyone gets distracted at some point. And many distractions are internal rather than external, such as restlessness or boredom. Find out some tricks for side-stepping the common pitfalls when dealing with internal distractions in this section.

Overcoming boredom or agitation

Boredom and agitation are connected to energy states. Boredom is associated with low levels of energy and agitation with high levels of energy. Mindfulness is about noticing both. A side-effect of mindfulness can be to cultivate a more balanced energy level within yourself.

One way of dealing with the emotion of boredom is to become curious about it. Consider the questions in Worksheet 9-6 when boredom next arises for you when you're practising mindfulness meditation.

Worksheet 9-6	Monitoring My Boredom
What thought preceded the feeling of boredom?	
What's happening to the feeling of boredom from moment to moment?	
Can I feel it in my body? Where exactly? Does it become more or less intense as I breathe?	
What do I desire to do instead?	
What happens when I connect my attention to the sensation of breathing?	
What happens if I accept the feeling of boredom, just as it is?	
What happens if I imagine my breath going into and out of the boredom?	
What happens when I take a step back from the emotion of boredom?	

Observing boredom is useful, because when you don't observe it, it can take over and lead you to stop practising mindfulness. Just accept that boredom will come and go, and that's okay. If you focus on getting rid of boredom all the time, that can be counter-productive from a mindfulness standpoint. The key is acceptance and curiosity about the feeling.

Restlessness is excessive trapped energy and an overactive mental state. If you've been rushing around on autopilot all day, it is difficult to stop, let go and be mindful. If you can slow down a bit during the day and be mindful from time to time, you're less likely to feel restless when it's time for you to meditate.

A way to try and combat restlessness is to begin your meditation with some mindful movement, such as mindful walking or mindful yoga. Gentle exercise helps to slowly calm your mind so that you're able to practise some sitting or lying down meditations.

The next time you practise meditation and you feel restless, fill in Worksheet 9-7.

Worksheet 9-7		Monitoring Restlessness		
Date and Time	How Restless Did I Feel? (1 = Calm, 10 = Extremely Restless)	Where in My Body Did I Feel Most Restless? Did the Feeling Have a Shape or Size?	What Thoughts Popped into My Head?	What Happened as I Continued to Be Mindful of My Breathing Together with the Feeling of Restlessness?

Ultimately, whether your restlessness grows or diminishes as you do this practice doesn't matter. What's important is your resolve to continue to practise mindfulness despite the feeling. Try to sit and stay put despite what the mind says. All feelings have a beginning and an end. The feeling will pass as long as you can be patient with it. Persevere and keep curious about your experience, like a scientist doing a new experiment for fun.

If you find yourself feeling bored or restless very often, consider what you eat and how much you exercise too. A balanced diet with plenty of fruit and veg helps you to be more mindful and balances your energy levels. Try to do some physical activity daily. Even brisk walking for 20 minutes a day or two lots of ten minutes can make a significant positive difference and ease excessive boredom or frustration. Combine the walking with some mindfulness, and that's even better.

Dealing with unusual experiences

At some point, you may well have some form of unusual experience when practising mindfulness meditation. You may experience a feeling like floating or being very heavy, automatically stretching your limbs, feeling itchy or restless, feeling your body expand or even feeling shocks in your body or visualising vivid images.

Don't be concerned if you have an unusual meditation – you're not alone. It's normal and it will pass, like every other experience.

If you do have an unusual meditation experience, jot it down in Worksheet 9-8.

Worksheet 9-8	Recording Unusual Meditation Experiences	
Unusual Experience	*My Thoughts, Feelings and Bodily Sensations*	*Effect of Acceptance, Self-kindness or Curiosity on the Experience Itself*

If you have an unusual experience, simply allow it to unfold, unless the experience is overwhelming for you, in which case stop and have a break. Remember, you're in charge – not the mindfulness teacher or audio track you're listening to, or anyone else. If you feel you need professional support, you can find a mindfulness therapist to help you through the process.

Handling difficult emotions

Mindfulness is a powerful way of handling difficult emotions. As a human being, you'll always experience emotions. In your mindfulness practice, emotions continue to arise and pass away, just like in everyday life. However, as you turn your attention inwards, you have a greater possibility to notice and process emotions that you may have suppressed in the past.

If you have a strong, difficult emotion such as deep sadness during your mindfulness practice, the temptation may be to fight the emotion or run away from it. Consider the last time you experienced a difficult emotion – how did you deal with it? Perhaps you escaped the emotion by distracting yourself by socialising, overworking or exercising. None of these activities are bad in themselves, but your underlying desire is to escape from the emotion. The question is, was it effective? Did your method work in the long run? If so, that's fine. But if not, you may like to try the mindful approach.

Mindfulness teaches a healthy way of being with emotions. Strangely, the secret is counter-intuitive – you need to just be with the emotions instead of trying to get rid of them. The act of avoiding emotions gives them power and makes them more of a problem. By allowing the emotions to simply be, they become less of a problem.

Your difficult emotion, maybe anger, sadness or boredom, is like a neighbour you don't like who really wants to come into your home. The neighbour keeps knocking on the door. You have three options:

- ✔ Your first option is to get annoyed and shout at the neighbour to go away. Your neighbour shouts back and you get into an energy-draining argument.

- ✔ The second option is to pretend the knocking isn't happening. But no matter what you do, you can hear it in the background. That's frustrating.

- ✔ The final option is to stop the struggle and simply let him come in. You don't have to like him, but you find the best way to deal with him is to acknowledge him and allow him to be there.

That's the idea with acceptance of emotions – you let go of the battle with your emotion, step by step.

Emotions are natural experiences to feel, not problems to avoid.

Try filling out Worksheet 9-9 to help develop your mindfulness approach when dealing with difficult emotions.

The man who tried to control the lake

There was once a man who used to go down to a large, calm lake and sit by it for pleasure. The lake was always still and the expanse of water was beautiful and vast. One day the man went down to the lake and saw some ripples in it. The man was upset – he liked the lake to be still and calm. In his frustration he began to pat the water, trying to make the lake still, but this caused more ripples. He tried harder and harder, but the problem just got worse. Finally, he gave up. He accepted that the lake was full of ripples and just watched. To his amazement, as he accepted the imperfection of the lake, the wind started to die down and the lake calmed itself naturally. The man discovered that acceptance was the key, not trying harder to get rid of the ripples.

Try dealing with your own emotions in the same way. Instead of trying to fix them, let them be and watch them. The winds of your emotions may reduce or may not – but watching them is certainly easier than constantly trying to control the inevitable.

Worksheet 9-9	Evaluating my Difficult Emotions

What am I feeling? (For example, anger.)

_____

How intense is it on a rating of 1 to 10, with 10 being strongest?

_____

What is my current attitude towards the emotion? (For example, wanting to shout at someone, cry, distract myself with television.)

_____

What mindful attitude can I bring to the emotion? (Such as curiosity, acceptance, kindness, affection, just noticing it more carefully, not fighting with it, allowing it space to be there.)

_____

Where exactly do I feel the emotion as a physical sensation in my body? What is its shape, size, texture and colour?

_____

_____

What thoughts run through my mind together with the emotion?

_____

_____

What happens if I imagine my breath going into and out of the emotion in my body, bringing warmth and friendliness to it as best I can?

_____

_____

When it all gets too much

Managing strong emotions mindfully sounds easy in theory, but takes a bit of practice in reality. Essentially you need to create a shift in your attitude towards your emotions. You need to try to allow the emotion to simply be. Imagine your emotion is a tennis ball and your attitude is the way you grip the ball. You're aiming to rest the ball in the palm of your open hand. You don't need to throw the ball, or grip it tightly. Just gently let it rest in your palm.

If the emotion is overwhelming for you, you can move your attention away from the emotion. Try feeling the sensation of your feet on the floor, or feeling your breathing. If you are feeling your feet, just simply notice what it feels like to notice the sensation of your feet on the ground. Alternatively, focus on your breath. Simply notice your in-breath and out-breath rather than your emotion. And when you're ready, gently go back to the emotion.

Managing difficult thoughts

Thoughts and emotions are interconnected and often interact with each other. But they're also different. Thoughts are like sounds or images in your mind. Emotions are experiences felt within your mind and body. In mindfulness, we take a slightly different approach to thoughts than we do to emotions, as you'll discover.

Some difficult, negative thoughts may arise when you practise mindfulness as it's often when you're more mindful that you actually notice them. Mindfulness can be a bit like turning on a light in the dark, untidy room of your mind. Suddenly you start to notice all the things that are wrong rather than the beauty of the room itself.

Mindfulness doesn't create negative or positive thoughts. Mindfulness is about awareness. You simply notice your thoughts. If you have negative thoughts that have been running in the background of your awareness, you may notice them a bit more now, but they have less impact on you if you're mindful of them.

Here's how to manage difficult thoughts in a mindful way:

1. **Take a step back from your thoughts**. You have many ways of doing this such as:

   - Notice the type of thought (maybe you're worrying, planning, judging, self-criticising).

   - Say to yourself: 'I notice I'm having the thought that I'll mess up the presentation tomorrow' or 'This is just a thought, not necessarily a fact'.

   - Ask yourself: 'Am I confusing a thought with a fact?'

   - Imagine your thoughts are projected on to a cinema screen and you're sitting back in your seat, away from the screen, watching the film.

   - Watch or visualise clouds passing. Then place your thoughts on those imaginary clouds, so that you can see them come and go from a distance.

   Experiment to see what works for you. Be curious. You're not trying to avoid or get rid of the thoughts – just to take a step back from them.

2. **Turn your attention back to your focus**. If you're meditating, your focus may be your breathing or bodily sensations. If you're not meditating, you can focus on something external. This focus could be your work, the breeze as you walk or the sound of the music in the coffee shop, for example.

Mountain meditation

Listen to the mountain meditation (Track 4 at www.dummies.com/go/mindfulnessworkbookuk) to help you to deal with strong emotions.

Sitting comfortably upright, take a couple of deep breaths. Each time you breathe out, have a sense of letting go. Each time you breathe in, feel nourished. Then let your breath return to normal, and close your eyes.

Visualise a beautiful, majestic mountain; serene, stable, balanced and ancient, full of inner strength and poise. Imagine a mountain with its snow-capped peak high above the clouds in the clear, blue sky. Notice the wind and rain don't affect the stability of the mountain. As day turns to night, the mountain is unmoved. You notice the changing seasons, and the heat beats against the mountain, and yet the mountain is able to stay strong. Cold winds whistle past the mountain, rain turns to snow, and yet the mountain remains unshaken and accepting...

Notice the stability and groundedness of the mountain and play with the idea that your being can merge with this image of the mountain. You are strong, stable, still, balanced and grounded. You are present, despite the changing seasons of your thoughts and emotions. You accept their presence, without being moved. You simply notice the landscape of your inner experiences that is naturally in constant change, just as the mountain does as the seasons change.

Table 9-1 shows negative thoughts about mindfulness that you need to be particularly careful to step back from, rather than believe. These thoughts can lead you to stop practising mindfulness altogether. We give you some antidote thoughts that you can use to manage them.

Table 9-1	Combating Negative Thoughts about Mindfulness
Negative Thought	**Antidote**
Mindfulness isn't working for me.	Mindfulness is a long-term process and way of being, not a quick fix. I'll keep trying to be mindful, treating myself kindly and respectfully.
I can't stop my thoughts from racing.	Mindfulness isn't about stopping thoughts. Mindfulness is about awareness and as I become more aware, I'm bound to notice more thoughts, especially at the beginning. That's okay.
I can't sit still.	I can practise mindful movement, or be more mindful in my daily activities. Mindfulness is about awareness rather than position. Alternatively, I can try to sit still and notice the urges to move within my body.
I can't do it.	I'm not trying to do anything, in a way. I'm just noticing and watching what's happening. Step by step, I'll learn to become more mindful. I'll learn at my own pace.
I'm wasting my time.	How do I know I'm wasting my time? This is just my mind speaking. It will take time to notice the benefits of mindfulness, but I will give myself a couple of months of practice before I decide whether this is for me.

For a range of ways for managing negative thoughts in general, check out Chapters 11 and 12.

Learning mindfulness (like life in general) will always present difficulties and obstacles. Perhaps you're pretty nasty to yourself through excessive self-criticism when things don't work out how you want them to. The way to deal with this harsh inner voice is to listen to it, give it space to unfurl and bring to it a sense of curiosity in a gentle, warm way.

I (Jo) used to be very self-critical of everything I did. When I first practised yoga, for example, I thought about how bad I was at doing the poses. The voice telling me I'm bad at yoga comes back occasionally, but now I simply notice it and usually smile when I hear it. The negative thought usually dissipates quickly after that and I can carry on with my yoga (which I am now better at through steady practice!).

Difficulties can be terrifying when you're running away from them, but the more you turn and face them, the more they lose their power. It's like camping and being terrified of the dark and the noises in the woods. But when you shine a torch around you realise there's nothing to be afraid of.

If a strong difficult thought or worry comes up in your meditation, fill in the answers in Worksheet 9-10.

Worksheet 9-10   **Dealing with Difficult Thoughts**

What effect is this difficult thought having on your body?

What effect is it having on your emotions?

What happens if you listen to the difficulty with empathy?

What happens if you say to yourself, 'It's okay, whatever the emotion is, it's ok. Let me feel it'?

What happens if you accept it just as it is?

What happens if you breathe into the difficult thought and stay with the sensations?

(continued)

What happens when you say to yourself, 'I'm having the thought that . . .'?

_____

What happens when you gently return to the focus of meditation?

_____

Part IV
Enjoying the Rewards of Mindfulness

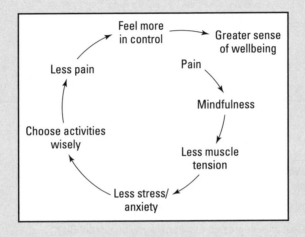

In this part . . .

- ✔ Welcome more happiness, energy and creativity into your life.
- ✔ Manage stress and anger with mindfulness.
- ✔ Deal with depression and anxiety with mindful CBT exercises.
- ✔ Discover how mindfulness can help with pain relief.
- ✔ Coach children in mindfulness.
- ✔ Go to www.dummies.com/go/mindfulnesswork bookuk to listen to audio meditations.

Chapter 10

Boosting Your Happiness Mindfully

In This Chapter

▶ Understanding what makes people happy

▶ Combining mindfulness and positive psychology

▶ Cultivating positive feelings

▶ Enjoying ways to increase your creativity

The Dalai Lama's book *The Art of Happiness* begins with this quote:

I believe that the very purpose of our life is to seek happiness [. . .] Whether one believes in religion or not [. . .], we all are seeking something better in life. So, I think, the very motion of our life is towards happiness.

After making such a bold statement, the Dalai Lama was asked if happiness is a reasonable goal for most people. He answered, 'Yes. I believe that happiness can be achieved through training the mind.'

Mindfulness practice offers that training. Through a combination of mindfulness meditation and day-to-day mindful awareness, you can train your mind to be happier.

In this chapter, you take a good, honest look at happiness and find out what it's all about, including what the researchers suggest - from sitting up straight to getting absorbed in a hobby. You discover how the art of mindful living, being positive and getting creative can all help move you towards living a happy life. To find out more, dive into this chapter – and smile!

Looking into the Concept of Happiness

The secret of happiness, you see, is not found in seeking more, but in developing the capacity to enjoy less.

— Socrates

Happiness has been a topic of interest for thousands of years, from the ancient Greek philosophers to modern-day psychologists and neuroscientists, and the eternal question 'What constitutes a happy life?' continues to be explored. To help you address this question for yourself, we ask you to clarify your own ideas about happiness by answering a few questions and then thinking about what your answers mean for you.

Discovering your ideas about happiness

People are just as happy as they make up their minds to be.

— *Abraham Lincoln*

To help discover what's important to you, answer and think about the questions in Worksheet 10-1.

Worksheet 10-1	Reflecting on My Happiness

Generally speaking, how happy are you?

What sorts of activities make you feel happier?

How important is happiness in your life?

How important is money as a factor for your happiness?

How important are relationships with friends, family or a partner for happiness?

If you were to describe your ideal life that would lead you to feel very happy, what would that consist of?

Having reflected on the above questions and your answers, now consider the following statement:

> A life of wellbeing is not about doing one thing; it's about a range of different things that together lead to a life of wellbeing. When you're cooking a meal, you don't just have one ingredient, you have a whole load of different foods that make up the meal – that's what makes the meal tasty, nutritious and balanced. In the same way, a life of wellbeing consists of a range of different elements that work together for you.

In a moment we ask you to list your typical elements, but to get your creative juices flowing, here's what we came up with, for us:

- ✔ Meditation and yoga.

- ✔ Being grateful for what we have in life.

- ✔ Spending time with friends and having fun.

- ✔ Exercising and keeping a healthy diet.

- ✔ Letting go of things that don't really matter.

- ✔ Doing work that we enjoy and having goals, but not getting too concerned if we don't achieve those goals on time.

- ✔ Laughing at ourselves and not taking ourselves too seriously.

- ✔ Being a good, supportive friend.

- ✔ Helping others who need it.

- ✔ Convulsive giggling.

Your list may well be very different. For example, if you have a family, the time you spend with them may be important for you. Or you may have particular hobbies that you really enjoy.

Now create your personal wellbeing recipe in Worksheet 10-2.

Worksheet 10-2	**My Wellbeing Recipe**

1.

2.

3.

4.

5.

6.

7.

8.

9.

10.

Ask yourself whether you give enough time and attention to these different areas. If not, take a small step today, for just one of those elements, to help it grow.

Challenging your ideas about happiness

Consider the following list. Which of the items do you think would make you happier in the long term? Prepare to be surprised:

- ✔ A relationship.
- ✔ More time off from work or more money.
- ✔ Having a baby.
- ✔ Losing weight.
- ✔ Knowing what you want to do with your life.
- ✔ Ending a physical disability.

Amazingly, according to findings from years of careful scientific research, none of these outer circumstances would make you significantly happier. In fact, changes in outer circumstances result only in a maximum of a 10 per cent increase in wellbeing. In addition, as you can see from Figure 10-1, 50 per cent of your happiness is fixed by your genes. But you can determine the rest, a massive 40 per cent, by your inner attitude and chosen activities. In other words, making the right choices allows you to boost your long-term wellbeing.

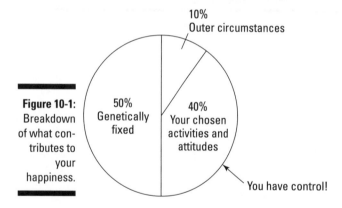

Figure 10-1: Breakdown of what contributes to your happiness.

Using Mindfulness with Positive Psychology

For much of its history, psychology focused on mental illness and other psychological problems, often overlooking what makes people happy. Today, however, we have *positive psychology* – the study of happiness and wellbeing – and it's not airy-fairy, namby-pamby, artsy-fartsy (how come so many dismissive statements are hyphenated!) nonsense. Positive psychologists use the latest scientific approaches and techniques to research what makes people happier and more fulfilled. Not surprisingly, mindfulness has been found to be one of the key factors in a happy life.

Flourishing with mindfulness and positivity

The latest wellbeing theory from the founder of the positive psychology movement, Dr Martin Seligman, consists of five elements, summarised by the mnemonic PERMA. Dr Seligman believes that these elements together help to develop a life of wellbeing:

- ✔ **Positive emotion:** Feelings such as joy, hope, curiosity and love fall into this category. These emotions are important to enjoy in the present moment and are an essential element of wellbeing. You can't feel happy all the time – in fact, trying to hold on to happiness rather than letting it come and go can cause you problems. Instead, mindfulness helps you to become aware of these emotions when they arise without you getting attached to them.

- ✔ **Engagement:** This element is a fascinating one. When your attention is fully focused on a task, hobby, work or person, you go into a state of mind called *flow*. In this state, you're fully in the present moment, lose track of time and forget about almost everything else, including your own sense of self. The more often you get into this state, the more likely you are to experience wellbeing. Through mindful awareness, you cultivate your ability to focus and thereby get into this sort of engaged state more often.

- ✔ **Relationships:** Positive relationships form the core of a life of wellbeing. We don't mean only a partner, but your friends, family, colleagues – people you regularly interact with. If you give time and energy to cultivating good quality relationships, you're much more likely to live a life of greater wellbeing. This fact isn't surprising because humans are social beings. Mindfulness helps you to be less reactive and more empathic, guiding you towards developing more positive relationships.

- ✔ **Meaning:** This category is about dedicating yourself to a cause that's bigger than yourself – perhaps belief in God or working to improve humanity's lot in some way, whether large or small. You may be a road sweeper and reflect on how you're creating a cleaner environment in the neighbourhood to create a personal sense of meaning. On the other hand, you can be the leader of a nation and if you just focus on how to have more power you're going to lack meaning in your life.

- ✔ **Accomplishment:** Achieving a goal that's valuable to you contributes to your wellbeing. Maybe you want to get married, learn how to speak Spanish or win an award in your area of speciality. Through mindfulness, you're able to clarify which goals are important to you and focus on those that are achievable and enjoyable to do. Crucially, mindfulness also emphasises the importance of the journey to the achievement, rather than just the outcome.

Use the questions in Worksheet 10-3 to boost your long-term wellbeing in each of these five areas.

Worksheet 10-3	Improving My Wellbeing in Five Areas

Positive emotions

What activities do you enjoy and need to do more of?

_____

Engagement

Think about activities that you've done in the past that make you feel fully connected. Is it a sport, a particular hobby or a job? What activities absorb your attention?

_____

How can you do them more often?

_____

Relationships

Do you have several positive relationships, with your friends or family? If not, what do you think you need to do to forge positive relationships? For example, spend more time with the people, read or attend a workshop on relationships or ask someone good at relationships for some tips? Regular meditation can also help improve your relationships (check out Chapter 6).

_____

Meaning

How does the work you do every day help others?

_____

What small acts of kindness can you do that other people would appreciate?

_____

Accomplishments

You need to keep this one in balance. For many people, wellbeing is linked exclusively to achievements, whereas in fact it's just one element.

Do you feel that you're moving towards achieving your dreams in life? What small steps can you take to achieve them?

_____

In Worksheet 10-4, put your own examples of things you have done this week that fit the five ways to happiness.

Worksheet 10-4	Identifying Activities that Help Me to be Happy	
Day	**Main Activities**	**What Aspect of PERMA Did They Fulfil?**
Monday		
Tuesday		
Wednesday		
Thursday		
Friday		
Saturday		
Sunday		

Practising gratitude

Don't cry because it's over, smile because it happened.

— *Dr Seuss*

Dr Seuss comes up with a gem here. When challenging circumstances happen in your life, the normal response is often to focus on the hurt, the pain and the disappointment. But why not consider all that went well? Surely that would be a more balanced perspective.

The human brain has evolved to focus on and remember what's gone wrong rather than right. This protective tendency dates back to cave-dweller days, when if you forgot about all the surrounding dangers, you ended up a goner pretty quickly. This evolutionary past still lingers in the modern human brain. When something goes wrong, such as your car breaking down or your girlfriend not calling you, that's what you most strongly remember that day. You forget about all the good things and miracles that are happening right in front of your eyes. As a result, you can easily take things for granted. For more on this phenomenon, called the negativity bias, see Chapter 2. Gratitude practice is a great antidote, helping you to put things in perspective.

According to research in positive psychology, an attitude of gratitude is a powerful way to increase your wellbeing. Science agrees. Researchers at the University of Connecticut found that gratitude has a protective effect against heart problems. And those who did have a heart attack but considered the benefits gained from the heart attack, had a lower risk of having another heart attack.

Not only that, but also grateful people are:

- ✔ More energetic or hopeful.
- ✔ More spiritual or religious.
- ✔ More forgiving.
- ✔ More likely to exercise and sleep better.
- ✔ Less materialistic.
- ✔ Less likely to be depressed, anxious, lonely, neurotic or envious.

If you fancy being like that, you can by thinking about what's going well in your life, and being thankful for it.

Since I (Jo) started practising mindfulness, I see things in a different way. A few weeks ago, early in the morning, the water in my flat stopped flowing as I was about to start work. I had a million things to do that day and had to wash with a large bottle of water. Instead of getting annoyed and frustrated as I may have been before practising mindfulness, I was grateful that I was able to buy a bottle of clean water to shower with and grateful that I usually had clean running water. When I got back home from work, the water was back on and it made me smile. Now I always include running water in my gratitude practice.

Recording things and people you're grateful for

If you like writing, one fairly easy way to develop your sense of gratitude is to note down what you're grateful for. You can include things that seem so natural that they're trivial, such as clean air, drinking water or a warm bed, as well as more obvious things such as your partner or family, your health or your friends.

Reduce depression in five minutes a day

In one study by a positive psychologist at the University of Pennsylvania, a group of severely depressed patients were asked to do one simply positive psychology exercise everyday: to write down three good things that happened that day. For example, 'My friend Jo called me', 'I managed to get out of bed before noon' or 'My favourite programme was on TV today'. After just over two weeks of doing this, 94 per cent said they experienced relief and they went from being in the most extremely depressed category to 'mild to moderately depressed'.

If you suffer from depression, ask your doctor if this exercise may be useful for you.

Research seems to suggest that you don't want to write gratitude entries so regularly that you get bored. Doing so, say, once a week on a Sunday is fine. Alternatively, you may be the kind of person who enjoys making diary entries several times a week, or even daily. If so, choose a time of day where you have a few minutes to reflect, such as first thing in the morning or just before going to sleep (the practice may help you have a good night's sleep too).

Try to be creative in your diary entries, however, and avoid it becoming too routine. Shamash encourages his clients to think of more unusual times to practise gratitude, and in a way that fits with their lifestyles. If you put the exact same things down, at the same time every day, you may be doing the practice mechanically rather than consciously. Instead, bring some mindfulness to the practice and reflect on what other things you're grateful for in your life. Perhaps completing the diary entry at different times of day may help – even at a time when you're not feeling that great.

When I'm (Shamash) feeling a bit low, I usually do some mindfulness practice, reflect on a few things that are going well and then decide on the best thing to do next. That lifts my mood sometimes, and if not, I just practise mindful acceptance of the emotion within my body and then carry on with my day, as best I can.

Complete Worksheet 10-5, once a week for a period of six weeks, and see what effect the process has on your wellbeing.

Worksheet 10-5	**My Gratitude Diary**			
Week	*What I'm Grateful for This Week*	*How Do I Feel, Having Written This?*	*How Well Did I Sleep This Week?*	*Generally, How Happy Do I Feel This Week?*
1				
2				
3				
4				
5				
6				

Another gratitude practice is to thank people who've done something for you. It may be a family member, friend or perhaps a colleague at work. You can also express your gratitude in different ways, such as writing a letter and posting it to them, or even better, reading it out to them in person.

Use Worksheet 10-6 to help you think of a few people with whom you can do this gratitude practice and reflect on doing so.

Worksheet 10-6	My List of People to Thank	
Person I Want to Thank	**What I Want to Say**	**Thoughts, Feelings and Bodily Sensations that Arose After I Thanked Them**

Finding your own way to gratitude

Don't feel that you have to write down your thankfulness every day. Instead, practise gratitude in whatever way works for your character and lifestyle. Here are a few suggestions. Take your pick and see which you most prefer:

✔ Think about a few things you're grateful for while you're travelling to work, coming home or whenever you have a few moments.

✔ Find a gratitude partner and together share what you're grateful for. You can then remind each other and have the added benefit of socialising and sharing positive moments together.

✔ Share what you appreciate with a visitor. When a friend comes to see you, you can show the person your stamp collection, your young child's first drawing or your favourite local theatre.

✔ Notice when you're not feeling great and use that as a reminder to count your blessings.

✔ Send a gratitude email every week thanking people for what they do. Even a couple of sentences are fine. That's makes for a great start to the day.

Savouring the now

Here's a quote that a friend shared with the Learn Mindfulness Facebook page. (You're welcome to join the page if you're on Facebook, and share insights and observations with the community of several thousand.)

WISE WORDS

First I was dying to finish high school and start college. And then I was dying to finish college and start working. Then I was dying to marry and have children. And then I was dying for my children to grow old enough so I could go back to work. Then I was dying to see them marry and have children. Then I was dying to retire. And now I'm dying, and suddenly I realised, I forgot to live. Please don't let this happen to you. Appreciate your current situation and enjoy each day.

— Author Unknown

This quote can be a real wake-up call. If like many people you find yourself constantly planning for a future but never really enjoying the present moment, perhaps you can try the practice of savouring the now. This practice is essentially mindful, but with a slight twist – the idea is to tune into the pleasantness of an experience in the moment. Savouring present-moment experiences is one of the core hallmarks of leading a life of wellbeing, and so it's worth having a go.

In this section, we suggest three ways to savour and enjoy life more.

Enjoying ordinary, everyday experiences

Life contains many pleasures and overlooking them or moving quickly on to something else is all too easy. Try slowing down and savouring pleasurable experiences. Instead of gulping down that cafe latte while trying to read a newspaper, really taste the flavour, enjoy the warmth of the cup and connect with the aroma. When going for a walk, literally take time to stop and smell the roses. Taking time and some effort to connect and luxuriate in your senses can make ordinary experiences more enjoyable.

A friend of Jo's takes great pleasure in pairing up socks – she absolutely loves it! To you this may be a boring task, but to her, it's pure bliss. She sits down, puts all the odd socks in a box and slowly pairs up each one. When she's finished, she feels contented and happy.

Glad to be alive

I (Shamash) remember meeting my friend a couple of days after he'd been in a car accident. He was lucky to be alive. While we were having dinner together, he was in a hyper-aware state of mind and was savouring every single experience. He talked about the stunning beauty of the lights in the restaurant, the vividness of the colours and the rich tastes in the food. Perhaps the shock of the accident had thrown him fully into the here and now, and he was savouring every moment. The hyper-aware state wore off after a week or so, but his descriptions reminded me of the beauty of savouring the now.

Savouring the moment with others

Enjoying the here and now with friends or family can heighten the feeling of pleasure. Going on a walk and looking at a lake, a flower or a stunning view together. Or you can just be at home and be in the moment as you cook together. Many people talk about a different but positive feeling when they meditate with others, which seems strange, because for many people meditation is a very personal experience.

Practising mindfulness meditation in the now

When you meditate regularly, you develop a brain that's more connected with the present moment. With mindfulness meditation practice every day, you're more likely to be able to focus your attention in the present moment and savour pleasurable experiences, instead of being overly highjacked by your thoughts.

One of Jo's favourite things to do is to cook dinner for friends, something she tries to do mindfully. She gets all the ingredients together and feels the sensations in her body as she creates the meal. She gets to share it with others when it's finished too, or sometimes a friend who takes pleasure in cooking helps her prepare the meal, and she can share the first process as well.

Complete Worksheet 10-7 with some activities that you can really savour and note your reflections in the right-hand column.

Worksheet 10-7	List of Activities to Savour
Activity I Want to Savour Today	*Observations (Consider the Thoughts, Feelings and Bodily Sensations You Experienced)*
My walk to the train station from home.	I enjoyed listening to the birds as I walked. I thought, 'That's lovely,' and felt joy and a relaxing feeling and warmth in my chest. My shoulders dropped a bit too.

Being kind to other people

Be kind, for everyone you meet is fighting a harder battle.

— *Plato*

Recently, on a BBC television programme, three keys to wellbeing were suggested: be mindful, be grateful and be kind. What a wonderful suggestion! We cover mindfulness and gratitude in the earlier sections 'Savouring the now' and 'Practising gratitude'. Now, we take a look at another form of wellbeing: kindness.

When you perform an act of kindness for others, you get many benefits in return:

- ✔ **You feel great.** Just think about the last time you did something nice for others. How did it make you feel? Perhaps you gave someone a lift, looked after someone with the flu or listened to your friend to help ease his worries.

- ✔ **Others feel great.** By being kind to someone else, that person is likely to appreciate it and feel good too. Again, just think of the last time someone did a favour for you – it often feels great when someone thinks about you.

- ✔ **You feel part of a greater whole, connected with others.** When you're being kind to other people, you're reminded that all people are interdependent on each other. Instead of seeing yourself as an isolated individual, you recognise yourself as being an important part of the whole. As a result, you're more likely to be a good friend, partner or colleague and thereby improve your relationships – a core factor in wellbeing (see the earlier section 'Flourishing with mindfulness and positivity').

- ✔ **You focus on how you can help rather than your own little worries.** When you're helping others, you stop worrying about your own concerns. Your attention is engaged in how you can help others. You're more likely to think about how fortunate you are – and naturally you begin to feel grateful and positive.

- ✔ **You feel more confident.** When you're being kind to others, you see yourself in a more positive light. You think about your usefulness and feel more optimistic. This feeling is heightened if you're volunteering for a particular cause too.

You don't have to do some huge gesture of kindness; any small act counts. For example, I've (Shamash) been writing this book at my local coffee shop. I enjoy the company of others as I write. On my birthday, I invited the regular coffee drinkers to a local pizza place. We shared a meal together and a few laughs. I was happy to pay the bill, which wasn't a big deal, and my new-found friends were very grateful, and so it was a win-win situation all round.

Using Worksheet 10-8, keep a list of your acts of kindness and your subsequent feelings.

A New York kind of Friend

The American TV show *Friends* has an episode where the character Phoebe tries to do a selfless deed. She wants to do something for someone and for it to be completely selfless. However, everything she does for someone else makes her feel good, and she concludes that no such thing as a selfless deed exists, because each one benefits her wellbeing also. She's right! You're likely to feel good when you're kind to others.

Worksheet 10-8	My List of Kind Acts
Kind Action	*How It Made Me Feel*

Developing Positive Emotions Mindfully

In mindfulness, positive emotions are cultivated without grasping them and difficult feelings are accepted without fighting them. Mindfulness isn't about chasing positive emotions. Primarily, it's about accepting your present-moment feelings, with a sense of warmth if possible. More positive feelings occur as a side effect. The great thing about mindfulness is that you don't need to try and be happy all the time – you can just relax and be yourself, however you're feeling.

Being mindful of your body posture

You may have noticed how your emotions affect your body posture. If you're feeling blue, you're more likely to look down and walk slowly with hunched shoulders. But if you're feeling confident, you probably stand more upright with your shoulders back, and you walk a little more quickly and purposefully.

Interestingly, new research is showing that by adjusting your body posture, you can impact how you feel. In other words, not only do your emotions affect your body posture and movement, but changing your body posture and movement can have an effect on how you're feeling:

1. **Sit with a slumped posture on a chair.** Become aware of your breathing or the sensations of your feet on the floor for a minute.

2. **Notice how you're feeling and what you're thinking.** Label the emotion internally in your mind. Notice where you feel your emotion in your body, if anywhere.

3. **Sit in a more upright way.** Really open your chest with your shoulders back. Relax your facial muscles and jaw if you can. Sit in a confident, dignified way for a minute or so.

4. **Notice how you feel and what you're thinking now.** Become aware of how you're feeling. Be curious. Do you feel exactly the same or have your feelings changed in some subtle way?

After completing the exercise, answer the questions in Worksheet 10-9.

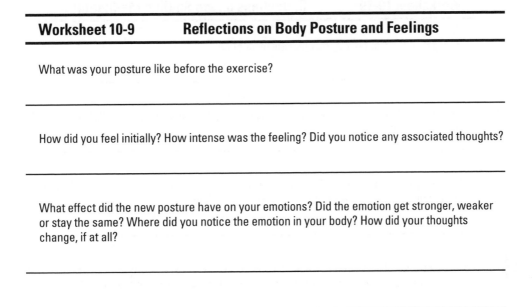

| Worksheet 10-9 | Reflections on Body Posture and Feelings |

What was your posture like before the exercise?

How did you feel initially? How intense was the feeling? Did you notice any associated thoughts?

What effect did the new posture have on your emotions? Did the emotion get stronger, weaker or stay the same? Where did you notice the emotion in your body? How did your thoughts change, if at all?

Say 'cheese!': Flexing your smile muscles

Have you noticed that people who smile tend to be surrounded by a lot of people (and it's not because they're thinking, 'What's that wise guy smiling about?')? The reason is that being in their company is pleasant. After all, you broadcast your emotional state from your facial expression. Some researchers have discovered links between how intensively people smile and the quality of their relationships, and even claim to be able to predict how long people will live from old photographs of people smiling.

Also, when you focus on smiling, you reduce your stress levels, encouraging more peaceful and relaxed sensations. By putting a smile on your face, you automatically begin to lift your mood. You don't even have to be genuinely smiling – begin by just faking it and see what happens!

Have a go at this smiling meditation and record your findings. Hold a gentle smile on your face as you do this meditation:

1. **Find a place where you can comfortably practise smiling and where you feel comfortable.**

2. **Begin by taking a few slow, deep breaths (you can keep your eyes open or closed).**

3. **Say to yourself, 'I'm aware that I'm breathing in' (or just 'breathing') as you breathe in.**

4. **Say to yourself 'I smile at my out-breath' (or just 'smiling') as you breathe out.**

5. **Continue repeating Steps 3 and 4 for a few minutes.**

Now answer the questions in Worksheet 10-10 and reflect on what you discover.

Worksheet 10-10   Reflections on the Smiling Meditation

How did you feel at the beginning of the meditation?

How did you feel during the mindful smiling practice? What did you like or dislike about it?

How did you feel at the end of the practice? Did you feel lifted at all? Would you like to try this more regularly for a week or two, to see what effect it has?

Here are some alternative phrases to say to yourself as you smile and breathe in and out. Try each one for a few minutes or longer and see which ones you like:

✔ Grateful for my in-breath . . . grateful for my out-breath.

✔ I smile as I breathe in . . . I open my heart as I breathe out.

✔ Breathing in is wonderful . . . breathing out is wonderful.

✔ Present moment . . . wonderful moment.

✔ Breathing in, I'm happy . . . breathing out, I'm smiling.

Smiling while simultaneously thinking a negative thought is pretty difficult to do. The mere act of smiling seems to drain the thought of some of its power.

Boosting Creativity with Mindfulness

Although the precise nature and origin of creativity is mysterious, one thing's for sure: when you have a calm mind, creativity naturally reveals itself, which makes you feel happier too. Here's an example: as we mention in the earlier section 'Practising mindfulness meditation in the now', Jo loves to cook mindfully, looking at recipes and thinking of ways to adapt them and make them extra yummy. She can't say where the ideas come from, they just pop into her awareness and leave when they've served their purpose, but her calm, focused state of mind seems to promote her creativity. If she's under too much pressure and running on autopilot, she's far less likely to be creative.

Mindfulness can develop creative solutions

Many of the business clients I (Shamash) coach initially have sessions to relieve anxiety, stress or depression. However, in the long term, they find that they also get the added benefit of more creative and effective solutions in their work and personal lives. Those business clients that continue to see me long term use the sessions to keep up with their regular mindfulness practice and ask questions about the deeper, more personal experiences that they face. Together we explore creative ways of meeting their challenges in the long term, to help maximise their wellbeing as well as that of those close to them. These results show the powerful creative output possible from mindfulness practice, which you can access too.

Creating the space for creativity with mindfulness

Nobody can say for certain how mindfulness leads to creativity, but here's our theory on the process. When you practise mindfulness:

1. **Your normal conscious thoughts start to lose their grip on your awareness.**

2. **Your more creative, unconscious brain is able to work more effectively and create new connections and ideas.**

3. **You make a mental space when your conscious mind calms down in which the new ideas are revealed.**

Mindfulness provides many other creative benefits too:

✔ **Clarity:** Regular mindfulness leads to a clearer mind. You can then see problems for what they are and spot solutions quickly. If your mind is overwhelmed with thoughts, you're unlikely to see any creative ideas.

✔ **Insight:** Mindfulness is sometimes called 'insight meditation' for good reason. By looking inwards, you're able to see connections and solve problems in novel ways, whereas without looking, you can't see the creative solution at all.

✔ **Focus:** When your attention is in the right place, creativity often flows. If your mind is wandering too much, you can't expect yourself to be creative in a productive way. Yes, letting yourself daydream can help with creativity, but having the ability to focus can be even more helpful.

✔ **Perspective:** Creativity is about seeing things from a different perspective or viewpoint. Mindfulness is particularly good at developing this ability because it's about stepping back from your thoughts and emotions rather than getting caught up in them. You can step back to help solve whatever problem you're working on, to help you see your task in a new light.

One of my (Shamash) most creative moments popped into my head in the middle of a mindfulness retreat. I was meditating away, not even considering any new project, when without warning a new title for a book came into my head, as clear as day. It took me by surprise. I didn't have to write the idea down – it was such a strong thought, it stuck in my head. After the retreat, I emailed the publisher and they agreed! I'll be writing that book next!

You don't have to sit down and meditate to practise mindfulness, although that's powerful. You can also go mindful walking in a local park, eat your lunch slowly and mindfully or drink your afternoon tea with your phone switched off and without your usual colleagues. All these strategies can get your creative juices flowing.

Use Worksheet 10-11 to find your own way to creative solutions.

Worksheet 10-11	My Creative Solutions

Write down a challenge in your life, for which you want a creative solution (remember to be specific about the challenge).

Decide how you're going to practise mindfulness today to help you let go of the problem (for example, mindful jogging this afternoon).

What possible new solutions popped into your head while you were meditating?

Encouraging creative solutions through meditation

Occasionally I (Shamash) use visualisations alongside mindfulness meditations and exercises with my clients. Some people are more visual that others, and enjoy them. Here's a visual mindful meditation that you can use to help find creative solutions to a challenge you may be facing. And remember: if creativity itself makes you happy, then solving problems creatively will doubly do so!

1. **Remove all possible distractions.** Find a quiet, cosy place to sit or lie down.
2. **Stretch briefly to help relax your muscles.** Perhaps tense all the muscles in your body for a few seconds and then let them go.
3. **Close your eyes and take three slow, deep mindful breaths.** Feel your breath coming in and as you breathe out, have a sense of letting go.
4. **Let your breathing be natural, as best you can.** Feel the physical sensation of your breathing for a few minutes.
5. **Imagine yourself in a peaceful place.** Take your time to choose a place where you feel relatively calm and relaxed and then stay there.
6. **Be mindful in your peaceful place.** Notice what you can see, hear, smell, taste, touch, feel and so on.

7. **Visualise meeting someone or something who represents creativity, wisdom and kindness.** It can be a wise friend, a spiritual person, a religious figure who you admire, an animal or some other being. Take your time to meet this person and say hello.

8. **Share your problem or challenge with this person.** Explain it as clearly as you can and ask for some creative solutions. Listen mindfully to the solutions that this person or being comes up with. Ask follow-up questions if you want until you feel that you've finished having the conversation.

9. **Say goodbye to this creative, wise and kind being when you're ready.** Remember, you can always go back and ask the being more questions. Return to feeling your breathing, gently open your eyes and stretch your body.

Now answer the questions in Worksheet 10-12.

Worksheet 10-12   Reflections on Solving My Problem Creatively

What did the creative and wise being suggest?

_____

What do you like about those ideas? What do you dislike about those ideas? What's the best idea?

_____

_____

What do you think the obstacles are to that idea?

_____

How can you overcome those obstacles?

_____

What do you think is the best solution to this challenge?

_____

If you think that it's a good solution, what's the next step you need to take? When will you take that step? Do you need help to take it? If so, who can you ask?

_____

_____

Chapter 11

Using Mindfulness to Reduce Stress, Anger and Tiredness

....

In This Chapter

▶ Managing stress mindfully

▶ Discovering mindful ways to cool your anger

▶ Enjoying ways to increase your energy

....

*A*s a human being, you're bound to experience the effects of stress, anger and tiredness from time to time: from demanding bosses and crying children to bad drivers and thoughtless friends, it comes with the territory of living. The question is, how can you handle these problems and what can you do to ensure that you don't suffer excessively from them?

Fortunately, mindfulness has some novel approaches to tackling these three difficulties. As we describe in this chapter, the awareness that mindfulness offers helps you to see where you may be creating or exacerbating the symptoms of stress, anger and fatigue. We also reveal ways for you to work through the feelings effectively, so that you don't make life even more difficult than it already is.

Using Mindfulness to Manage Stress

Mindfulness may seem to be a strange way to cope with the stress in your life. Perhaps you're wondering how becoming more aware can help you cope with, say, an elderly parent, a challenging job or a busy family life.

The fact is that awareness is the starting point for managing *any* change, which is why mindfulness is so important. You can't expect to change how you manage stress while you remain unaware if or how exactly you're generating the stress. That would be like trying to walk from your home to your friend's place in the middle of the night with no torch – you're going to get lost and what's more, not even know whether you're getting closer or farther away.

In the same way, the awareness that mindfulness offers helps you to notice what's causing you stress, and the thoughts and emotions that are associated with it. You can then see how the stress arises in the first place and what you need to do to move away from excessive stress. In other words, you switch on your torch and make your way to where you want to go.

Understanding stress

Consider the word 'stress' and write down what other words or thoughts come into your mind in Worksheet 11-1.

Worksheet 11-1	Words I Associate with Stress

This exercise helps to show you how you perceive stress. Some people see stress in a negative way; others think of stress as positive and motivating. To help clarify the situation, we find that using the following terminology is useful:

- ✔ **Pressure:** A helpful state when at the right level. Leads you to feel awake and motivated and drives you to take positive action in your life to achieve your goals.

- ✔ **Stress:** An unhelpful state created by too much pressure. Stress can also be generated by having too little pressure.

Think of yourself as being like a guitar string and the pressure you experience in life as the tension in the string:

- ✔ If the string is too loose, you don't get a decent sound. In other words, you're not under any pressure and feel bored.

- ✔ If the string is too taut, the sound produced isn't pleasant and the string can easily break. In other words, being under stress from too much pressure can lead to burnout – physical and emotional exhaustion – in the long term.

- ✔ If the string is at just the right tension, you get a beautiful sound. In other words, when you feel the right amount of pressure in your life, you feel motivated, focused and energised. You're likely to be in a state of flow (check out Chapter 2 for more details on this state).

How your interpretation can contribute to stress

The problem of excessive, sustained stress and associated damaging symptoms arises when you *interpret* pressure as being too much to be able to cope with.

When I (Shamash) was training to be a science school teacher, I experienced high levels of stress. I had to prepare lesson plans and experiments, learn how to teach, mark books, study new topics, have meetings with senior teachers, write reports and risk assessments, and more. I began to think that I was unable to cope with all the demands I was facing

and felt highly stressed. But remember, that was only an interpretation. If I'd thought and believed: 'I can handle this. I'll just do it step by step,' I probably wouldn't have experienced the high stress. Or if I'd noticed the thought 'I can't cope' as just another thought, rather than a fact, I'd have felt less stress. Stress is rarely just from an external source – stress often requires an internal interpretation by you that you can't handle the situation. Change your attitude to the situation and your stress levels can change.

Figure 11-1 illustrates the effects that increasing pressure can have on your performance in daily life. When you have too little pressure, you feel bored. When you have too much pressure, you feel anxious and stressed; if this situation continues over the long term, you can experience burnout.

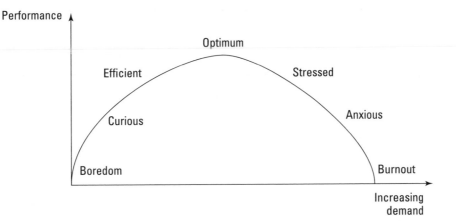

Figure 11-1:
Effects that stress and pressure have on your everyday performance.

For protection, all human beings are hard-wired to have a stress reaction when faced with a dangerous or threatening situation. When the stress reaction switches on, your body prepares itself to run, fight or freeze to avoid the danger. So, if you're being followed by an aggressive person, your heart starts to beat faster, your muscles tense, your senses heighten and you feel energised. Your body turns off your digestive system and immune system because you don't need to bother digesting your breakfast or fighting the flu if you're about to be attacked.

The problem is that the stress reaction doesn't just get switched on in physically dangerous situations that require running or beating someone up. Stress is activated when you realise that you're behind on your book deadline (that'll be us!), when you think about how annoying your boss is or when your partner says something unkind to you. But hang on a minute – that's crazy! You don't need your immune and digestive systems to shut down while talking to your partner. In fact, even the more reasonable, intelligent and wise part of your brain shuts down in a stress reaction. You're placed into a state of mind looking for threats.

So although the stress reaction is fine for extraordinary physical threats, it's a malfunction during normal life. Not only is chronic stress unhelpful in your everyday tasks, but also it's dangerous: having your immune system turned down over long periods of time can cause many illnesses. We don't mean to stress you out more than you already are – but remembering how dangerous long-term, high-level stress can be is important, as is taking swift action to reduce stress before it creates more problems for you.

Consider what happens to you when you're under high levels of stress and note down what you find in Worksheet 11-2:

Worksheet 11-2	How I React to Stress
Body	
Mind	
Emotions	
Behaviour	

This exercise helps you to identify your stress. If, in the future, you show any of the warning signs that you've listed above, you know that you're experiencing stress and can take preventative measures. See Chapter 8 for more on creating a stress reduction action plan.

Measuring your stress levels

When beginning the process of getting back in control of your stress, the first step is to record your levels of stress for a few weeks. Use Worksheet 11-3 to get you started this week and see what you discover. We provide a sample entry for you.

Worksheet 11-3			Recording My Stress Levels			
Date and Time	Cause of My Stress	Level of Stress on a Scale 1–10	Body Sensations I Noticed	Emotions I Felt (and Where in My Body)	Thoughts Arising in My Mind	How I Managed the Stress
Tuesday morning	Having to do all the housework.	8/10	Tense shoulders and jaw	Irritation, frustration. Tense shoulders.	John should have helped me out yesterday evening. I've got too much to do. I'm late for work.	Nothing much. I just carried on with the work but felt annoyed.

Having filled in Worksheet 11-3 for one week, consider the questions in Worksheet 11-4 to help increase your awareness:

Worksheet 11-4	**Considering My Stress**

What patterns did you notice about your stress?

What were your most helpful ways of managing the stress?

Responding rather than reacting to stress

In mindfulness, we make a clear distinction between *reacting* and *responding* to situations. Here's what we mean:

- ✔ **Reaction:** An automatic thought and action to an event in your life (for example, a source of stress).
- ✔ **Response:** Where you reflect for a moment and make a conscious choice about your behaviour in a particular situation.

Victor Frankl puts it well:

Between stimulus and response there is a space. In that space is our power to choose our response. In our response lies our growth and our freedom.

The stimulus can be a situation causing you stress or perhaps just a stress-inducing thought. If you're not mindful of the space between the stimulus and your response, the result is an automatic reaction. If your automatic reactions to situations are unhealthy, you may well feel even more stressed.

To reduce your stress, notice the gap between the cause of your stress and your reaction.

Imagine for a moment that a friend meets up with you and has forgotten your birthday. An unmindful *reaction* may be along the following:

1. **Automatic thoughts:** 'He should have remembered! How rude!'

2. **Feelings:** Anger, frustration, disgust.

3. **Body sensations:** Rapid beating of heart; raised temperature.

4. **Action may be:** To ignore your friend for a few days, or to lash out with angry words.

Zen and the Art of Dentistry

When you go to the dentist and are given an anaesthetic injection, you're told not to eat anything for a while afterwards. The reason is partly because your mouth has been made numb and so you're not *aware* of the sensations inside your mouth. As a result, you can easily hurt yourself by biting your tongue or the inside of your mouth. This simple example reveals the importance of awareness. Mindfulness offers that awareness – so that you don't accidently hurt yourself by getting too stressed. You notice the early warning signs and naturally take action to prevent your mind spiralling into something worse. That's one of the reasons why mindfulness is such a powerful way of reducing stress.

A mindful *response* to the same situation, however, may result in a different situation:

1. **Having the initial automatic thought:** 'That's so rude!' together with its associated feelings and bodily sensations.

2. **Noticing the space:** The moment before you react automatically by saying something.

3. **Practising mindfulness:** Awareness of the thoughts popping into your head and telling yourself, 'That's just a thought.' You may also recall, say, that your friend has been really stressed with his house move recently, and so may have forgotten for that reason. You apply your own inner wisdom.

4. **Making a mindful choice about how to respond most effectively:** You may stop and feel a few breaths, or do a mini breathing space meditation (see Chapter 6). You feel the sensation of anger in your body, together with your breathing. You see your thoughts as just thoughts – not necessarily facts. You then reflect, 'Is it worth getting angry over this? I've forgotten friends' birthdays before. And he's so busy at work at the moment.' You may still choose to be angry, but you can also make a choice to respond by simply reminding your friend, or dropping a few hints!

As we mention in the earlier sidebar 'How your interpretation can contribute to stress', your emotional reaction is based on your interpretation of events, not the event itself at all. Events need to be interpreted before the stress response is switched on (see Figure 11-2).

Figure 11-2:
The role of interpretation in stress.

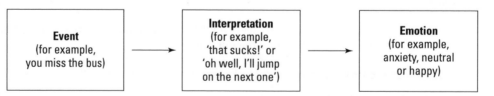

Event
(for example, you miss the bus)

Interpretation
(for example, 'that sucks!' or 'oh well, I'll jump on the next one')

Emotion
(for example, anxiety, neutral or happy)

Use Worksheet 11-5 to become more mindful of your stress reactions (we provide a sample entry to get you started).

Worksheet 11-5		Noting My Stress Reactions	
Stressful Situation	*My Interpretation of the Situation*	*My Thoughts/Emotions/ Bodily Sensation/Actions*	*How Can I Be More Mindful Next Time?*
Too many meetings today.	I'm not going to be able to cope!	I can't cope/anxious/tingling stomach/procrastinating.	Say to myself, 'It's just a thought.' Do things one step at a time. Do some deep, mindful breaths every hour.

Using the breathing space meditation to manage stress

You can use the breathing space meditation that we describe in Chapter 6 to help you manage your stress. The meditation is a short approximately three-minute mindful exercise. By practising it at times of stress, the following positive things can happen:

- ✔ You become aware of how stressed you are.

- ✔ You notice your thoughts, feelings and bodily sensations separately rather than as a single combined and often overwhelming experience.

- ✔ You begin switching off your automatic 'doing' mode of mind and turn up your more conscious 'being' mode of mind (see Chapter 4 for more on these modes).

- ✔ You have time to step back from your thoughts and emotions – a core mindfulness skill that can help to ease excessive stress.

- ✔ You're able to take a break from the stressful situation.

- ✔ You can *respond* to your stress by making a mindful choice rather than *reacting* automatically and compounding the issue (along the lines we discuss in the preceding section).

Practise the breathing space meditation three times a day for a week and jot down what you notice afterwards in Worksheet 11-6.

Worksheet 11-6   **How I Feel After Doing the Breathing Space Meditation for a Week**

Stepping back from your thoughts and emotions to reduce stress

Taking a step back from your thoughts and emotions is a great way to manage your stress response. When you do so, the thoughts and emotions lose their power to affect you, and you're able to watch them without being overly involved in them.

Figure 11-3 shows the benefits of stepping back.

Identifying or being stuck with your own thoughts and emotions. Not really accepting. Trying to fight or run away from your experience. No breathing space.

Mindful response to stress. Aware of thoughts, feelings and body and accepting that this is your experience already. Taking a step back from your experience.

"I'm stressed. I hate it"

"I feel anxious. It's horrible. I can't get rid of it"

"I'm tense in my body. I just can't relax"

"I'm watching stressful thoughts. I'm separate from them. They're not all true. I watch them"

"I notice anxiety. I fully accept it, here and now"

"I'm aware of tension in my upper shoulders. I'm curious and separate from it"

Figure 11-3: Stepping back to reduce your stress levels.

The following exercise is a really handy way of managing difficult emotions. You can try using the process a few times with mild stress. After you get the hang of the method, you can use it for more extreme sources of stress. The technique is based on the easy-to-remember acronym: RAIN.

Go through the following process in Worksheet 11-7 and afterwards note down what effect each step had:

Worksheet 11-7	The RAIN Exercise

---

1. Recognise: Become familiar with your current thoughts and feelings. You may be thinking, 'I can't believe this queue is so long!', and you may be feeling anxious. Ask yourself, 'What's happening for me right now?' Research shows that the act of labelling the emotion that you're experiencing in your mind is beneficial.

What did you notice?

---

2. Accept: Acknowledge that, *at this moment now,* this is your present experience. Denying the fact of the present-moment feeling doesn't help you to get rid of the feeling. For example, the feeling of anxiety already exists and is a fact. Stop fighting with your present-moment's reality.

How did this step go?

---

3. Investigate with kindness: Become aware of how this emotion is being generated by your thoughts. Notice where you feel the emotion in your body. These difficult sensations can be challenging to be with, so we recommend that you bring as much warmth and kindness to this step as you can. Look at the emotions as you'd look at a young child in pain – with compassion.

What did you notice when you investigated with kindness?

---

4. Non-identify: This stage is about stepping back and looking at your inner experience from a wider perspective. This step follows naturally from the previous three. You step back into awareness and watch your experience without the idea, for example, 'I'm anxious.' Instead you aim for the sense of *watching* anxiety without *being* the feeling – you're resting in open awareness without clinging on to experience.

What was this stage like for you?

Cooling the Flames of Anger

I (Shamash) rarely get angry. The last time I got into a state of anger that was out of control was probably over ten years ago. This level-headedness is partly due to my mindful approach to life, which I discovered as a student at university. I get frustrated and irritated from time to time, but not really angry. You too can use mindfulness to help you to manage your feelings of anger if you need to.

We regularly hear stories from clients who are now using mindfulness to soothe their feelings of anger about the damage that rage has caused them: relationship breakups, lack of progress at work and even ill-health in extreme cases. This section helps you to get to grips with the feeling of anger and how to manage it.

Understanding anger

Anger is a natural human emotion and has evolved throughout nature. The feeling acts as a form of protection. Watch two dogs as they approach each other – if either of them feels threatened, it growls and shows its teeth, and suddenly you have two angry dogs. Underlying anger is in fact a feeling of fear – the dog is scared that it may get attacked and so anger arises as a form of protection. The fear turns on the physical fight-or-flight response and the animal prepares for the threat – to fight or run for its life.

Humans experience anger for a similar reason – to protect themselves from other animals, or other humans! However, you may not need to get angry as often as you do. For example, imagine you get angry when someone cuts in front of you while driving. You may start swearing in your car or at the other driver. This reaction is probably because you feel threatened. You may have begun to have images or words in your mind about what *could* have happened. These *hot thoughts* cause feelings of anger. But your anger doesn't usually lead to other drivers improving their skills and can result in traffic accidents if you then begin to drive recklessly yourself, as a form of revenge.

Mindfulness helps you to become aware of your thoughts and emotions at an earlier stage. Eventually, through regular mindfulness practice, you may begin to find that the feeling doesn't rise up quite so often – and if anger does arise, you notice the feeling in your body in a dispassionate way, as if you're an observer of the sensation rather than *being* the sensation. In other words, instead of, 'I'm so angry!' you say to yourself, 'I'm observing anger arising in my body. I feel some tension in my shoulders and heat in my upper chest.'

The angry chief meditates

Shamash works with corporate clients on the phone because often they're too busy to meet in person. A while back he started working with the CEO of a large firm. This man had recently had to take time off work due to stress. As part of his process of rehabilitation, he decided to practise mindfulness over the phone. Through the mindful exercises and meditations, he started to notice that he suffered from flashes of anger quite regularly – a feeling he hadn't noticed before.

Every morning, Shamash gave him a guided mindfulness exercise that he listened to using his phone on the train. The length of the track was precisely the right time for his journey. Each lunchtime, he did a three-minute mini meditation. After a couple of months, he was integrated back into work and his feelings of anger began to stop self-perpetuating. Other feelings arose and dissipated through his accepting attitude. He found time to start jogging every day and began to leave work earlier. He also started to notice himself being kinder to his colleagues – listening to their issues and offering support rather than just half-ignoring them. This change goes to show the positive knock-on effect of mindfulness meditation on other aspects of your life. Shamash now just coaches him every two or three weeks. The CEO continues to practise, and he's coping much better.

Measuring your anger levels

Before you decide whether or not you need to deal with your anger, take a week to assess what your anger levels are like by creating a diary (see Worksheet 11-8). You may feel that you already know how angry you get, but taking time to stop and record your anger levels can be one of the most important steps you take to manage your anger. Shamash's clients find it very helpful.

Worksheet 11-8			My Anger Diary		
Date and Time	**Who or What Caused My Anger?**	**How Angry Did I Feel? (Scale 1–10)**	**What Sort of Bodily Sensations Did I Notice?**	**What Thoughts Did I Have?**	**What Did I Do?**
14 Dec, 8 a.m.	Person on the train takes up all my space.	8	My face felt hot, my shoulders and jaw tense.	'That's so rude, he should give me more room!'	I looked crossly at him, and eventually got up and walked to a different seat.

See if you can notice any patterns. Consider:

- Do you always get angry about the same things?
- Do you often carry out the same actions when feeling angry?
- What ways of coping with your anger seem to be the most effective for you?
- Do the particular thoughts you have create an impact on your anger?

Using mindful approaches to ease anger

If you find that you're excessively or often angry and want to get your emotions under control, the following Worksheets have some practical, mindful ways of managing your anger. Give them a try and see if they work for you. They're based on being mindful: non-judgemental, curious, kind and taking a step back from the experience.

Practising mindfulness meditation regularly helps you to become more aware of your internal world. You notice the bodily sensations, thoughts, emotions and behaviours leading up to and during your feelings of anger. Inner experiences seem to slow down allowing you to notice what's going on, instead of suddenly feeling very angry. You can then make a more informed choice about how to deal with your anger. You may choose to express it or you may choose to do something else.

Worksheet 11-9   **Managing My Anger with Meditation**

Have you tried meditating? What effect has it had on your anger?

_____

_____

Exploring anger and your body

The next time anger arises for you, feel the sensations in your body. Notice as much as you can. Does your heart beat faster? Do you feel hotter? Do your hands tremble? What happens to your breathing rate? Does your entire body feel more tense? By bringing a sense of curiosity to your experience, you begin to stop fighting with the emotion, which just adds fuel to the anger flame. Bring a kindness and warmth to the feeling – as if you're concerned about your own baby. We call this approach practising _non-reactivity_ in your body. Record your observations in Worksheet 11-10.

Worksheet 11-10   **Managing Anger Using Non-reactivity**

What did you observe? What effect did this approach have?

_____

_____

Exploring anger and your thoughts

When you're next angry, notice the kind of hot thoughts (which we define in the earlier section 'Understanding anger') arising in your mind. What are you thinking? Are you experiencing lots of 'should have' or 'it's not fair' types of thoughts? Are you swearing in your mind, or out loud? Become curious about your thoughts. See if you can imagine them on clouds floating past. Or if you prefer, imagine them on leaves floating by in a stream, or on the carriages of a train travelling past you.

Worksheet 11-11   Managing Anger through Using Your Mind

What did you observe? What effect did this thought experiment have? What did you discover about your judgements?

_____

_____

Exploring anger and your emotions

During an anger episode, try to note what emotions you're feeling, exactly. Are you experiencing any other feelings apart from anger? Do you feel scared or threatened? Where do you feel the emotion in your body? How is the emotion changing, if at all, from moment to moment? What happens if you feel the sensation together with your breathing?

Worksheet 11-12   Managing Anger by Exploring Your Emotions

What did you observe? What effect did this approach have?

_____

_____

Exploring anger and your behaviour

The next time you're angry, make the effort to try and notice your behaviour. How are you acting? What are you saying? How is your body moving? What does your tone of voice sound like? How is your behaviour different to other times?

Worksheet 11-13   Raising Awareness of Your Behaviour

What happens when you watch your behaviour with curiosity?

_____

_____

Here are five mindful tips for managing your anger:

- ✔ **Communicate:** If someone has caused you to feel angry, communicating with them effectively is key. When the full force of the anger has dissolved a little, try to say things like, 'I felt this when you behaved like this,' instead of 'You have done this,' and so on. Doing so means that you're taking responsibility for your own feelings rather than accusing others.

Your tone of voice has a stronger effect that your words. If you speak in an angry tone, the other person is likely to react angrily, leading to rising anger levels rather than a reasonable conversation. Speak softly rather than with anger if you can.

- ✔ **Don't expect to change straight away:** Managing anger is a difficult process, so be patient with yourself. Forgive yourself when you go back to your usual automatic patterns. You can't expect to change the habits of a lifetime in a few weeks or months.

- ✔ **Be mindful in your everyday life:** Notice things, people and your own thoughts and feelings. When you do, you're more likely to notice when anger arises.

- ✔ **Use your breath to anchor yourself:** When the anger is overwhelming and you're about to react, remove yourself from the situation and focus on your breathing. Return to the situation when your breath has calmed you down and you're back in control of yourself.

- ✔ **Walk around the room and feel the contact of your feet with the ground when the anger arises:** With this approach you're neither running away from the anger nor immersing yourself in the feeling too much. Be balanced in your attention.

The most important point is to try and discover the cause of your anger by watching your thoughts.

Raising Your Energy Levels with Mindfulness

Everyone loves to be full of energy! Imagine waking up with a clear mind and relaxed body, getting all your tasks finished and still having the energy to play with the children or socialise with friends. But if you don't have energy, even the simplest task feels like a drag. You're more likely to be annoyed rather than cheerful, feel less capable of finishing things and life just isn't so much fun.

Well, fear not! Mindfulness provides many ways to adjust your lifestyle to help raise your energy levels. We can't guarantee that you'll be leaping out of bed full of beans straight away, but step by step you may well find yourself living life with more vigour when you do the mindful exercises in this section regularly.

Discovering your daily energy levels

Managing your energy levels starts by assessing exactly how your energy fluctuates in a typical week (see Worksheet 11-14). You may think that you know your energy levels, but many people surprise themselves with what they discover, so we encourage you to have a go. We provide a sample entry to show you the sort of thing we have in mind.

Worksheet 11-14			My Energy Level Log	
Day	*Morning*	*Afternoon*	*Evening*	*Daily Insights*
Monday	Low, but went up towards lunch.	Very sleepy.	Felt quite drained, but lifted when Jane popped over.	Interesting to see just how low my energy was at the start of the day, but seeing my friend really changed it. Maybe it's to do with my mind-set.
Monday				
Tuesday				
Wednesday				
Thursday				
Friday				
Saturday				
Sunday				

Consider the questions in Worksheet 11-15 to increase your energy-level awareness:

Worksheet 11-15   Evaluating My Energy Levels

At which part of the day was your energy highest?

_____

_____

_____

At which part of the day was your energy lowest?

_____

_____

_____

What small step can you take to boost your energy levels?

_____

_____

_____

Use your observations from Worksheet 11-14 to see what helps to raise your energy levels. Then consider utilising them to boost your energy levels. For example, if a light salad at lunchtime kept you going in the early afternoon, consider eating salads every lunchtime for a week and see what happens.

Identifying activities that drain or boost your energy

Some activities act like holes in a bucket – leaking your energy away. You can stop those energy leaks by identifying and then avoiding lifestyle and mental energy drainers and carrying out energy-boosting activities instead. Examples of your energy drainers could be excessively watching television, missing out on your daily exercise or working overtime.

Here are some useful physical energy boosters:

- ✔ **Exercising regularly:** Ensure that you perform some physical activities every day.

- ✔ **Eating sensibly and regularly:** Ensure that you have time to eat your meals and avoid eating too much sugar or fat in each meal.

- ✔ **Going to sleep and waking up at the same times each day:** Doing so helps to regulate your body clock and ensure that you get enough rest at night.

- ✔ **Working in a balanced way:** Working too hard is a common energy drainer; seek balance in your working life.

- ✔ **Doing what you enjoy:** Following your passion in life is energising and uplifting. Consider what you value and look for ways of fulfilling that need.

The following list contains some great mental-energy boosters:

- ✔ **Being mindful through the day:** When you focus your attention on the present moment, you're not thinking excessively about the past and future, so you give your brain a break from over-thinking. Your brain uses *more energy than any other organ in your body* – about 20 per cent of all the body's energy. By living in the moment, you're less likely to having cyclical thoughts and save lots of energy for more interesting things, like arranging your stamp collection (apologies to any philatelists)!

- ✔ **Practising regular meditation:** Meditation (such as those in Chapter 5) is an extended period of mindfulness and five or ten minutes a day can help. You give your brain a much needed rest from the incessant 'doing' mode of mind.

- ✔ **Managing negative thinking:** Everyone has negative thoughts popping into their heads. If you believe them all to be true, your energy is sucked right out. Work at noticing these thoughts as just thoughts, sounds or pictures in your mind (refer to Chapter 8 on seeing thoughts and decentring from them). Remember, these thoughts aren't necessarily reality, so take a step back and gently refocus your attention on whatever you need to be mindful of next. Just think of the amount of energy you can save that's currently wasted by generating unnecessary, difficult emotions.

- ✔ **Carrying out relaxation exercises:** Stress is a big energy drainer because it's designed for a short-term energy burst followed by a long rest (check out the earlier section 'Using Mindfulness to Manage Stress' for much more on stress). By doing mindful exercises, such as the body scan meditation in Chapter 5, you reduce the stress levels you're under and so have more general energy through-out the day. Relaxation exercises can also help in this area. See *Relaxation For Dummies* by Shamash Alidina (Wiley) for many relaxation techniques for you to try out.

In Worksheet 11-16, note down what things you've done to uplift you during the week. Choose one energy-boosting tip a day and note its effect. Remember to ensure that you do these energy boosters in a mindful way to enhance their effect!

Worksheet 11-16		Making Efforts To Lift My Energy		
Day	**Morning**	**Afternoon**	**Evening**	**Insights/ Observations**
Monday				
Tuesday				
Wednesday				
Thursday				
Friday				
Saturday				
Sunday				

Using technology can be an energy drain. Give yourself a day of being totally technology-free every week or fortnight if you can. Even a morning or afternoon without looking at a screen can be hugely beneficial. The most mindful people have the discipline to switch off their phones, televisions and other devices on a regular basis.

Practising meditations to boost your energy

Here are three meditations that Shamash developed to help boost people's energy. Use Worksheet 11-17 to rate your energy level before and after each meditation and see whether the practice has a positive effect for you. Usually the positive results of these exercises are cumulative, so you may require a few weeks of daily practice before you notice a change. But if you're lucky, you may notice a boost of energy straight away!

Worksheet 11-17	Boosting My Energy		
Meditation	*Energy Level Before (1 = Low Energy, 10 = Maximum Energy)*	*Energy Level After (1 = Low Energy, 10 = Maximum Energy)*	*Insights/Observations*

Enjoying an energising breath meditation

In this meditation, you use a combination of relaxation, mindfulness and a gentle smile on your face to lift your mood and energy levels.

1. **Adopt an upright position.** Ensure that your back is relatively straight and your chest is open with shoulders back. Having a particularly open, erect, dignified posture can really help to energise you.

2. **Take three deep in- and out-breaths.** Really feel those breaths moving in and out of your body.

3. **Place one hand on your chest and one hand on your belly.** On your next in-breath, ensure that you breathe down in your belly. The hand on your chest needs to remain relatively still, if possible.

4. **Breathe out slowly from your mouth.** Feel the physical sensation as you do so.

5. **Imagine yourself being energised as you breathe in.** If you're a visual person, imagine golden light entering into your body, nourishing all your cells with soothing, uplifting energy. If you don't like golden light, choose whatever image works for you – you're in control.

6. **Keep a light smile on your face throughout this energising breath meditation.** Doing so can help to boost your energy.

7. **Guide your attention back each time your mind wanders.** Do so with kindness and gentleness.

8. **Bring the meditation to a close after ten minutes or so.** Slowly open your eyes.

Feeling grateful during a body scan meditation

This meditation is based on the body scan exercise in Chapter 5. The aim is to focus your attention on your body and try to release some muscle tension. You then use gratitude after you're feeling more grounded to reduce your negative viewpoints and boost your energy levels.

1. **Lie down on your back in a warm, quiet place.** If that's not comfortable, whatever position works for you is fine.

2. **Feel your own natural breathing.** Notice the physical sensation of each breath, mindfully.

3. **Begin scanning the physical sensation in your body (as we describe in Chapter 5), starting with your head.** You need to spend only a few minutes doing this.

4. **Become aware of any tension in each body part.** Imagine your breath going into and out of the tension to soothe the tightness. If the tension doesn't leave, that's okay – just be aware of the sensation and move on to the next part of your body.

5. **Think about things for which you're grateful.** What's going well in your life? Perhaps remember that at least you've got this book and have time to practise this meditation. Spend a couple of minutes reflecting on this reality.

6. **End this meditation with three deep, mindful breaths.** Slowly stand up and have a good stretch before getting on with the rest of your day or evening.

Making a mindful morning cuppa

In this meditation you make your morning cup of tea mindfully. Ideally you're drinking herbal tea, but if you like a bit of caffeine in the morning, fair enough. The idea is not to multitask for this period of time, but to focus on each step:

1. **Place the tea bag in your cup and pour in the hot water.** Notice the different aromas that are released and listen to the sound of the water filling up the cup. Watch as the steam gently rises.

2. **Sit down after making your tea and look out at your garden if you have one.** If not, sit somewhere pleasant and comfortable.

3. **Hold the warm cup of tea in your hand.** Feel the warmth of the cup. Notice the weight of your tea. Feel a few of your breaths as you wait for the tea to cool down.

4. **Bring the cup of tea slowly to your lips and take a sip.** Savour the flavour and warmth of your tea. Enjoy the moment as best you can. Be aware of swallowing the tea and perhaps even feeling the tea travel down into your stomach. Be mindful of this nourishing moment – this is a time for you to enjoy.

5. **Notice when your mind wanders off.** Kindly and gently, with a little smile, guide your attention back to your tea-drinking experience.

6. **Take a moment after finishing your tea.** Be grateful that you've made the time for this process, no matter how the experience was for you.

All mindfulness meditations can lead you to feel more energised because they help to reduce your worrying thoughts, to accept rather than fight the present-moment's experience and often ease muscular tension as a side effect.

Use the three-minute breathing space meditation from Chapter 6 throughout the day, whenever you have the time, to help you refocus and re-energise.

Chapter 12

Reducing Anxiety and Depression with Mindfulness

Depression and anxiety are common forms of mental distress: the World Health Organisation estimates that 350 million people suffer from depression worldwide. The causes of depression and anxiety are complex and can be a combination of biological, psychological, social, genetic, environmental and spiritual (belief) factors. The good news is that the evidence that mindfulness is an effective treatment of these conditions is growing rapidly. The latest forms of psychological treatment for a wide range of mental-health conditions have mindfulness and acceptance at their heart.

In this chapter we show you how you can use mindfulness for the rest of your life to help you deal with difficult thoughts or feelings that arise from anxiety or depression. As the spectrum for these problem is vast, in particular we aim this chapter at mild to moderate cases, providing plenty of exercises and tips to help you lift your mood. Specifically, we describe an approach called mindfulness-based cognitive therapy that can help prevent recurring depression.

Feeling depressed or anxious is a normal part of being human. However, they become classified as clinical conditions when they last for an excessively long time or are more strongly felt, affecting your sleep and having a significant impact on your daily activities. Depression is characterised by low mood, low self-esteem and loss of interest in normally enjoyable activities. Anxiety disorder is characterised by excessive feelings of fear, uneasiness or too much worry. If you suspect that you're suffering from clinical depression or anxiety disorder, get in touch with your GP who can assess you and, if necessary, refer you for the appropriate treatment. If you do decide to use mindfulness alongside medical advice, ensure that you keep your doctor or health professional informed.

If you need emotional support or are experiencing suicidal thoughts and can't get in touch with a doctor or health professional, contact the Samaritans (www.samaritans.org) or Befrienders Worldwide (www.befrienders.org). Their staff will listen to you non-judgementally.

Dealing with Depression the Mindful Way

When you say to someone, 'I'm depressed,' you may mean that you're feeling a bit down or fed up – experiencing a low mood that passes. *Clinical depression* is different: a low mood along with other symptoms lasting for at least two weeks. Clinical depression is very common, affecting two out of three people at some point in their lives.

When you feel depressed, you may well feel that you should 'pull yourself together' or 'snap out of it', and yet find that doing so is very difficult if not impossible.

As the statistics show, depression is very common and nothing to be ashamed of.

Understanding depression

Most people know when they're feeling depressed, but due to the many possible physical symptoms of depression, they can visit the doctor thinking that they have a physical problem. They can be unaware that the problem originates in depression.

Many different symptoms of depression exist. Here are the two main ones:

- Low mood.
- Lost of interest in previously enjoyable activities.

Additional symptoms can include:

- Changes in sleep pattern.
- Changes in food intake.
- Loss of energy or slower physical movements.
- Poor focus or indecisiveness.
- Thoughts about death.
- Feeling excessively guilty or worthless.

Depression tends to be a recurring condition. The first experience of depression is often linked to a major life event, such as the death or illness of a loved one, divorce, separation or unemployment. However, further episodes of depression can seemingly occur out of the blue – perhaps even without a major challenging event happening. The more times you have an episode of depression, the greater the likelihood of recurrence. That's why experts developed the mindfulness-based treatment for depression that we describe in the following section – to help people reduce the chance of depression recurring.

Tackling recurring depression with mindfulness

Three top therapists and scientists, Mark Williams, Zindel Segal and John Teasdale, were looking for a new way to treat recurring depression. They investigated whether a mindfulness course with cognitive behaviour therapy (CBT) would reduce such relapses and help people to manage their mood in a more helpful way.

Their aim was to combine ancient mindfulness approaches with modern psychological therapies to see whether they'd be effective. The result is the 8-week course called mindfulness-based cognitive therapy (MBCT), some exercises from which we describe in the later section 'Combating Depression with Mindful CBT Exercises'.

The scientists began by researching depression and discovered an interesting fact. When you experience clinical depression, links are created in your brain between your low mood, your negative thoughts and your achy and tired body, and perhaps even your body posture and movement (see Figure 12-1). When the episode of depression has subsided, although you may feel fine, those latent links are still dormant in your brain. If you then experience a small difficulty in your life, the connections in your brain can trigger off the depression again, with a small, low mood spiralling into full-blown depression. The more times you experience depression, the stronger these connections can get and the greater the chance of depression recurring.

Figure 12-1:
Links between negative thoughts, low feelings, uncomfortable body sensations and sluggish behaviour.

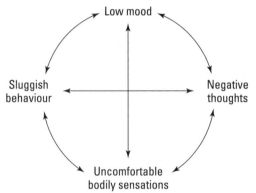

But here's the good news! The same scientists discovered that mindfulness provides several very helpful skills that can prevent a low mood from spiralling into major depression (see Figure 12-2).

Figure 12-2:
Mindfulness can cut the connection between low mood and other thoughts, sensations and behaviour.

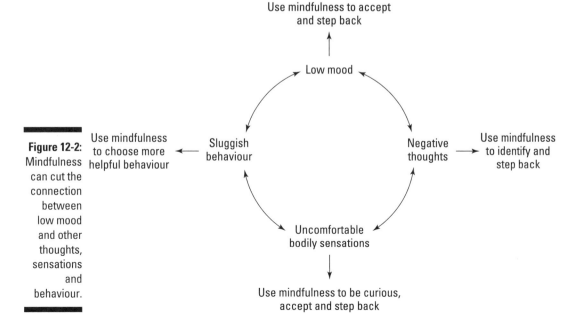

The key mindfulness skills that can help are:

- **The ability to step back from your thoughts.** This skill prevents one of the key factors that drives depression, which is *rumination* (repetitive unhelpful, cyclical thinking). You can find yourself caught in a thinking spiral that goes round and round as you try to think yourself out of your emotion, which doesn't work. Mindfulness helps you to notice what you're doing, and so step back from this unhelpful pattern.

- **The ability to approach difficult feelings, thoughts and sensations instead of avoiding them.** Your natural tendency may be to avoid uncomfortable experiences within yourself, but avoidance ends up strengthening difficult emotions and causes you to try and run away from an experience. See the emotion as being like a relatively harmless dog from which you run away – the faster you run, the faster the dog chases you. However, if you approach the dog, usually the animal is calm and co-operative.

- **The ability to notice the onset of depression and take mindful action.** If you aren't aware of your negative thoughts or low mood, you can end up taking automatic, unhelpful action, such as fighting the experience. Mindfulness helps you to spot the warning signs (which we discuss in the later section 'Creating a personal early warning system for depression') and take a more positive, helpful course of action. Perhaps you choose to carry out the breathing space meditation from Chapter 6, some gentle, mindful walking (see Chapter 6) or even just a shift in attitude from trying to change your experience to accepting the present-moment's experience mindfully, just as it is.

Mindfulness helps to reduce the 'what ifs' and the 'if only' thoughts in your life:

- 'What if' thoughts are worries about the future.
- 'If onlys' are regrets about the past.

When you live more in the present moment, the only moment that exists, you have less time to wander excessively to those other thoughts. Of course, nothing's wrong with thinking about these things occasionally – as the unicyclist said: it's just a matter of balance.

Combating Depression with Mindful CBT Exercises

In this section we describe several practical exercises taken from the 8-week MBCT course that has been clinically proven to prevent the onset of recurring depression. For more about the whole course, read Chapters 7 and 8 in this book or pick up a copy of *Mindfulness-Based Cognitive Therapy For Dummies* by Patrizia Collard (Wiley). Always consult your doctor first if you think you may be suffering from clinical depression.

Interpreting your thoughts and feelings

The purpose of this exercise is to show you that the way you think about a situation affects how you feel. Read the following paragraph and imagine yourself in that scenario, waiting for a friend. Take your time, and particularly notice the thoughts and feelings that arise for you. You may spot a difference in how you feel; for example, if you think, 'He's always late,' you may not feel too bad, but if you think, 'I must have got the date wrong,' you can feel anxious or low.

Imagine that you've arranged to meet a friend at a local coffee shop at 4 p.m. You arrive a few minutes early, grab a drink and sit down to wait, but 4 o'clock arrives without any sign of your friend. How do you feel about this? What do you think? Where do you experience this feeling in your body? Time passes. Now it's 4.10. Still no sign of your friend. How do you feel and what do you think? Then it's 4.15 . . . 4.20 . . . 4.30, and still your friend hasn't arrived. What do you think? How do you feel?

That's the end of the exercise. Now complete Worksheet 12-1.

Worksheet 12-1		Recording My Thoughts and Feelings		
Time	*Feeling*	*Thoughts*	*Location and Description of My Bodily Sensations*	*Action I Took (If Any)*
4.00				
4.10				
4.15				
4.20				
4.30				

Now consider the following questions in Worksheet 12-2.

Worksheet 12-2   **Linking Thoughts and Feelings**

Do you notice any link between the kind of thoughts that pop into your head and the emotions that you feel?

_____

Do you notice any patterns about the location(s) in your body where you feel the emotions?

_____

Did you find yourself judging yourself or the other person? Are you judging yourself now?

_____

Did you take any action or simply wait in this situation?

_____

Imagine that you were in a really positive mood just before this situation happened. Would you have seen the situation differently?

_____

The thoughts that pop into your head are thoughts, not necessarily facts. Don't take them too seriously, because they're often different in different mood states or influenced by what you were doing earlier, or even how hungry you are. Practise questioning your own thoughts instead of always believing them to be true because doing so can be tremendously helpful for managing your mood. Also, understanding this fact only intellectually is quite different from experiencing the truth of it in reality. That's why practising these exercises and watching your thoughts as you go about your daily life is so helpful.

Discovering the landscape of depression

Carrying out this exercise allows you to see the process of depression as being separate from you – so helping you to not identify with the illness.

In Worksheet 12-3 we list some negative-thinking patterns associated with depression. Go through the list and consider which ones you're experiencing.

This exercise is obviously not to make you feel worse about yourself. The purpose is to show you that *the depression* is creating these thoughts – not you.

Worksheet 12-3	Identifying Negative Thinking Patterns	
Type of Thinking	*Example*	*My Specific Thought*
All or nothing thinking.	I didn't call my friend today . . . I'm a useless friend.	
Over-generalisation.	I'm always tired.	
Labelling yourself.	I'm a loser. I'm rubbish.	
'Shoulding'.	I should be working harder. I shouldn't ever say 'X'.	
Emotional reasoning.	I feel so pathetic . . . I am pathetic.	
Jumping to conclusions.	Mind reading – he probably thinks I'm an idiot. Fortune telling – I'll be stuck in this job forever.	
Diminishing the positive.	He said he enjoyed talking to me, but he's probably just saying that out of politeness.	

If you find yourself thinking in any of these ways, try taking the following steps and record the effect in Worksheet 12-4:

1. **Become aware of the thought instead of trying to avoid it.**

2. **Do the three-minute breathing space meditation from Chapter 6.**

3. **Notice how you now feel.**

For example, do you feel as if a bit more space exists between yourself and the thought? If not, have another go at the breathing space meditation and infuse the practice with a bit of gentleness, kindness and curiosity if you can.

Worksheet 12-4	Effect of the Breathing Space Meditation

Practising an alternative viewpoint exercise

In this exercise you discover how your emotional state affects your thoughts, emotions and reactions.

Imagine the following two scenarios:

✔ **Scenario 1:** You go into your local bank. You check your balance and the cashier is rude. He doesn't give you his full attention, doesn't smile and keeps giving you the wrong information. The whole process takes much longer than you expect. As you finally leave the bank, you notice a friend and want to talk to her. However, the friend says that she's really busy and rushes off. Notice what you think and feel at that moment.

✔ **Scenario 2:** You go into your local bank. You check your balance and the cashier is friendly. He gives you his full attention and is helpful. The whole process is efficient and simple. As you finally leave the bank, you notice a friend and want to talk to her. However, the friend says that she's really busy and rushes off. Notice what you think and feel at that moment.

Now fill in Worksheet 12-5.

Worksheet 12-5	Monitoring How Thoughts and Emotions Change Depending on My Mood		
Scenario	*Thoughts*	*Feelings*	*Bodily Sensations*
1			
2			

Notice how your thoughts and feelings about your friend seem different, even though she behaved in exactly the same way. This exercise is a practical way of showing that your emotional state can affect the kind of thoughts that pop into your head, which can in turn feed back into your emotions. Again, it demonstrates why you shouldn't always take your thoughts too seriously – especially if you're in a low mood.

Decentring from your thoughts

De-centring (that is, stepping back) from your thoughts gives you space to see yourself, or whatever situation you're in, more clearly. This skill is particularly helpful when you find yourself caught up in damaging rumination (something we describe in the earlier section 'Tackling recurring depression with mindfulness').

In Worksheet 12-6 we itemise a few of the ways in which you can decentre from your thoughts. Try each one out and see what effect they have on your state of mind when you're ruminating.

Worksheet 12-6 — Recording the Effect of Decentring Thoughts	
Approach	*How Well I Managed to Step Back From My Thoughts*
Carrying out the three-minute breathing space meditation (see Chapter 6).	
Imagining leaves floating down a stream and placing my thoughts on those leaves for a few minutes.	
Saying to myself, 'Thoughts are just thoughts, not necessarily facts,' when difficult thoughts come up, and then re-focusing on whatever task I need to do next.	
Visualising clouds passing through the sky and placing my thoughts on the clouds for a few minutes.	
Visualising bubbles floating through the air and imagining my thoughts inside those bubbles.	
Imagining sitting on a train and watching the scenery going past and placing my thoughts onto that scenery.	
Trying the mountain meditation (Chapter 9).	
Saying to myself, 'I'm having the thought X.'	

In mindfulness, you don't need to be too concerned about whether a thought is true or not. Just consider whether it's helpful to you in your life. For example, thinking, 'I'm useless,' isn't usually a helpful thought, so use a decentring approach to distance yourself from it. Being aware of what's really happening in the present moment is more important that constantly judging yourself and others.

Creating a personal early warning system for depression

As you become more mindful, you begin to notice some typical warning signs that depression may be coming. For example, you may start to feel tense in your chest, begin criticising everyone, feel irritable all the time or avoid meeting up with friends. When you notice these early warning signs, you can take action to nip the process in the bud instead of fighting or running away from the feeling.

To help you take wise action when you notice yourself slipping into a low mood, creating an early warning system especially for you is useful. In this system, you list all your typical early warning signs and mindful action strategies that you can try out to cope.

Here are some examples of mindful action strategies that may well work for you:

✔ Carrying out the three-minute breathing space meditation in Chapter 6, or simply experiencing your breathing for a few minutes.

✔ Doing whatever work you need to do next in a really mindful way, fully connecting with your senses.

✔ Going for a walk or jog.

✔ Phoning or meeting up with a friend or other positive, supportive person.

✔ Practising your favourite hobby with mindful awareness.

These activities can be something that gives you a sense of mastery or a pleasurable activity, as we mention in Chapter 8. You can create your own system using Worksheet 12-7.

Worksheet 12-7			My Early Warning System for Depression	
My Early Warning Signs				*My Mindful Action Strategies*
My Thoughts	*My Feelings*	*My Bodily Sensations*	*My Behaviour*	

Calm down, dear, it's just an email

I (Shamash) checked my email recently and received a message from a colleague of mine. I'm working on a new online mindfulness radio show (http://mindfulnessradio.com) where I interview different mindfulness authors every week and play the show on air. My colleague listened to the show that I shared out of excitement, and instead of being positive and supportive about my latest episode, he wrote a long list of criticisms. I immediately felt quite shocked at his response and was just about to write a short message back while in a slightly emotional state, but then I stopped.

I realised that I had a moment of choice and decided not to respond emotionally. I focused on my bodily sensations with a sense of self-kindness. I felt a slight tightness in my shoulders and chest, which seemed slowly to release as I began to accept the feeling. I became aware of my breathing. I watched as my breath gently became more calm and smooth. I decided that I wouldn't reply to the email until I feel calmer. In a different state of mind, I can now see that email as a helpful set of constructive tips that I can use to improve my service. The email from him is the same, but with a different interpretation and I had a different emotional and behavioural response.

On a good day you can catch your thoughts like this before they spiral into unhelpful judgements and actions that you may later regret. But at other times you won't manage this, and on those days a mindful attitude is to forgive yourself and resolve to try again in the future.

Calming Anxiety with Mindfulness

Anxiety is a natural human response. For example, if you're about to give a presentation, have an interview or sit an exam, anxiety is likely to arise and in fact helps you to focus your energy and attention on the situation. If your worries and fears are excessive, however, and interfere with your normal everyday life and sleep, you may be suffering from an anxiety disorder.

If you're preparing for an exam and are feeling anxious in the run up to the test, that's normal, healthy anxiety. If you're constantly worrying, plagued by irrational fears, avoid everyday situations because of your anxiety or experience sudden rapid heart-pounding panic, you may be suffering from an anxiety disorder.

Many different causes of anxiety disorder exist, with the main ones thought to be genetic factors, challenging life situations, recreational drugs and/or caffeine.

In this section we provide some mindful approaches for calming your excessive or misplaced anxiety and debilitating fears.

Defining anxiety disorder

Anxiety becomes an issue when it interferes with your daily activities – your work, your relationships and your home life. At this point, anxiety goes from being motivating and energising to becoming a disorder that requires help from a doctor or therapist. Mindfulness can help with managing an anxiety disorder, but check if your health professional agrees first.

Anxiety disorders often have physical symptoms, a by-product of the fight or flight response by the body (explained in Chapter 11). For this reason, most people think they have a physical illness rather than anxiety.

The common physical symptoms of anxiety disorders are shortness of breath, upset stomach, pounding heart, headache, insomnia, fatigue, sweating, muscle tension or tremors. Emotional symptoms of anxiety disorder include irrational fear, excessive worry, feeling tense, lack of focus, expecting the worst, restlessness and irritability.

Consider the questions in Worksheet 12-8. If you answer 'yes' to a few of them and the symptoms don't go away, you may have an anxiety disorder.

Visit your doctor if you're also suffering from a lot of physical symptoms to check that you don't have a medical condition such as a thyroid problem, asthma or hypoglycaemia. Then, if anxiety seems to be the cause, ask your doctor to refer you to an experienced therapist who knows how to treat anxiety disorders. CBT is a proven, effective way of managing anxiety disorders. Some CBT therapists may also use mindfulness – ask them if that's what you're looking for. Visit the UK CBT register at www.cbtregisteruk.com for a list of accredited CBT therapists in the UK.

Worksheet 12-8	Am I Suffering from an Anxiety Disorder?
Symptom	*Yes/No*
Do I feel constantly tense or worried?	
Do I suddenly find my heart is pounding in a panicky state?	
Do I avoid situations that create a feeling of anxiety for me?	
Do I think something bad will happen if I don't do things in a certain way?	
Do I feel overwhelmed by a fear that I know doesn't make sense, but I can't seem to get rid of it?	
Does anxiety affect or interfere with my daily responsibilities?	
Do I feel something dangerous is just about to happen, almost all the time?	

Managing anxiety with mindfulness

Here are some of the key ways in which practising mindfulness can help you to manage anxiety:

- ✔ **Approaching feelings instead of avoiding them.** Anxiety perpetuates itself through your avoidance of the feeling, which is a natural response because the sensations are unpleasant. But avoidance is generated by a sense of fear, which in turn creates more anxiety. By approaching and accepting the feelings step by step, mindfully in the present moment, you can create a healthier relationship to the anxiety.

- ✔ **Refusing to identify with your anxiety.** Mindfulness shows you how to observe sensations and emotions without identifying with them; that is, recognising that you and the anxiety are separate. When you separate from the feeling you can watch it arise and perhaps pass away too. Essentially, you're finding out how to widen your perspective and take a step back from your experience.

✔ **Stepping out of automatic unhelpful thoughts.** Anxiety is characterised by worry. When you become mindful, you notice unhelpful thought patterns earlier and so can shift your attention to somewhere else, such as your breathing, the sensations in your feet or on to whatever task you need to do.

✔ **Developing the ability to tolerate difficult physical sensations or emotions.** Through mindful practice, you become better able to be with difficult experiences without reacting to them. When you're able to do this with your anxiety, you're less likely to make the feeling worse.

✔ **Generating a sense of control.** Mindfulness offers you a moment of choice about how you meet your feeling. As a result, you begin to feel in control, which can positively reduce your sense of anxiety too.

Here's a practical exercise that you can try out to manage your anxiety when it arises. It's called the STOP exercise and stands for: Stop, Take a breath, Observe and Proceed.

1. **Stop.** If you're in the middle of some work or other activity, take some time to stop if you can. If you feel that you're so busy that you can't even spare a few minutes to stop, you probably really do need to stop. The act of stopping whatever you're doing may not be easy, but does have a positive effect.

2. **Take some mindful breaths.** In this stage, take a few slow deep, mindful breaths. Feel the breath as it moves down into your belly. Ensure that your stomach is expanding as you breathe in and contracting as you breathe out. In this stage you're recentring your attention instead of becoming lost in a sea of thoughts, emotions and bodily sensations.

3. **Observe.** When you're ready, notice your bodily sensations. In particular, if you can, shift your attention towards the physical discomfort. See if you can allow the bodily sensations to be just as they are. Feel them together with your breathing, with a sense of kindness instead of judgement. You're a human being and feeling anxiety is quite natural. Use your breathing as an anchor, to help support your attention on the bodily discomfort. Then, after observing your body for some time, you can move onto emotions and thoughts. Just watch the thoughts and emotion and give them the space to pass away in their own time, if they want to.

4. **Proceed.** Gently bring your attention back to whatever you need to do. As you shift your attention back to the outer world, give full attention to your senses instead of getting too lost in thought, if you can. Continue your daily activities with a greater sense of acceptance and acknowledgment of your feelings as they are, knowing that all feelings are temporary and do pass away in time.

Promising research on using mindfulness for anxiety

Research conducted by the University of Massachusetts Medical School discovered that practising mindfulness yielded positive results for anxiety. The researchers taught an eight-week mindfulness course to a small group of patients with generalised anxiety disorder. They found significant reductions in anxiety and panic immediately after the course, after a three-month follow up and even after three years. Many of the group were still practising mindfulness after three years, probably because they were finding it helpful. Cognitive behavioural therapy has the best evidence-base for treating anxiety disorders, but mindfulness is gradually beginning to show promising results too. Many more years of research are required before the evidence is more conclusive, however, because conducting quality research is such a slow process.

Now complete Worksheet 12-9, particularly when your anxiety levels feel overwhelming, and write down what effect the STOP exercise had.

You're not trying to get rid of the anxiety. You're trying to shift your attitude towards the anxiety, to one of acceptance, curiosity and non-judgement.

Worksheet 12-9	Practising and Appraising the STOP Exercise
Date and Time I Practised the STOP Exercise	*Effect the STOP Exercise had on My Thoughts, Feelings, Bodily Sensations and General Attitude*

You can use this STOP exercise for all sorts of different situations where you need to ground yourself, not just when you feel inappropriate anxiety. You can even use the practice a few times a day, no matter how you're feeling, to improve your ability to focus and turn off your automatic-pilot mind.

Here are a few daily tips for managing anxiety mindfully:

- ✔ **Take time every day to practise some mindfulness meditation.** Ideally about 20 minutes a day at least, but even a few minutes are better than none at all.

- ✔ **Carry out the STOP exercise or the mini breathing space meditation (from Chapter 6) three times a day.**

- ✔ **Do one thing at a time rather than multitasking.** When you're doing that one thing, give the activity your full attention. For example, as I'm writing now, I switched off the Internet and phone, cleared my desk and shut the door. This approach prevents the temptation to be distracted, which can lead to greater anxiety.

- ✔ **Practise gratitude.** Think about what's going well in your life before you go to bed, when you wake up in the morning or at any other time during the day.

- ✔ **Spend time doing an enjoyable pastime mindfully every day.** This activity can be gardening, cooking, knitting, walking in nature, stroking your cat or polishing your car. When you give the activity your gentle, mindful attention, you soothe your mind and improve your ability to shift your attention away from believing unhelpful thoughts.

In Worksheet 12-10, write down one thing you're going to commit to doing this week from the previous list that you think may help to manage your anxiety. After the week is over, note down what effect it had and try another item for the following week.

Worksheet 12-10	Managing My Anxiety

What I'm going to do this week to try to manage my anxiety:

_____

_____

I noticed the following effects:

_____

_____

_____

Discovering Acceptance and Commitment Therapy (ACT)

Another interesting form of therapy that uses mindfulness is ACT – Acceptance and Commitment Therapy. Developed in the early 1980s by Steven Hayes, ACT is grounded in quality science and yet has elements that echo ancient eastern ideas. The evidence is growing rapidly and so far seems to show that ACT is effective for social anxiety, depression, obsessive compulsive disorder (OCD), borderline personality disorder, workplace stress, chronic pain, weight control, diabetes management, smoking cessation and more.

ACT helps you to accept what's out of your personal control and commit to action that improves your life. ACT achieves this by:

✔ Using mindfulness skills to deal with difficult thoughts and emotions.

✔ Helping you to determine your *values* (what's truly important for you) and offering ways to help you move towards living by your values.

The mindfulness part comprises four principles:

✔ **Defusion** – Using techniques to let go of difficult thoughts, beliefs and memories. Fusion is about being stuck and so *defusion* is about becoming unstuck from your thoughts by seeing that thoughts are just sounds and images in the mind. For example, if you have the thought, 'I'm rubbish at everything,' you can imagine that sentence in front of you with curiosity. Then you imagine Mickey Mouse repeatedly saying the words in a high-pitched voice. Finally, you imagine the character dancing around and saying, 'I'm rubbish at everything.' This is just one of many ways to defuse.

✔ **Acceptance** – Making space for painful thoughts, feelings and sensations without struggling against them. Acceptance isn't admitting defeat or resignation or thinking that the experience is going to exist forever. Acceptance is letting go of the fight with your *present-moment* experience.

✔ **Present moment** – Being in contact with the here-and-now experience with curiosity and a sense of openness.

✔ **Observing yourself** – Stepping back as the observer or witness of your experience as spacious, open awareness. You discover how to watch thoughts and emotions arise and pass away as an observer instead of identifying with the experience.

The main difference between the ACT approach and other mindfulness approaches is the emphasis on action and less of a focus on long meditations. The idea is to use mindfulness skills to help you manage your difficult thoughts and emotions as you move towards taking action based on your core values. Shamash uses some ACT approaches when coaching clients because doing so helps them to clarify what's most important in their lives and commit to taking action in those areas, so that life feels more rich and meaningful.

To find out more about ACT, try *Get Out of your Mind and into your Life* by Steven Hayes (New Harbinger Publications) or *The Happiness Trap: How to Stop Struggling and Start Living* by Russ Harris (Trumpeter).

Mindfulness is not the only way of managing anxiety. You can also try exercise, relaxation (for example, deep breathing or yoga), adjusting your diet, cutting out alcohol, nicotine and caffeine, joining a support group or reading self-help books on anxiety recommended by health professionals. See what works for you!

Coping with your fears

Here are a few tips for coping with your anxiety and fears from the UK's National Health Service. Many of them are about acceptance and moving towards your fears, which is also of course the mindful way:

- ✔ **Take time out for a break.** Even a 15-minute walk around the block or a hot bath can help give you some space to see the big picture.

- ✔ **Ask yourself, 'What's the worst that can happen?'** It's usually not that bad, and not as scary as you thought.

- ✔ **Face the fear.** For example, if you're scared of parties, go to parties and stay for some time. Eventually the fear subsides.

- ✔ **Welcome the worst instead of running away from it.** If you're terrified that your panic may cause a heart attack, trying thinking yourself into a heart attack. It's impossible and your fears around this dissipate.

- ✔ **Don't expect perfection.** Life is messy; sometimes, aiming for 80 per cent perfect can help.

- ✔ **Visualise a calm and peaceful place for you.** For example, imagine a beach and notice the colours, smells, sounds and feelings.

- ✔ **Get some sleep.** If at night you can't sleep and find yourself trying to fall asleep – stop. Instead, try and stay awake! The effort of trying to sleep can make you feel anxious and actually prevent you from sleeping.

- ✔ **Reward yourself when you do overcome your fears.** If you have a fear of enclosed spaces but still managed to get into the lift, have some tasty chocolate as a treat, watch that new DVD, take a walk in a beautiful place or get your nails done! Whatever makes you happy.

Chapter 13

Healing Your Body Naturally

● ●

In This Chapter

▶ Uncovering the mind-body connection

▶ Discovering your natural capacity for healing

▶ Applying proven mindful attitudes for pain management

● ●

The natural healing force within each one of us is the greatest force in getting well.
– Hippocrates

Health is about more than just the absence of disease. It's about living a life of wholeness, meeting challenges skilfully and positively and being kind and understanding
towards yourself when you fall short of this aim. In fact, the word 'healing' means to make
whole.

In this chapter, you discover the close connection between your mind and body, which
helps you change how you relate to your body, especially when ill or in pain. Disease (perhaps think of it as 'dis-ease', a lack of ease) is more than only a physical condition. Just as
your physical experience (of pain) impacts on your mental state (say, as frustration), so
using your mind in a skilful way (via the mindfulness approaches we discuss) allows you to
have a positive impact on your body. For example, rather than feeling broken or damaged
after a bout of disease, you can explore the possibility of feeling more complete, or whole,
despite your illness. We also describe how you can deal with the difficult feelings of physical pain to minimise your suffering rather than compounding it.

In these ways, you may even create conditions for your symptoms to reduce or diminish
altogether, as other users of mindfulness have found.

If you suspect you're suffering from a medical condition, or are experiencing pain, always
visit your doctor. And if you plan to use mindfulness together with your medical condition,
always check that's okay with your doctor first.

Meeting the Mind-body Connection

Healing is a matter of time, but it is sometimes also a matter of opportunity.
– Hippocrates

Although Western medicine viewed mind and body as being separate for hundreds of years,
many of the top universities around the world now study and teach *mind-body medicine:*
using the fact that your thoughts and emotions impact on your physical health and wellbeing. Mind-body medicine includes looking into and using practices such as yoga and mindfulness meditation.

One way in which mind-body approaches including mindfulness help you to heal is that when stress is reduced, your immune system works more efficiently (see the later section 'Boosting your immune system to reduce your stress'). But mindfulness is about more than just stress reduction; it's a journey to knowing yourself better – an opportunity to get in touch with your own body and mind in a more accepting and kind way. Certainly mindfulness helps to reduce stress, but it also generates a positive relationship with yourself. Therefore, even if you do find yourself ill, you're able to respond to that challenge in a healthy, helpful way.

The mind and body impact each other all the time. To show you what we mean, here's a simple little experiment. Take a minute to think about something that you find scary, whether it's giving a presentation in front of a big audience or the sight of spiders. Really immerse your mind in recreating the experience – as if you're present and it's happening to you. It may be an experience you had in the past or you can make something up. Think about it or imagine yourself in such a situation for about a minute.

Now in Worksheet 13-1, write down what effect this visualisation had on your heart rate and breathing rate. Did you notice any other changes in your body?

Worksheet 13-1   **Testing the Mind-Body Connection**

The chances are that your heart rate started to go up and your breath became a little more rapid and shallow. Perhaps you even started feeling a bit warmer.

'So what?', you may think. Well, this small example has big implications. It shows that the thoughts and images in your mind impact on your emotions, which in turn have an effect on the physical mechanism of your body.

In addition and most importantly, it suggests that if you can manage your mind effectively, you can create a positive effect on your body.

Placebos really working

The power of belief in a treatment has a measurable physical effect on the brain. A research study at UCLA Neuropsychiatric Institute on the placebo effect on depression, comparing several weeks of taking anti-depressants compared to placebos, found that patients on the placebo had increased brain activity in different parts of the brain compared to the anti-depressants. So, the placebo effect caused physical effects in the body.

Another experiment tested the effect of placebo for pain relief. Participants were given a placebo injection in their jaw and told they were being given a drug for pain relief. The placebo caused pain relief in many of the patients. The researchers found that the patients' minds naturally released pain-relieving hormones (endorphins) into their bloodstream.

One of the most powerful ways of showing the effect of the mind on the body is called the *placebo effect*. A *placebo* is a dummy pill (for example, a sugar pill) or treatment (such as an injection, a liquid or a procedure) that a person believes will help treat a particular condition. The placebo has no medicine in it and so taking it should have no effect. But incredibly, in about a third of all cases, people recover! Sometimes believing that a pill is going to make you better works just as well as a real drug! See the nearby sidebar 'Placebos really working' for some examples of placebo effectiveness.

Have a go at using the power of your mind to lower your stress. Try the mindful exercises in Worksheet 13-2 and note down their effect on your heart rate. This exercise is just for fun, so don't take it too seriously. You'd need to do the test many times to get an accurate result, but play with it and see what happens!

Worksheet 13-2 Measuring the Effect of Mindfulness on My Heart Rate

Mindfulness Exercise	Heartbeats per Minute Before	Heartbeats per Minute After	How Relaxed I Felt Before	How Relaxed I Felt After	Did the Exercise Help to Reduce My Stress?
Practise mindful breathing for ten minutes (Chapter 5).					
Do breathing space meditation for ten minutes (Chapter 6).					
Listen to the sounds around you in a mindful (non-judgemental) way for ten minutes (Chapter 9).					
Practise the mountain or lake meditation from Chapters 3 and 9 (listen to the guidance on the audio to help you).					

If you find that your stress level goes down after the mindfulness exercise, that's great! But don't worry if it didn't. In mindfulness, you can never make relaxation the goal (you probably have enough goals in your life to worry about). Mindfulness exercises are a time to put aside all aims and goals, and instead just to be with your experiences, no matter what happens. It's a time to just be.

Using the Power of Your Mind in Healing

As we explain in the previous section, the mind and body are closely linked. So, if you use your mind in a healthy way, you can have a significant positive effect on your body. Mindfulness is one way of cultivating a positive mind state and thereby aiding the healing process in your body, as well as ensuring you don't fall ill so easily in the first place.

Boosting your immune system to reduce your stress

Stress is a modern epidemic. What used to be considered clinical levels of anxiety in the 1950s in young people are now average. Many possible reasons exist for the high levels of stress in modern society – constant busyness, 24-hour digital connectivity, the breakup of the traditional family, lack of community support, higher demands of productivity, less job security in the workplace, worries about identity theft, climate change and a bleak financial outlook and so on and on.

When you're feeling stressed, your body releases stress hormones (*corticosteroids*) into your bloodstream that affect many of your bodily systems: your blood pressure rises, your immune system receives less energy and your natural capacity to heal is diminished. By using mindfulness to reduce your stress, your immune system is boosted and you're more likely to get better, faster.

Chronic, that is long-term, stress makes you more likely to get ill, because the stress hormones suppress your immune system, making your body more susceptible to attack from disease. Chronic stress also raises your heart rate (because this is part of the fight-or-flight system) and may increase your chance of getting coronary heart disease. Another effect of the stress response is an inhibition of your digestive system, linking chronic stress to problems such as gastric ulcers.

Think about the different times in your life when you experienced high levels of stress: perhaps it was exams, losing your job, money problems or loss of a loved one. What physical changes did you experience? Did you become ill? If so, how? Fill in your answers in Worksheet 13-3. Doing so may reveal some patterns and show you the link between stress and disease in your own experience, to help motivate you to take steps to reduce your stress levels.

Worksheet 13-3	Discovering How to Identify Warning Signs for High Stress	
Situation That Caused Me Stress	*Level of Stress (High, Medium or Low)*	*Physical Changes or Type of Illness*

Taking a break to aid healing

The only disability in life is a bad attitude.

– *Scott Hamilton*

Healing takes time. If you're too driven by work and so on, you're more likely to delay the healing process. Trust your instinct and give yourself some space. For some diseases – such as the flu – if you give your body a break, it can often heal itself. For a personal anecdote on this subject, see the nearby sidebar 'Slowing down to keep going'.

Slowing down to keep going

At one point in my life, I (Jo) went through a particularly stressful time, moving house, changing jobs and dealing with a relationship breakup. At the time I always felt exhausted, but battled the exhaustion by continuing to work all hours and fit in the gym when I could. But I was still exhausted and finally went to the doctor; he diagnosed me as being anaemic. I took the prescribed iron tablets and continued with my working regime, but I was still exhausted.

Only when I let go of some of my working hours and gym time did I truly start to get better. I ate healthier meals, relaxed more, made time for meditation every day and then when I felt strong enough, slowly introduced my routine back – but not so much that I felt exhausted. When I returned for a check-up with my doctor a couple of months later, the anaemia had disappeared. I made time for my healing and have never suffered with anaemia since.

The Dalai Lama sums the situation up with this quote about knowing your limits and taking time to heal and be healthy:

> *Man [. . .] sacrifices his health in order to make money. Then he sacrifices money to recuperate his health. And then he is so anxious about the future that he does not enjoy the present; the result being that he does not live in the present or the future; he lives as if he is never going to die, and then dies having never really lived.*

Answer the questions in Worksheet 13-4 if you're currently unwell and seeking some kind of healing. Do so relatively quickly rather than thinking too much – try trusting your gut instinct.

Worksheet 13-4 **My Health/Activity Balance**

Do you think that you're giving yourself enough space and time to heal?

_____

What are you doing too much of? For example, working, socialising, sleeping, exercising.

_____

What are you not doing enough of? For example, resting, relaxing, walking, socialising, talking, meditating.

_____

_____

After some reflection, if you still agree with the statements you made, begin to make the necessary changes in your life. Start with tiny steps and let a trusted friend know your goals, so that person can encourage you along the way.

Refusing to define yourself by your illness

Modern man is sick because he is not whole.

– *Carl Gustav Jung*

One of the things about ill health is that you can all too easily identify yourself with the disease. If you suffer from anxiety, which causes much physical and mental discomfort, you may say, 'I'm anxious.' Or for other conditions, you may say something along the lines of 'I'm depressed', 'I'm stressed' or 'I'm sick.' Without knowing it, by using the words 'I am' and what describes the state, you're identifying with your illness. In effect, you're saying that you *are* the illness.

Such identification has problems because thinking that you *are* an illness or disease can make you feel more helpless and down. For example, rather than saying *you* are ill or *you* have cancer, you can say *your body* in unwell or *your body* has cancer at the moment. To show an alternative mind-set, a helpful model is to think of yourself as having three selves:

✔ **Your physical self:** Your physical body, with its arms and legs and head and all the other bits and pieces that make up the physical you.

  If you think that your physical body constitutes you, consider this: if you lose part of your body- for example, an arm or leg in an accident – do *you* cease to exist? Of course, your life changes and perhaps your attitude and outlook, but do you change as a person? Most people say 'no'.

✔ **Your thinking self:** Your mind, thoughts and emotions. When lost in a train of thought, you're identifying with your thinking self. Whenever you engage your mind to consider something, you're connecting with your thinking self. No doubt this part of yourself is very familiar to you.

  If you think that your thinking self is you, when your thoughts change do *you* change? Most people think not.

✔ **Your observing self:** The part of you that watches your physical body, your thoughts and emotions, and the world around you. You *are* the observing self all the time. Another way to describe it is as pure awareness. You can't directly experience your observing self, just like you can't directly see your own eyes, but you know you have eyes because you can see the world around you. Similarly, you'd be unaware of your experiences without the observing self.

  Think of your observing self as clear sky and your experiences as clouds. The clouds come and go, just like thoughts, emotions, sensations and experiences in the world come and go, yet the sky (your observing self) remains the same. Understanding the observing self can be difficult because this witnessing aspect of you is beyond concepts, words or ideas. Instead, the observing self is what watches concepts and ideas as they arise. Reflect on this fact for a few minutes.

Here are a few useful hallmarks of the observer self. The observer self:

✔ Is always present.

✔ Is always watching your experience without getting involved or affected by the experience.

✔ Stays the same throughout your life, right from yourself as a young child.

✔ Is your essential, true self.

✔ Isn't your thinking self or feeling or physical self but the part of you that's *aware* of thinking and feeling and everything else.

✔ Gives you a sense of freedom and space, especially from difficult emotions, thoughts or sensations.

✔ Isn't something you have to believe or disbelieve. It's just something you deduce though your observation.

You can get a sense of the observing self in the following meditation:

1. **Find a position that feels comfortable for you, in a place you won't be disturbed.** Switch off any potential distractions such as your phone and give yourself time for this exercise.

2. **Become aware of your breathing.** Feel your in-breath and out-breath. Notice yourself watching the breath (the observer) and the breath itself – in some ways, totally separate from each other.

3. **Notice your physical sensations.** Turn your attention to your body as a whole. And notice yourself observing your body. Again, be aware of *you* and *your experience* as two separate things.

4. **Become aware of sounds around you.** Some may be loud, others quiet. You're observing the sounds arising in awareness. You are the listener and the sounds are what are being listened to.

5. **Turn your attention to your thoughts and emotions.** Notice the range of different thoughts. Be aware of how your attention often gets caught in a train of thought. Yet still, you have a sense of watching your thoughts arise, one after another.

6. **Let your awareness be fully open to any particular experience.** Allow yourself to be aware of whatever is predominant in your awareness. Get a sense of being the observer self (awareness), with experiences arising within your awareness.

7. **Notice in all these experiences how you were watching, observing, looking or listening to the experience.** You are the observer.

After the meditation, answer the questions in Worksheet 13-5.

Worksheet 13-5   Reflecting on the Observing-Self Meditation

How did you find this experience?

_____

What did you notice?

_____

Did you get a sense of what it means to discover the observing self?

_____

Quite often, if you've suffered from a prolonged physical or emotional illness, you feel broken. You may think that something about you is permanently damaged and can't be fixed. But when you begin to identify with the observing self from time to time, you may not feel quite the same. You can acknowledge an aspect of your being that's untouched by your illness, difficult thoughts and emotions. You can then see this aspect of you as being always pure, perfect, complete and whole (remember that *healing* means *to make whole*).

One of the most effective ways to step back into your observer self is to practise mindfulness meditation as often as possible. Even a few minutes, several times a day, is helpful.

Using Mindfulness to Manage Your Pain

Everyone experiences pain – it's part of life – and remember that it serves a purpose: to protect your body from harm. If you stopped feeling pain, within hours you'd probably be covered with bruises and have inadvertently cut yourself.

Sometimes pain is experienced as a warning signal that something is wrong: for example, a headache may indicate that you need to drink more water; a pain in your back may signal that you need to rest, correct your posture or perhaps go for a walk. By listening to your pain and taking corrective action, you can take better care of your body, which can lead to healing in both the short and long term.

In essence you can experience two types of pain:

- **Acute pain** arises in the short term to indicate a problem. For example, a headache that lasts for a day. That may mean you need to drink more water or relax more.

- **Chronic pain** lasts over the long term. Your nervous system's pain signals can keep on firing for months or years. Chronic pain can occur for a variety of different reasons: it may be triggered by a disease such as cancer or arthritis, or may just start by itself. An estimated 1.5 billion people suffer from chronic pain worldwide, so it's a huge problem.

In this section, you discover that mindfulness is a powerful and transformative treatment for pain, especially the chronic type. Some research shows that people suffering from chronic pain report up to a 50 per cent reduction in pain following a course in mindfulness.

Understanding how mindfulness can help with pain

Pain can bring your life to a standstill. You can't do the activities you used to take for granted and may have to stop making long-term plans. Your pain can become your main focus above and beyond any other considerations. One of the recommended techniques for pain management is the mind-body approach, including mindfulness (check out the earlier section 'Meeting the Mind-body Connection' for more details).

 The idea of using mindfulness for pain relief may appear strange to you. After all, the experience of pain is very physical, so why use mindfulness as if pain is a psychological issue? Well, although the physical pain is real, pain has a direct impact on your emotional wellbeing too, which feeds back into the physical discomfort.

When you experience prolonged periods of pain, you can ignore other signals from your body, which often sets up a pain cycle. You feel, say, mild levels of stress, anxiety or pain, but ignore them and keep going. At some stage you then inevitably feel high levels of pain and crash out with no energy or focus at all. You end up avoiding daily activities, fearing the high levels of pain, and find that you see family and friends less often.

Mindfulness helps you to become more aware of the initial warning signs from your body, so that you can take appropriate action before the pain gets worse. At the same time, mindfulness ensures that you don't shy away from activity altogether, out of fear of the pain returning. Figure 13-1 shows how mindfulness helps you manage the pain cycle.

Figure 13-1: How mindfulness helps manage the pain cycle.

To help understand how mindfulness assists with pain management, view pain as comprising the following three experiences:

- ✔ **Your physical pain:** This is your physical experience of pain – the actual sensation that you directly feel in your body. Most people think of this as being the only dimension of pain.

- ✔ **Your emotional reaction:** These are the emotions that arise for you as a result of the pain, such as anger, frustration and anxiety. This reaction to a challenging physical sensation that you don't want to have is perfectly understandable.

- ✔ **Your mental reaction:** These are the thoughts that arise in your mind. They can be negative thoughts about your past, present or future such as, 'If only I hadn't done X. I can't do anything – I'm useless. I hate this. I can't stand this anymore. What's going to happen to me? How can I survive if this continues forever? What's the point?' These thought stories may be familiar and yet keep repeating in your head. They can also be so subtle that you don't really know that they exist – but they take a real toll on you.

As you can see, two of the three pain components aren't physical but connect to your mind and emotions. These problems are in fact *emotional suffering*. When you understand the difference between pain and emotional suffering, you can use mindfulness to reduce the latter and prevent your experience getting worse.

Pain is an inevitable part of life, but suffering isn't. Mindfulness provides you with ways to alleviate your suffering.

Easing the emotional suffering of pain with mindfulness

Mindfulness is about separating the physical sensation of pain from the emotional suffering that's automatically generated in your being, and so you discover how to bring your awareness to the pain with mindful attitudes. In this section, we describe some ways to manage your pain mindfully.

Living in the moment

When suffering from pain, you can find yourself thinking about the past and how good it used to be, and the future and how bleak it may seem, and get caught up and repeatedly re-engage with these stories. But one of the key benefits of using mindfulness for pain is discovering how to live in the present moment – the only time that really exists. You can 'be' with almost any pain knowing that you only have to be with it for this moment and don't need to keep re-experiencing it. You can then begin to learn to live your life, moment by moment, with a sense of kindness for yourself, connecting with your senses and experiences around you, and creatively and flexibly exploring ways of coping with the pain.

Instead of being overwhelmed by thinking of the entire day that you need to face, break things down. Start with breakfast. Take the meal step by step. See if you can taste one single spoonful of food. And if so, try the next one. Then move on, say, to your shower. Notice the temperature of the water for a few moments if you can. By breaking down your tasks and maintaining your attention in the moment, you may not feel so anxious about the day as a whole.

Aim to just be your best rather than beating yourself up for not managing to be mindful perfectly – that's just not possible. Doing what you can is perfect.

Moving from anger to kindness

You may quite understandably hate your pain. You want to fight it and make it go away. But unfortunately you can't win the battle that way because fighting your pain turns on your stress response. Your muscles begin to tense up and you release stress hormones into your bloodstream (for more details, turn to 'Boosting your immune system to reduce your stress' earlier in this chapter). Tensing your muscles is bound to increase your physical pain, which leads to a vicious circle.

Mindfulness encourages you to consider meeting the pain with a sense of kindness. This attitude may seem counterintuitive, but it is really helpful in beginning to relieve the stress of bracing against the pain.

When you're feeling your pain, gently turn your attention towards it. If you can, bring a tiny, or even minuscule, feeling of affection towards it. Now complete Worksheet 13-6.

Worksheet 13-6 **Bringing Kindness to Pain**

What happened to your experience and level of pain and suffering when you tried this exercise? Did you discover anything interesting?

Seeing yourself as the observer of the pain

As we describe in the earlier section 'Refusing to define yourself by your illness', you aren't just your physical body, your sensations or your thoughts or emotions. You're also the observer – pure awareness beyond thoughts and emotions – that allows you to experience things.

We invite you now to consider that dimension of yourself, as whole, complete and free from all suffering. See whether you can say to yourself, 'I'm observing the pain right now' rather than 'I'm in pain!' Have a little go at feeling the pain sensation itself with a sense of curiosity rather than just negative judgement. Try identifying yourself with the observer of the experience, rather than the experience itself. The sensation still exists, but perhaps you feel a little less of the tension and stress around the sensation. This exercise isn't easy, but have a go as an experiment. See what happens and then address the questions in Worksheet 13-7.

Worksheet 13-7 **Observing My Pain**

What happened to your level of pain and suffering when you tried this? What did you discover?

Keeping a mindful pain journal

Maintaining a journal of when, where and how much pain you suffer is useful for several reasons:

✔ You're carrying out a mindfulness activity in itself. When you notice what you're doing day to day and the level of pain you're experiencing, you can spot patterns and adjust your lifestyle to manage your pain more mindfully.

✔ You can more accurately report how your pain levels fluctuate to your doctor, who may then be able to identify more accurately what you need to manage your pain effectively.

✔ You're doing something (keeping a diary) that's emotionally healthy. You don't have to stick to the format in Worksheet 13-8; if you prefer, write about how you're feeling each day, expressing your fears and concerns without holding back. You may want to include motivating ideas, inspiring quotes and how your relationships are going. In this way you can ease your stress and have a positive impact on your pain levels.

Keep a pain journal by completing Worksheet 13-8 or your own preferred version.

Worksheet 13-8		One-Week Pain Journal		
Day	*Time*	*Level of Pain (0 = No Pain, 10 = Worst Ever Pain)*	*Description of Pain (For Example, Burning, Dull, Sharp, Aching, Tingling, Pulsating and So On)*	*What I Was Doing When the Pain Began*

The power of mindfulness lies in being with your moment-by-moment experiences, just as they are, instead of wanting them to be different.

Using meditations to deal with your pain

You can use all the mindfulness meditations in this book to help you cultivate a more non-judgemental, curious and compassionate awareness towards your pain. Here are a few to try, all described in Chapter 5 (we suggest you begin with the breath meditation):

- ✔ Mindfulness of breath meditation.
- ✔ Body scan meditation.
- ✔ Sitting (expanding awareness) meditation.
- ✔ Mindful stretching, yoga or t'ai chi.

Here's a guided meditation specifically for working with pain. You can read this meditation out, record it and then listen to it as you practise, or you can read one paragraph, do the practice for a few minutes and then read the next paragraph and so on. We use ellipses (. . .) to indicate times for you to pause and reflect.

You can purchase several audio recordings on mindfulness specifically for pain. We recommend ones by Jon Kabat-Zinn or Vidyamala Burch in particular.

1. **Find a position that minimises the pain for you.** You may like to sit up straight, need to lie down or adopt some other position that's best for you. Feel free to use cushions and blankets to make you feel at ease.

2. **Turn your attention towards your out-breaths.** You may be feeling all sorts of pain pulling at your attention, preventing you from being able to concentrate. That's understandable, so don't beat yourself up about it. Just try and feel your next out-breath (a half-breath) and feel it all the way out . . . If that was possible, try the next out-breath . . . Feel the breath all the way out, no matter how much your painful sensations seem to be calling out . . . .

3. **Have a go at feeling your next in-breath when you're ready.** Just feel your in-breaths . . . Sustain your attention for the whole duration of your in-breath, as best you can . . . Notice if that was possible . . . If so, try the next in-breath, feeling it despite any painful sensations seeking your awareness . . . .

4. **Feel each in-breath and each out-breath, if you can.** . . . Being mindful of your breathing, one half-breath at a time. Taking things slowly, half-breath after half-breath . . . in-breath followed by out-breath. Your pain is still present but your focus is on your breath. . . .

5. **Bring an attitude of curiosity and discovery.** See what happens as you practise being with the breath . . . gently sustaining your breath with a certain sense of determination . . . .

6. **If your attention is overwhelmed by the sensation of pain, try shifting your focus.** Perhaps move your attention towards your difficult sensation and experiment breathing into it, imagining that your breath can go in and out of the pain . . . Allow your breath to wash over the painful sensation . . . like the tides of the ocean . . . breathing into and out of the sensation of pain. In this way, you're feeling your breathing and your painful sensation together, as a whole, allowing them to co-exist in your awareness . . . .

7. **Don't try and get rid of the sensation of pain, make it diminish or change it.** Just bring mindfulness to painful sensations, an awareness with non-judgement – just feeling the sensation itself . . . Allowing your breath to wash over the pain, just as the ocean washes over the shore. Sustaining your attention in this area, and just seeing what happens . . . .

8. **Bring a quality of warmth, kindness, gentleness and tenderness to your intense, unwanted sensation, a quality of befriending.** . . . You may discover that the sensation isn't fixed but changing, fluctuating, subtly moving. Try to discover the changing nature of the feeling of pain if you can . . . .

9. **Reflect on the following question: Is my *observing self* in pain or just my *physical self*?** You may get a sense of yourself as awareness, as free of the pain itself. If so, take time to explore it . . . noticing what happens . . . Perhaps you can see your awareness as being bigger than your pain, because your awareness contains not only your pain, but also your breathing and perhaps some other bodily sensations . . . .

10. **If you experience a whirlwind of thoughts and emotions during this meditation, such as, 'Why am I feeling this pain?', 'When will this end?', 'My life is ruined', 'I can't stand this' and so on, notice that these are thoughts and not necessarily a reflection of reality** . . . You may notice that when these thoughts

arise, you also experience an echo within your body. The thought stories that you tell yourself are very likely having an impact on your experience. See if you can notice this . . . Emotions are fuelled by thoughts and you may feel them in your body. Watch all this happening as best you can. Seeing this subtle yet relentless process puts it out in the open, and opens up the possibility of meeting your mind and its ways . . . .

11. **Notice that the word 'pain' is a thought.** How often does the word 'pain' arise in your mind while you're feeling your pain? . . . You may like to explore the possibility, maybe just for a breath or two to begin with, of feeling your pain without the thought. Begin to see what effect the word 'pain' has on your difficult sensation . . . .

12. **Practise opening your awareness to other experiences, as best you can.** Even if only for a few moments, see whether you can step back into the open, spacious awareness and watch whatever experience is most predominant for you. This may very well be your painful sensation, or it may be your thoughts, emotions within your body, or even sounds or other experiences. Bring the qualities of curiosity or interest and open-heartedness to your experience and take things moment-by-moment . . . .

13. **Bring this meditation to a close when you're ready.** See if you can continue to keep a mindful, spacious open-hearted awareness into your next activity.

After having a go at the meditation, answer the questions in Worksheet 13-9. Don't worry about answering them in detail; whatever you can manage is great!

Worksheet 13-9   **Reflecting on the Pain Meditation**

Did you manage to get yourself into a suitable, comfortable position? Would you experiment with a different posture next time, and if so, which one?

_____

_____

Were you able to focus on one half-breath at a time? What did you notice?

_____

_____

Did you explore the effect of feeling the sensation of discomfort in your body, together with your breathing? What happened when you did this?

_____

_____

(continued)

What sort of thoughts and emotions arose for you? Did you explore seeing thoughts *as thoughts* rather than looking at your experience *from* thoughts? And what sort of emotions came up and where did you feel them in your body?

_____

_____

How much did you manage to accept your feelings of pain at the end of the meditation, compared to the beginning? Did you spot any shift in the way you related to your pain, and if so, how? The tiniest change is what you're looking for – a very small step is perfectly fine.

_____

_____

Chapter 14

Bringing the Benefits of Mindfulness to Children

*I*n some ways children are more mindful than adults. They live in the present moment rather than frequently reliving the past or worrying about the future, and they're naturally curious and excited about new experiences. They're like mini mindfulness gurus wandering around. You can introduce mindfulness to any children over the age of about five, up to about 17 years old. The earlier you start, the better.

As children grow up, they form a sense of personal identity – a sense of I, me and mine and perhaps a connected selfishness. Developing this identity is obviously necessary and healthy, but can cause problems for children when they're trying to relate to others and carve out happy, productive lives. Like all humans, children are also part of a bigger whole, and their journey is to move towards this realisation as they grow up. Every person needs to go through this process – developing a sense of interconnection with other people and nature and the sense of awe and wonder with the universe as a whole. Mindfulness can help children to begin this inner journey and help them manage the challenge of constant change that they face as they grow up.

Teaching mindfulness to children involves much more than just guiding them in a few meditations. Mindfulness includes instilling a set of values around self-compassion, gratitude and curiosity. In this chapter, you discover not only how to introduce mindfulness to children and several appropriate exercises, but also the importance of being mindful yourself in all dealings with youngsters. Setting the right example by living in a mindful way lies at the heart of developing mindfulness in children. We hope that this chapter is useful not only for parents and other family members, but also for teachers and indeed any adults in contact with children.

Mindful Parenting: An Art of Living

Parenting can be one of life's most rewarding experiences. Watching your child grow and nurturing them with the best you can offer can be deeply satisfying. But raising children certainly isn't easy. You may be nervous about what to expect and find yourself worrying all the time. You may be confused by the wide range of recommendations for ways to bring up your children. The constant busyness of dealing with school, meals, poor behaviour and activities as well as the rest of your life may feel overwhelming.

A calm word works wonders

Jo used to work at a college where some of the children came from quite underprivileged backgrounds. When they had misbehaved, the teenagers were sent to the office she worked in where her colleague dealt with them. They often arrived angry, shouting and frustrated, but instead of shouting back at them, he used to request them calmly to sit down, make them a cup of tea and ask them to tell him what had happened and why they were angry. More often than not, they told him or burst into tears. He tried to remember the way they were treated at home, with busy, stressed parents who often shouted at them. Because he took the time to really listen and give them the attention they deserved, they nearly always calmed down.

Feeling stressed with the challenges of family life is to be expected, at least from time to time. You soon discover that you need to offer love, but also much more. You have to build up your skills at juggling the demands so that you feel a little more in control instead of being dragged along by the challenges you face.

The concept of mindful parenting can help you immensely. *Mindful parenting* is about caring for yourself as well as your children: taking time to nourish yourself with mindfulness meditations when you can, having at least a little bit of quiet time every day and developing realistic expectations rather than stringent demands on yourself. Mindful parenting is also about developing your relationship with your partner if you have one, as well as with your children.

This section isn't just for parents, but for anyone who regularly looks after children. Take a peek at the sidebar 'A calm word works wonders' for an example.

Caring for yourself

Being a mindful parent involves caring for yourself and Worksheet 14-1 contains a few suggestions for doing so. Read each idea and write underneath whether you like it or not. If you do, state when you plan to do the activity.

Worksheet 14-1 Looking After Yourself

Make some time each week to do an activity you enjoy in a mindful way.

Manage your time. Make some time for yourself, for your family, for your partner and for your friends. And remember to say 'no' to people who want to take this time away from you.

Practise a mindful physical activity, such as swimming, walking, running or even housework, at least a few times a week. Do so with mindful awareness instead of rushing through the process. Chapter 6 contains more on mindful everyday activities.

Eat as healthily as you can and in a mindful way. In other words, give your meal your full attention and gratitude and notice when you're eating to soothe your emotions rather than satisfy your hunger. But remember to be kind and not berate yourself when you do eat to avoid your difficult emotions. Nothing's wrong with giving yourself a little treat every now and then.

Have some daily quiet time for reflection, meditation and rest. Even a few minutes are valuable.

Discovering your strengths and weaknesses: Completing a mindful parenting questionnaire

In some ways mindful parenting is simultaneously an ancient and a relatively new way of parenting. You may like to use Shamash's mindful parenting questionnaire in Worksheet 14-2 to get an idea of how mindful you are as a parent.

The purpose of this questionnaire isn't to criticise yourself. Instead, use the result as a guide to build your mindful parenting skills in ways that work for you. All the mindfulness exercises throughout the book can help you do this as well.

Circle the answer in Worksheet 14-2 that pops into your head after reading each question. Note the number beside your chosen response and total them up. Don't be too analytical – just trust your gut feeling.

Worksheet 14-2　　Discovering How Mindful You Are as a Parent

Do you find yourself rushing around and multitasking when you're with your children?

Often rushing (1)　　　Sometimes rushing (2)　　　Rarely rushing (3)

Do you find yourself judging and criticising yourself about how well you're doing as a parent, or constantly judging your child?

Often judging (1)　　　Sometimes judging (2)　　　Rarely judging (3)

Are you self-compassionate and compassionate towards your child? If you do something wrong, are you understanding of yourself or do you criticise yourself for making the mistake? When your children accidently make a mistake, can you see the world from their shoes or are you uncaring?

Often compassionate (3)　　　Sometimes compassionate (2)　　　Rarely compassionate (1)

Are you curious about yourself and/or the world around you? Do you find yourself asking questions about your thoughts/emotions/body or about certain topics that interest you? Do you encourage curiosity in your child?

Often curious (3)　　　Sometimes curious (2)　　　Rarely curious (1)

(continued)

Are you quite a forgiving person or do you hold grudges for a long time when someone does something of which you disapprove? Do you forgive your child when appropriate?

Forgiving when necessary (3)   Sometimes forgiving (2)   Rarely forgiving (1)

Do you live your life automatically and mechanically with your children, or are you conscious and deliberate in your approach?

Often automatic (1)   Sometimes automatic (2)   Often conscious and aware (3)

Are you a grateful person? Do you often reflect on how well things are going in your life and appreciate what you do have?

Often grateful (3)   Sometimes grateful (2)   Rarely grateful (1)

When talking to others, are you focused and attentive?

Focused (3)   Sometimes focused (2)   Often distracted (1)

Do you have some quiet time every day to practise mindfulness meditations or something similar, such as another meditation, yoga, t'ai chi or perhaps some form of mindful physical activity?

Have daily quiet time (3)   Sometimes have quiet time (2)   Never have quiet time (1)

Do you accept your emotions when they arise, or do you always try to avoid them in some way?

Always accept emotions (3)   Sometimes accept emotions (2)   Rarely accept emotions (1)

Now add up your score:

- ✔ A score of 10–15 indicates that learning mindfulness approaches can have a great, positive effect on your life. Applying the exercises in this book can create transformative benefits for you and your children.
- ✔ A score of 16–24 indicates that you're already quite mindful but deepening your mindful parenting skills in some areas can enhance your life. You may find some of the exercises in the book significantly beneficial for your life.
- ✔ A score of 25–30 suggests that you're already significantly mindful as a parent and you need simply to fine-tune your skills in a few areas. You may like to consider helping other parents lead more mindful lives too.

Feeling inspired by parenting tips

In this section we provide some tips on mindful parenting. After reading each tip, you may want to consider writing down some of your reflections on how well you're doing in that area, and how you specifically hope to develop this skill. In this way, you can build mindful parenting skills.

Listening to yourself and your child with full attention

Make sure that you listen to what your children say and note their tone of voice and body language. In this way, you hear their words and understand their emotional state and what they really need at this time.

Listening to yourself is also important. From time to time, carry out the breathing space meditation (from Chapter 6) to assess how you're feeling and what you need to function most effectively.

Balanced acceptance produces results

Richard Branson, the founder of the Virgin Group, was beaten regularly by his teachers as a child for poor achievement at school. However, he was dyslexic and doing his best. The teachers didn't accept his poor progress and thought corporal punishment would work, in line with the culture of that era. Fortunately, his parents were very loving and accepting of him as he was and encouraged him to excel in sports and as an entrepreneur, giving him challenges and praising him along the way. The rest is history.

Practising balanced acceptance for yourself and your child

You're bound to have expectations for your children. If those expectations are too high, however, you make yourself and them unhappy. Your children need to feel accepted for who they are and what they can achieve. Of course, this doesn't mean that you never encourage them to improve. Getting the right balance is key – hence we use the term 'balanced acceptance'. Discipline and guidance are necessary, but from a platform of accepting the present moment you're better able to understand where your children are coming from. They enjoy being praised and accepted for who they are, just as you do.

Developing emotional awareness of yourself and your child

Raising children is challenging and can lead to heightened emotional states in all concerned. Mindfulness helps you to notice when emotions are running high so that you don't automatically react to them. Instead, you mindfully make a choice as to the best action to take.

Mindfulness also involves being aware of the emotional state of your children so that you can best meet their needs as they arise and prevent them spiralling into worse behaviour. You can do this by noticing your own emotions whenever you can, labelling them in your mind and being aware of your physical state (most emotions have a bodily sensation associated with them – check out Chapter 5 for the body scan meditation, which helps you get in touch with your body and emotions). Practising mindfulness meditation helps you to better identify emotions, step back from them and so respond with discernment.

Building compassion for yourself and your children

Parents can be their own harshest critics. If you don't manage to be as good a parent as you hope, be compassionate and kind towards yourself. By being more understanding and remembering that no one's perfect and everyone makes mistakes and you're just having a bad day, you feel a bit better and become a better parent.

Compassion for your child grows out of this self-compassion. You're then more understanding when your child makes a mistake, is hurt or needs some comfort. Imagine the world from your children's point of view whenever you can to help to deepen your compassion for them.

Coaching Children in Mindfulness

Introducing mindfulness to children has many benefits: it can enhance their focus and attention, improve memory skills, deepen self-awareness and self-acceptance, and lead to a sense of inner calm.

Childhood isn't often carefree and easy. Many children lack the luxury of playing creatively without concern for time slipping by. They may have lots of activities to attend and feel constantly rushed. If they hear their parents or relatives arguing or sharing anxieties, they may also begin worrying about the issues. Even world news can be an anxiety for children. Disturbing or violent images or stories can lead to unrealistic fears about the world and their own safety. Pressures from school add to the stress. The constant comparisons they make with their peers, the need to impress and feel accepted, and ever-looming exams are further sources of anxiety.

High and sustained levels of stress in childhood can lead to mental-health conditions. Depression strikes children at younger ages than in the past, and, according to one US study, about one in eight children suffers from an anxiety disorder. Mindfulness is a gentle yet powerful way to show children ways to find some respite from a fast-paced and stressful world.

Introducing mindfulness to children is one way to help them manage their stress and find moments of joy, calm and focus. Using mindfulness together with a range of other relaxation strategies can help you and your children lead healthier and happier lives. For more, check out *Relaxation For Dummies* by Shamash Alidina (Wiley).

Setting the right example

The best way of teaching mindfulness to children is being mindful in your interactions with them. Children learn from what they observe, so let your relationship with them be mindful and wise, as best you can.

Worksheet 14-3 features a series of example situations. Write down how you may typically react to them and consider what you can do to make your responses more mindful in the future. A *mindful response* is one in which you don't react automatically. Instead, you notice what's happening, take a step back to see things from the wider perspective, decide whether or not to take an action and then respond in a conscious and controlled way.

Worksheet 14-3   Discerning Mindful Responses to Tricky Situations

---

You ask the children to do something and they refuse to do it.

Your typical reaction:

_____

Mindful response:

_____

A child is being very slow in getting dressed or going to bed.

Your typical reaction:

_____

Mindful response:

_____

A child receives a bad report from school.

Your typical reaction:

_____

Mindful response:

_____

A child throws a tantrum.

Your typical reaction:

_____

Mindful response:

_____

A child is complaining about something.

Your typical reaction:

_____

Mindful response:

_____

The children leave their room untidy.

Your typical reaction:

_____

Mindful response:

_____

A child wants to watch TV or play computer games all day.

Your typical reaction:

_____

Mindful response:

_____

If you struggle to respond mindfully, which is totally understandable, you can use the STOP exercise that we describe in detail in Chapter 13: Stop, Take a breath, Observe your (and the child's) feelings and then Proceed.

Responding mindfully rather than reacting mindlessly isn't simply a decision you take. You need to be living in a mindful way on a day-to-day basis as best you can. This approach means having mini mindfulness breaks from time to time, reserving some daily quiet time or developing your mindful awareness in a way of your choice. Then you're more likely to respond consciously and wisely to your children.

Using approaches that children enjoy

When introducing mindfulness exercises to children, make them fun, especially for children below the age of about 12. Here's one way of doing so that you may find useful.

Using Worksheet 14-4, make a list of activities that the children enjoy: for example, hide and seek, computer games or riding a bike. Then come up with some creative ideas for making those games more mindful and focused. For example, you can go riding a bike with them occasionally and point out the feeling of air against the skin, the importance of being grateful that they have a bike (many children don't) or how long they can feel the sensation of their breathing together with the view ahead before they get distracted.

Worksheet 14-4	Discovering Ways to Make Fun Activities More Mindful
Activities that the Child Enjoys	*Creative Ways I Can Make the Activity More Mindful*

We recommend limiting the amount of time children spend watching TV and using computer games and mobile phones. Playing with other children, getting plenty of exercise and having quality time with parents or guardians is the best way to nourish young children's brains, making them more likely to be mindful as they grow up.

Sharing Mindfulness Games with Children

To get you started and your creative juices flowing, we provide a series of mindfulness games, exercises and meditations to try out with your child, or your class if you're a teacher. They're just suggestions, of course, so please feel free to adapt them to meet the needs of specific children's interests and attention spans. Some children can handle longer games, others need very short games to begin with.

We suggest ages for each mindfulness games in this section, but that's for guidance only. You can adapt most of the exercises for different age ranges or the particular mood a child is in.

For each mindfulness game you carry out, you may like to keep a record of each child's progress. Fill in Worksheet 14-5 with any findings about each child's behaviour and create a similar table in a notebook so that you can note the effect of all the various meditations you try out. See if you can spot any helpful patterns.

Worksheet 14-5	Recording the Effects of Mindful Games on a Child's Habits and Behaviour for a Week						
Observations	*Monday*	*Tuesday*	*Wednesday*	*Thursday*	*Friday*	*Saturday*	*Sunday*
Game played.							
How long did the child sleep for?							
What was the child's mood like? On a scale of 1–10, 1 is very miserable or grumpy and 10 is very happy.							
What was the child's behaviour like? On a scale of 1–10, 1 is very bad and 10 is extremely good.							
How much energy did the child have? On a scale of 1–10, 1 is very low and 10 is very high.							

You can extend each mindfulness exercise for a few weeks or until the child begins to get bored or frustrated with it.

Dropping the pin game

This game works really well with a group of young children, say ages five to 10.

1. **Say, 'Everyone sit down really quietly.** We're going to see who's good at listening. At some point in the next few minutes, I'm going to drop the pin. You just need to sit still with your eyes closed and listen and see who can hear the pin drop. When you think you hear the pin drop, slowly raise your hand *really quietly* otherwise the others will hear you. No peeking – keep your eyes closed until I say so!'

2. **Give the children a few minutes of silence when everyone is settled and quiet.** Remind them that they need to be patient. Children who open their eyes or make a noise can lose a point (optional).

3. **Drop the pin and see what happens.**

4. **Repeat the game again but perhaps with a smaller pin, or drop the pin from a lower height so that it makes less noise.** Keep adjusting until hearing the pin land is really difficult.

Write your comments in Worksheet 14-6 concerning the aspects that work, what doesn't and how to improve the game in the future.

Worksheet 14-6	Comments on the Pin-Drop Game

Letting sleeping lions lie game

This game is suited to children from around five to nine and works well with children who need calming down! It has been slightly adapted from the classic children's game to make it a more mindful exercise.

1. **Tell the group of children that you're going to play sleeping lions.** Ask them to lie down on the floor and pretend to sleep very quietly, like a peaceful lion.

2. **Say that the best way to be really still and calm is to count their own breaths in their mind.** When they breathe in, they can say to themselves '1'. When they breathe out, they can say to themselves '2' and so on. When they get to 10, they start again.

3. **Inform the children that if anyone moves, they're out of the game.** See who can be completely still and not move a single muscle for five minutes.

4. **Walk around slowly, or just stand still and watch the group.** At the end of the exercise, ask the children how they managed to stay so still and if it helped to count their breaths.

Write your comments in Worksheet 14-7 on how the game goes and how you can improve it in the future.

Worksheet 14-7	Comments on the Sleeping Lions Game

Drawing a scene game

This game is a great way to teach mindful observation skills to children. It also helps develop their co-ordination and visual memory. You can adapt it for all ages.

1. **Ask the children if they want to play a drawing game that's really difficult and can only be done by children with super power-looking skills.** That should get them excited straight away!

2. **Take them to a place of natural beauty.** A park, lake or just in front of an attractive tree is ideal.

3. **Say, 'Okay, you have five minutes [can be less or more] to look at this scene.** Look closely at all the shapes and colours and observe well. Don't try too hard – your brain works better when it's relaxed. Just keep looking until I say stop. Then turn away from the scene and start drawing from your memory.'

4. **After they finish drawing, they can turn back and check how well they've done.** You can tell them that their brain gets better and better at this game if they play it regularly.

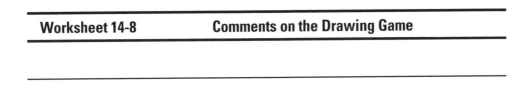

You can also get them to mark their work so they can assess their own progress.

Write your comments in Worksheet 14-8. State what works well and how you can improve or adapt the game.

Worksheet 14-8	Comments on the Drawing Game

Going to a happy place meditation

This visualisation-type meditation can stimulate what Shamash calls the children's 'inner senses' and may lead to a greater level of mindful awareness in their everyday lives. You can adapt it for any age.

1. **Ask the children to find a comfortable position.** Then tell them to gently close their eyes.

2. **Get them to imagine the most relaxing and happy place in the world for them.** It may be where they went on holiday, a place at home or school, or somewhere they make up. They can have other people in their happy place too, and be playing games with friends, being with their family or opening presents on their birthday.

3. **Pick the sense of sight and ask them to tune in to that sense for a minute or two.** Ask them to notice what they can see in their happy place. What colours? Who or what else can they see, for example, in the background? Is the sun rising or setting? In the same way, go through the other four senses.

4. **Encourage them to visualise the place as if they're really there.** Allow them time to immerse themselves in the experience. If they seem calm and engaged, slow the process down and give them time to linger in their happy place. If their eyes are closed and they're smiling, that's a good sign!

5. **Finish by asking them to feel their breathing.** Ask them to feel their breathing together with the visualisation. They can enjoy their breathing as they spend time in their happy place.

6. **Inform them that this happy place is inside of them, in their heart.** The core of their heart is always happy; it just gets covered up with other emotions sometimes. Emotions come to teach them something but always pass by. Whenever they feel upset or stressed, they can try going to this happy place, or some other happy place in their mind.

For older children, you can replace 'happy' with 'peaceful' or 'calm' if you prefer. This can work for adults too. As the age goes up, you can lengthen the time and do a longer mindfulness of breath at the end.

Write your comments in Worksheet 14-9 on how this meditation goes and how you can improve or adapt it.

Worksheet 14-9   **Comments on the Happy Place Meditation**

Watching thoughts as clouds

You can use this powerful visualisation for children of all ages. It helps them to step back from thoughts, a key skill in mindfulness. By doing this, children discover that they don't have to do whatever their thoughts tell them or believe that difficult thoughts are true.

1. **Get the children to lie down, adopt a relaxed position and close their eyes.**

2. **Ask them to imagine that they're lying down in a warm, sunny park.**

3. **Say that they're looking up at the sky and at the clouds that are passing.**

4. **Tell them to watch the passing clouds for a minute or so.**

5. **Ask them to notice their own thoughts.** Tell them that they're separate from their thoughts and can watch their thoughts pop up if they look carefully.

6. **Tell them that each time they have a thought, imagine placing the thought on a cloud and watch it pass by.**

7. **Keep reminding them to place their thoughts on the clouds.** If you're silent for too long, they get bored or lost in their thoughts for a long time.

8. **Finish by telling them that they can do this meditation whenever their mind is too full of thoughts, or whenever they feel like it.** They can even do it at night-time if they're struggling to fall asleep.

Write your comments in Worksheet 14-10 on what works and ideas for improvements or adaptations.

Worksheet 14-10   Comments on the Thoughts-as-Clouds Game

Carrying out random act of kindness

A random act of kindness is a selfless action that someone performs to help someone else, and often makes them smile. Simply describe to the children (of any ages) the benefits of being kind to others – it makes them happy and the other person happy too!

Here are some examples:

- ✔ Say good morning to people they meet, with a smile.
- ✔ Write a letter to their teacher or parent, saying how grateful they are and why they like them.
- ✔ Give one of their toys to a friend who'd really like it.
- ✔ Take a friend's dog for a walk when the family is on holiday (for older children).
- ✔ Help someone at school who's struggling in a subject that they're good at.
- ✔ Tidy up the house even when it's not their turn.

You can get children to come up with a new idea every day, and of course ask them how they felt after doing the act of kindness.

Visit www.randomactsofkindness.org for lots of ideas for sharing random acts of kindness, including lesson plans if you're a teacher.

Taking ten deep belly breaths

If you find some mindfulness meditations are difficult to teach to children, try this nice simple one, which is suitable for all ages.

1. **Get the children to lie down and if appropriate, lie down next to them.**

2. **Ask them how calm they feel, on a scale of one to ten.**

3. **Tell them that you're going to see who takes the slowest amount of time to take ten deep belly breaths.**

4. **Breathe in slowly together and ensure that the children's stomachs rise on the in-breath.**

5. **Pause for a few moments and then breathe out slowly, ensuring that the children's stomachs fall on the out-breath.**

6. **Continue until you get to ten breaths.**

7. **Ask the children to rate how calm they feel now on a scale of one to ten.**

They can do this exercise in a seated position, but that makes it a little bit more tricky to do the belly breathing, unless the children are naturally belly breathers.

Belly breathing turns on the relaxation response, so the children's stress levels automatically start to go down.

Sending love and happiness to everyone

This exercise is great for young children (five to ten years old) and adaptable for older children.

1. **Tell the children to lie down in a really comfortable way.** Provide lots of warm blankets and pillows, so they feel cosy.

2. **Ask them to place their hands on their chest and feel or imagine the warmth arising from their heart.** You can ask them to imagine a warm red or white ball of light, if they like that. This warmth represents the love and happiness that they're sending to themselves. They can even say to themselves, 'May I be full of love and happiness'.

3. **Get them to imagine that they're with their family and friends that they really like.** Again, they can send love and happiness to these people, imagining them smiling or laughing as the child sends them happiness. They can say or think, 'May my friends and family be filled with love and happiness.'

4. **Tell them to imagine sending love and happiness to all the people they know, whether they like them or not.** Everyone wants to be happy and feel loved, so they can imagine that their wish is granted and all people are happy. They can say or think, 'May all people alive be full of love and happiness.'

5. **Request that they now send love and happiness to all living beings on the earth: all the fish in the sea, the birds in the air and the animals and plants on earth.** Imagine sending them love and happiness. They can say or think, 'May all living creatures in the world be filled with love and happiness.'

6. **Bring this exercise to a close by allowing them to take a deep, mindful breath.**

Adapt this exercise for older children by using aspects of the loving kindness meditation from Chapter 5.

Practising the attitude of gratitude game

Developing an attitude of gratitude is great for children of all ages, and this exercise works best with younger ones aged five to 12 but is adaptable for all ages. Some studies show that children who kept a gratitude journal for around three weeks obtained higher marks at school at the end of the year.

In Worksheet 14-11, get the children to write down five things every evening that they're glad about: playing with a friend, having a nice dinner, getting a cuddle at the end of the day and so on.

Worksheet 14-11	**What the Children Are Glad About Each Day**
Day	**What Was I Glad About Today?**
Monday	
Tuesday	
Wednesday	
Thursday	
Friday	
Saturday	
Sunday	

Tracking children's moods and behaviour as they play the glad game is a great idea, and you can extend the process for three weeks if possible. How each child is benefitting from playing the game may not be obvious, so if they haven't mentioned anything positive don't be disappointed. Children take their own time cultivating gratitude and developing from it. For links to more free online resources to help you introduce mindfulness to children, visit www.learnmindfulness.co.uk/mindfulchild. Head to the bonus Part of Tens chapter, available online at www.dummies.com/extras/mindfulnessworkbookuk, to find children's books with a slant towards mindfulness.

Part V
The Part of Tens

Go to www.dummies.com/extras/mindfulnessworkbookuk for an extra Part of Tens chapter: '(Nearly) Ten Ways to Expand Your Mindfulness Experience'.

In this part . . .

✔ Discover simple yet incredibly effective ways to live life mindfully.

✔ Cultivate an attitude of gratitude.

✔ Dip a toe into acceptance and commitment therapy (ACT).

✔ Create a mindful space at home.

✔ Find a group to meditate with.

✔ Go to www.dummies.com/extras/mindfulnesswork bookuk for an extra Part of Tens chapter: '(Nearly) Ten Ways to Expand Your Mindfulness Experience'.

Chapter 15

Ten Tips for a Mindful Life

Here's one of our favourite chapters; a distillation of simple and practical ways in which you can live a more mindful life. If you only have time to read one chapter, make it this one. Then, you can dip into the rest of the book knowing some of the basic ways of integrating mindfulness into your life.

The simplest ideas and approaches can often lead to the deepest insights. Something as simple as mindfulness of breath, which is just feeling your breathing, can completely transform your life at the deepest of levels.

So, dive into this chapter with a sense of appreciation for the ancient tradition and modern science of mindfulness. You never know – your life may never be the same again.

Engage in Daily Mindful 'Me Time'

Mindful 'me time' means taking time out, every day if possible, to practise a mindfulness meditation or other mindful activity. If you're a constant giver – always thinking about others, perpetually active and never have a minute for yourself – this could turn out to be a valuable principle for you.

Regular mindfulness meditation is probably the hardest and yet most powerful way to become more mindful. You probably lead a busy life, and perhaps feel you can't find any extra time anywhere. But presidents and prime ministers have managed to find time to meditate, and so can you!

You can practise your daily quiet time at any time of day, and for any length of time. However, we recommend morning or early evening for ten minutes a day, which is a great start!

In your daily mindful time, you can do any of the following:

- ✔ Mindfulness of breath meditation (Chapter 5).
- ✔ Three-stage breathing space meditation (Chapter 6).
- ✔ Loving kindness meditation (Chapter 5).
- ✔ Have a mindful cup of tea or coffee (Chapter 5).
- ✔ Practise some mindful yoga or t'ai chi.
- ✔ Have a mindful bath or shower (see the nearby sidebar 'Bubble bath meditation').

You can be creative with mindfulness and make any activity a mindful one.

If you're struggling to motivate yourself to have some daily quiet time, remind yourself of these benefits of mindfulness:

- ✔ Reduced levels of stress, anxiety and depression.
- ✔ Higher levels of focus, resilience and wellbeing.
- ✔ Improved relationships with yourself and others.
- ✔ Greater feeling of calm and peace in your life.

If you still can't quite get into the daily habit, consider practising with a friend, joining a local group or doing an online mindfulness course at `www.learnmindfulness.co.uk`.

Complete Worksheet 15-1 to keep a record of your daily mindful 'me time' and see if you can get into the habit of practising regularly.

Bubble bath meditation

Even having a long bubble bath or shower can be a mindful experience. Find gorgeous-smelling bath salts or shower gel, unplug the phone and really enjoy the sensation of warm water on your skin. Feel how the water soothes your skin and muscles. Use the time to be mindful and let the experience nourish your being.

Worksheet 15-1		Daily Mindful 'Me Time'	
Day	*Mindful Practice*	*Length of Practice*	*Comments or Observations*
Monday			
Tuesday			
Wednesday			
Thursday			
Friday			
Saturday			
Sunday			

Meet People Mindfully

Relationships are so important. Humans are social beings, but getting on with others can sometimes be tough.

Mindfulness is a powerful way of improving the quality of your relationships with others:

- **Mindfulness helps improve your communication.** You're better able to listen to others when you're mindful. So you're less likely to miscommunicate and more likely to have good quality conversations and a deepening of relationships, whether with your boss, partner, parents or friends.

- **Mindfulness teaches you to respond rather than react.** So, for example, when someone says words that are hurtful, rather than instantly reacting to them, you're able to take a step back and respond after considering the options. Shouting and getting angry may not be the best way forward, and mindfulness gives you a choice rather than an automatic, habitual response. Chapter 6 has more on mindfully responding to others.

- **Mindfulness reduces your stress levels.** When stressed, you're more likely to interpret what people say as threatening. With less stress, you can speak to others with kindness instead of being aggressive and hostile.

Here are three little ways to improve your relationships mindfully:

- **Let go of judgement.** Each time you find yourself judging a person as you listen to them, try to let go of the judgement. You probably wouldn't like it if another person judged you, so try not to judge others. Chapter 3 has more on letting go of judgement.

- **Make someone a nice drink.** By doing an act of kindness as simple as offering to make a cup of tea, you feel better and so does the other person. Make the drink mindfully and offer it with a smile as a gesture of goodwill – don't look for thanks or anything else.

- **Be aware of your facial expression.** Be more aware of your expression when you're around others. Give people the gift of your beautiful smile. Everyone looks gorgeous when they smile. Smiles can keep spreading from person to person.

When people seem to be nasty to you, consider that you may not know their circumstances. I (Jo), studied a play in drama class where one of the characters was a mean lady who was rude to her servants. Our drama class all said what a horrible woman she was. But our teacher asked us to look at why she behaved the way she did. When we looked harder, we realised she had an impoverished background and had fought her way to the top for her children, to feed them and give them the best start in life. Studying this play definitely taught me not to judge people too harshly as you never know the full story.

Enjoy the Natural World

I (Shamash) was fortunate to go for a beautiful walk on holiday this morning, passing along a gurgling stream, walking across a sea of pebbles and up through a forest, along a path that wound up through to a clearing. I could see mountains, rivers and a small road with a few cars passing by. Above me, the mountain's summit was hidden by thick, white clouds that slowly drifted along. Every now and then a bird flew across the horizon. I could continuously smell the scent of forest vegetation as I gazed across the landscape.

How did you feel, reading that description? For me, just reliving the experience through writing about it made me feel calm. There's something special about nature that soothes the senses and settles the mind. Take time out to be in nature on a regular basis. Listen to the wind as it whistles past your hair. Watch the trees stand tall and straight. Smell the sweet perfume of a rose in bloom and feel the gentle rain as it touches your skin.

Spending time in nature is a way to rest your inner being – your deepest self.

If you have children, you could also explore nature with them together. As a child, I (Jo) remember catching and keeping a caterpillar. My mother and I watched its development from a small green caterpillar through the cocoon stage into a beautiful butterfly. I enjoyed setting it free and watching it fly away, thinking how truly beautiful nature is.

Here are a few tips for connecting with nature:

- ✔ Plan a rural holiday rather than a city break.

- ✔ Do some gardening.

- ✔ Have plants around your home and take time to look at them, water them and feed them.

- ✔ Notice the natural world on your commute. Look at the birds, trees and flowers. Watch how one season changes into another.

- ✔ Watch a sunrise or sunset when you can. And at night, take a few moments to look at the twinkling stars, the pale moon and reflect on the sheer size and beauty of the universe.

Although some of these activities may seem obvious, you may be so caught up in your worries, concerns and busyness that you sometimes forget to notice your surroundings. Remember to reconnect with nature.

Embrace Mindful Influences

You're constantly influenced by the people you spend time with, the newspapers and magazines you read, the television programmes you watch and the advertising you see. When you're mindful, you can be aware of unhelpful influences and seek experiences that lead to the kind of life you wish to lead, instead of being heavily influenced by external factors.

Here are some key influencers and ways to handle them:

- ✔ **The media.** Positive information and the millions of good deeds from around the world aren't widely reported as they don't grab people's attention. Believing everything's falling apart is easy if you constantly watch the news! Give yourself a break. Don't tune in to the news before work or last thing at night before bed. Doing so sets up your day with a negative start or ends your day on a downer so that you may not rest well. Instead, check the news or read the paper in the middle of the day or afternoon so it doesn't affect how you start or finish your day.

    Stop reading beauty magazines if you read them at all, as the airbrushed unreality can knock self-esteem.

✔ **Friends and family.** If you want to be more mindful in your life, find friends who value mindfulness. If you want to have a more positive outlook on things, spend time with positive people. Maintaining a positive outlook is tricky around negative people.

✔ **Books and music.** Read something inspiring every day; perhaps a page of a mindfulness book, a story of hard-won success or someone who's overcome a great difficulty or fought for something they really believed in. Enjoy a little bit of daily mindful inspiration!

Listen to uplifting or classical music to create a mindful atmosphere. Any music with a relatively slow rhythm can help you feel a bit more calm, centred and present.

Appreciate Your Blessings

Let us be grateful to the people who make us happy; they are the charming gardeners who make our souls blossom.

— *Marcel Proust*

Gratitude is a simple but hugely powerful emotion and habit. You have much to be grateful for, yet you may find yourself focusing on things you don't have. Switching your focus on your many blessings makes life more enjoyable.

Here are five tips to become more grateful in your life:

✔ **Keep a gratitude journal.** The act of writing down what you feel grateful for can really boost your levels of wellbeing. You begin to notice more things that are going well. Give it a try for a week. Head to Chapter 3 for a gratitude journal you can fill in.

✔ **Be mindful of your thoughts.** By noticing your thoughts, you may notice more times when you're thinking negatively about a situation. In this case, notice them as just thoughts and reflect on the question: 'What can I be grateful for in this situation?'

✔ **Make a commitment in front of your friends or family.** By letting those close to you know that you're making efforts to be a more grateful person, you'll feel more compelled to ensure that you put the time in to reflect on what you're grateful for. And your friends and family will remind you to be grateful too.

✔ **Hang out with grateful people.** Robert Emmons, Gratitude Researcher at the University of California says, 'If we hang out with ungrateful people, we'll "catch" one set of emotions; if we choose to associate with more grateful individuals, the influence will be in another direction. Find a grateful person and spend more time with him or her.'

✔ **Use reminders.** Stick gratitude quotes on your wall, mirror or computer, and bring a picture of your family to work – these things may all remind you to be grateful. For some inspiring gratitude quotes, check out www.learnmindfulness.co.uk/gratitudequotes.

For more on developing an attitude of gratitude, see Chapter 3.

Live in the Present Moment

The ability to be in the present moment is a major component of mental wellness.

— *Abraham Maslow*

Mindfulness is a practice and a way of living that encourages presence. By living in the here and now, you notice more about yourself and your surroundings, you feel more curious and alive, and discover new opportunities. By living in the moment, you create a better future.

Whenever you're connected with your senses or are aware that thoughts are popping into your head or emotions are arising in your being, you're in the present moment. Whenever you're worrying about the future or reflecting on the past, you're effectively no longer present.

Right now, as you're reading these words, this is all that exists. This moment is the only ultimate reality. Your thoughts about the past are just that – thoughts. Your plans for the future are just that too – plans. Nobody knows what's going to happen in the next few seconds, let alone tomorrow. So, by living in the moment, you're living in the only reality that you can be sure of.

Living in the present moment is a question of balance. You don't need to live every second in the present moment: that's impossible, unrealistic and perhaps even stressful! But mindfulness helps you to live more in the here-and-now to help you live with that same freshness as a young child does.

Living in the here-and-now is especially helpful when you're going through a tough time. You can take things moment by moment, rather than worrying about the whole problem. Say to yourself, 'I'll live my life one breath at a time and see what happens.'

Accept What You Can't Change

Acceptance. This is a powerful concept! Accepting that things can't always change has been shown to be hugely therapeutic in many studies.

The most transformative area for cultivating acceptance is your difficult, uncomfortable emotions. When you feel sad, anxious or frustrated, although you may not like the feeling, you can try not to avoid the sensation which, unless the feeling is mild or fleeting, can end up giving the feelings more power. You're fighting or running away from your feelings.

Instead, try accepting your emotions. Acceptance doesn't mean you have to like your emotions, or resign yourself to feeling bad for the rest of your life. No. Acceptance means that in this moment, this is how you feel, and that's okay. You acknowledge that this is the way things are at the moment.

Acceptance can go beyond just your emotions, of course. Any aspect of your life that just can't be changed, you need to accept. This acceptance leads to a clearer perception of the way things are and can often lead to a change in the future.

Head to Chapter 3 for more on acceptance.

Seeing Thoughts as Thoughts

Thoughts are just sounds and pictures that arise in your consciousness. And yet, problems with thoughts arise when you believe them all to be absolutely true.

By seeing thoughts as just thoughts, you become the master of them and can decide if a thought is helpful for you or not.

Mindfulness isn't about positive thinking. That's just putting another thought on top of any negative ones. Mindfulness is about seeing thoughts from a different perspective – from the bird's-eye view of mindful awareness. From this vantage point, thoughts are like words coming from a radio or images on a cinema screen. They're interesting, but they don't define you. Mindfulness empowers you to be in the driving seat rather than your thoughts.

To boost your ability in this skill, practise mindfulness of thoughts, described in Chapter 5.

Have Some Fun

Light-heartedness can be hugely helpful in putting the everyday hassles of life into perspective.

An injection of light-heartedness does just that – lightens the load on your heart. So we say, let there be a bit more fun in your life. Try to see the funny side of your situation.

The benefits of humour are:

- ✔ Your body relaxes. Physical tension in your body is released as your stress levels drop.
- ✔ You boost your immune system. Your ability to fight disease increases.
- ✔ You improve your heart health.
- ✔ You feel better!

But best of all, have fun and laugh just for the sake of it. Children don't think about why they want to have fun – they do it just because it feels so good! And you were a child once, so that same innate desire is still inside you.

Here are a few ways to bring more humour into your life:

- ✔ Spend time with funny, playful people. Their attitude is more catchy than a cold!
- ✔ Bring humour into conversations. Asking, 'What's the funniest thing that's ever happened to you?' is a great question to enliven a conversation!
- ✔ Make time for fun activities. You could go bowling, to a local comedy club or look up your local laughter yoga class! Yes, there really is such a thing!

Use the ACT Approach

Acceptance and commitment therapy (ACT) is a mindfulness-based therapy touched on in Chapter 12. You can use this ACT exercise whenever you're faced with a strong emotion or difficult situation that you need to deal with to help you live life more mindfully.

- ✔ **Accept.** Accept your reactions, feelings and thoughts by being present with your sensations, but taking a step back and watching them from a distanced perspective. Have an attitude of allowing or letting be. Hold the sensation in your body, notice what the feeling is actually like without judging it. Allow the sensation to rest in your being. Feel your breath and just be present with things as they are. You're making space for thoughts and feelings to be present without overwhelming you, if you can.

- ✔ **Choose.** Choose to move towards actions that can enrich and add meaning to your life. Have a sense of being together with your feelings rather than running from or fighting with them. When facing strong emotions, you may choose to go for a walk, talk to a friend or have a long bath. Let your choice be conscious and mindful rather than mindless and automatic.

- ✔ **Take action.** Take the action that you've chosen mindfully. Your choice may help you to soothe your emotions or deal with an issue. Be aware of how your choice, from a thought, turns into action. And make the activity mindful by connecting with your senses, your breathing or continuing to notice your thoughts and feelings that arise as you carry out the action. For example, if your girlfriend storms off in anger, you may choose to follow her and talk calmly to her.

Chapter 16

Ten Ways to Motivate Yourself to Meditate

. . . .

In This Chapter

▶ Discovering different ways to boost mindful meditation motivation

▶ Uncovering ways to make meditation more enjoyable

▶ Clarifying the benefits of meditation for your lifestyle

. . . .

People often say that motivation doesn't last. Well, neither does bathing – that's why we recommend it daily.

– Zig Ziglar

Getting into a routine of practising mindfulness meditation can be tricky if you have a very busy lifestyle and are continually on the go. Yet regular practice can actually help your busy lifestyle as you're more focused and more able to deal with stresses that are thrown your way. You may also find you have more energy from practising meditation. This chapter is your own personal pep-talk, giving you ten tips for increasing your motivation to meditate.

If you're struggling to practise meditation, let go of that inner battle. Instead, take a break from meditation. Don't try to meditate. After a while, maybe a month or so, try one of the tips below and see what happens. Meditation is here to help you – it's not just another thing on your to-do list that you don't get around to doing. Start slowly, gently and with compassion for yourself. One day, meditation will come to you.

Be still and look deep within. You'll find your motivation to meditate inside.

Overcome Difficulties

Quite often, the reason why you're not managing to meditate regularly is because of a particular problem or difficulty. If there was no problem with meditating, you'd be practising regularly! Consider the following common challenges, and if they apply to you, test out the suggested solutions.

Drinking peace meditation

Close your eyes and take a few deep breaths into your belly. Imagine you're standing at the edge of a beautiful lake. The sun is shining, reflecting off the water, giving a soft glow. It's a warm day and you can feel the sun on your skin, relaxing and comfortable. The grass is soft under your feet and you're looking out over the lake to the horizon. You begin to wade into the lake. The lake is warm, filled with fresh water, welcoming and peaceful. As you walk into the lake, the feeling of peace surrounds you. You cup your hands and collect water from the lake.

You begin to drink it. As you drink it, you can feel that feeling of peace entering your body. The peace continues down into your legs, your feet and toes, into your arms and hands. It continues through your torso into your lungs and into your head and neck. As you drink more and more, this peace has reached every corner of your body. You look around you and you're immersed in the peaceful water. You take a few more drinks of the cleansing water until you feel like you've drunk enough. Feel your breath. When you're ready, open your eyes.

Take time to really look at your life. Consider what you *really* want from your life, underneath everything else. If you take a close look, you'll find that meditation offers you a way towards your deep desires like peace, clarity or happiness.

✔ **Being creative with boredom.** You can choose from many different types and techniques of meditation. If you find the body scan meditation (explained in Chapter 5) too boring to practise, try some imaginative visualisations, such as the drinking peace meditation (in the nearby sidebar), or the mountain meditation (Chapter 9) or lake meditation (Chapter 3) on the accompanying audio at www.dummies.com/go/mindfulnessworkbookuk. Visualisations simply combine typical mindful exercises like feeling your breath or body together with imagining being in a certain place in your mind. Alternatively, try bringing a sense of curiosity to your boredom and ask yourself questions like, 'Why do I feel bored?', 'Where is the sensation of boredom in my body?', 'What does my boredom feel like?' and so on. Curiosity dissolves boredom pretty quickly!

Read books on mindfulness or meditation; they can be fascinating and motivating. Just be careful you don't spend all your time reading and never practise!

✔ **Making time in a busy day.** People commonly avoid meditation because they say they're too busy. Yet meditation can help you focus and get more done. If you really feel you don't have time to practise, take five or ten minutes to feel your breathing or simply drink a cup of tea mindfully – that's a meditation too!

✔ **Thinking you're doing it wrong.** There's no right or wrong way to practise meditation. You can't 'fail' or 'get it'. Mindfulness meditation is simply about present-moment awareness – not about stopping your thoughts or forcing yourself to relax. Whatever happens in meditation is your experience and is okay. You may achieve relaxation or you may not. Just be aware of your thoughts and emotions and treat the experience with kindness and curiosity. You aren't doing it wrong, because you can't.

In Worksheet 16-1, make a list of all the reasons why you may avoid meditation. Next to it, put your ideas on how you can counteract the avoidance.

Worksheet 16-1	Encouraging Myself to Meditate
Reasons Why I Avoid Meditation	*What I Can Do to Combat This*
No time to meditate.	Shorten the length of the meditation or meditate on the train to work.

Schedule Meditation

Forgetting to meditate is easy, especially if you have a busy lifestyle. Try this: schedule an appointment with yourself, like you would a meeting or a check-up at the doctor's. Seeing the reminder can be a source of motivation for you to do some mindfulness practice. Many business people love this tip as they use their diary so often.

Set a reminder on your phone, or on your calendar or diary to meditate every day. Or put a little note on the back of your bedroom door or on your bathroom mirror to get reminders.

If you don't want to do a long meditation, schedule a few short meditation practices. Doing so means that you're in a more meditative state of mind for the duration of the day.

Make a List of the Benefits

Drawing up a list of all the benefits you can have from regularly practising mindfulness meditation can motivate you to keep up a regular practice. Here are just a few reasons why practising mindfulness regularly can be beneficial:

✔ **Increases focus.** When you have a lot to do, meditation can help you to focus and therefore complete tasks more easily and with less stress.

✔ **Keeps you out of problem-solving mental traps.** When you're trying to find a solution to a problem, you can feel like you're banging your head against a brick wall. With mindfulness, solutions are easier to discover – you open up your ability to think creatively. You begin to access solutions from your powerful and intuitive unconscious mind.

✔ **Can ease pain.** People who regularly meditate find pain less unpleasant because they find different ways of relating to their pain. In fact, scientists found that meditation can cut pain perception in half. Turn to Chapter 13 for more about mindfulness and pain management.

✔ **Empathy for others.** Ever wondered why some spiritual leaders such as the Dalai Lama and others seem constantly happy and giggling, even though they may be going through a tough time? They practise loving kindness meditations, which create empathy for others and dissolve anger. Head to Chapter 5 for a loving kindness meditation.

These are just four benefits of practising mindfulness meditation – there are many more! Try writing the benefits you can think of in Worksheet 16-2 and how mindfulness meditation could specifically benefit you.

Worksheet 16-2	Benefits of Mindfulness Meditation
Mindfulness Meditation Benefits	*How Mindfulness Meditation Could Help Me*
Increases focus.	Will help me to complete my presentations at work.

Create a Mindful Space at Home

Having a quiet, relaxing place that you can go to in your home can really motivate you to meditate. If you have space, find a cosy corner in your home for soft cushions or beanbags, incense sticks and whatever makes you feel comfortable and relaxed to have as a space for meditation.

If you make a corner of your home attractive in that way, just seeing the place may draw you in to meditate. And if you practise meditation there regularly, just looking or imagining being in that place can put your mind into a more meditative state.

I (Jo), liked the colours in a yoga centre I went to. As I use my bedroom for meditation, I wanted to create the same calm effect that the yoga centre had. I didn't redecorate my whole bedroom, but just bought new bedclothes and a new lampshade for a bedside lamp to create a warm orange glow. Be creative and see how you feel.

Find a Group or Community to Meditate With

Meditating with a group of like-minded people is incredibly powerful and can really motivate you to meditate regularly. If you find a group or a community where you live that you can attend a couple of times a week, you'll be much more likely to stick to the practice of meditation. Try searching online for a mindfulness or meditation group near you. Try looking for groups on www.meetup.com, which is a website that connects groups of people with different interests.

If you can't find a physical group, you can join an online group to begin with. I (Shamash) have several thousand members on www.facebook.com/mindfulnessfordummies.

Make Meditation a Habit

Every day you follow some sort of routine of waking up, washing and brushing your teeth. You don't even think about it because you do it so often; your morning routine is a habit. Try to include your mindfulness practice in this way. Make it as natural as brushing your teeth in the morning and evening. Try to fit it in as part of your daily routine until it becomes habit.

The best way to get into the habit of mindfulness is to decide when you're going to meditate the following day. Then, on the day itself, you make sure that you do the practice at the designated time. If you can build up a certain sense of determination within yourself and do this for about three weeks, you'll be in the habit of the practice. Then, if you skip the meditation, you'll really miss it! Meditating has become an integral part of your day.

If you don't do your meditation when you decided to, simply be mindful about it. Instead of berating yourself, just be curious of the process unfolding. Notice how your emotions may have got the better of you. Be aware of the kind of thoughts that you have, driving you away from meditating.

Deal with Emotions

Sometimes upsetting and uncomfortable emotions and thoughts may rise to the surface in meditation. This situation makes feeling motivated to meditate more challenging.

 Mindfulness isn't about trying to get rid of these emotions, but about accepting and listening to them. If you feel you aren't ready to deal with that yet, try talking to a counsellor, a support group or even friends. Then, when you feel ready, resume your mindfulness practice.

Here are a few other tips for managing your emotions mindfully:

✔ Try labelling the emotion in your mind, such as 'anger' or 'sadness'. Research suggests this makes the emotion easier to cope with.

✔ Feel the emotion in your physical body.

✔ Notice the emotion with care instead of just avoiding it.

✔ Feel the emotion together with your breathing.

✔ Be with the feeling moment by moment instead of imagining the emotion will be with you forever.

Chapter 4 has more advice about dealing with difficult emotions arising in meditation.

Eliminate Distractions

Being surrounded by too many distractions makes meditating difficult. Find a quiet place away from the TV and computer, unplug the phone and switch off your mobile. Even take the batteries out of the doorbell if you need to! Make sure that you have your meditation time with as few disturbances as you can manage.

If you have children, try meditating while they're at school or in bed, or include them in your meditation, if possible.

When you become more experienced, you'll be able to deal with distractions in your meditation. You can then meditate on the train, bus or even standing in a queue with your eyes open.

Practise with Music

After silence, that which comes nearest to expressing the inexpressible is music.

– Aldous Huxley

You can listen to music while you're meditating if you find it too quiet on your own. Find some gentle music you can use and then play it over the guided meditations that come with this book.

Your whole meditation can even be to just mindfully listen to music. You can listen to soothing classical music on the radio or a CD for wonderful calming benefits.

Change Posture

If you feel particularly uncomfortable sitting cross-legged when you meditate, then don't. Choose a position that suits you. Don't expect to be an experienced Zen Buddhist monk sitting in the lotus position for hours for your first few experiences of the practice. That can demotivate you! If you need to lie down, lie down. If you feel very uncomfortable during the practice and want to move, then move. Remember, your practice is your own.

By getting into a posture that feels right for you, you're more likely to both enjoy the practice and gain greater benefit from it. This outcome can act as positive feedback to you, encouraging you to practise even more. Result!

About the Authors

Shamash Alidina, MEng MA PGCE, is CEO of Learn Mindfulness International, offering training and teacher training in mindfulness for both the general public, as well as life and executive coaches, yoga teachers, doctors, nurses, and other health professionals. His website offers online mindfulness courses and online mindfulness teacher training. He continues to grow his offers of audio CDs, books and more.

Shamash offers mindfulness workshops several times a year around the world and offers a limited number of one-to-one mindfulness coaching in person in London, or via phone/Skype.

Shamash has trained extensively in mindfulness at Bangor University's Centre for Mindfulness in the UK, and with Dr Jon Kabat-Zinn and Dr Saki Santorelli in New York. He holds a Masters Degree in Engineering (Imperial College) and a Masters Degree in Education (Open University), with a focus on Brain and Behaviour.

Shamash has appeared on television, radio and in magazines and newspapers including on the BBC and in the *Daily Express*. He hosts a mindfulness radio show at www.mindfulness radio.com which has several thousand listeners. He is an international speaker, addressing audiences at places like Cambridge University's conference on Mindfulness in the Workplace, the Mind and its Potential conference in Sydney and the Healthy Living Show in Auckland.

Shamash is the author of the international bestsellers *Mindfulness For Dummies* and *Relaxation For Dummies*.

See all Shamash's courses and workshops at www.learnmindfulness.co.uk or email him directly at shamash@learnmindfulness.co.uk.

Catch Shamash on the social networks at: www.twitter.com/shamashalidina, www.facebook.com/learnmindfulness and www.linkedin.com/in/learnmindfulness.

Joelle Jane Marshall holds a Film Studies degree, which included screenwriting and psychoanalytical study. She is developing workshops on Mindfulness and Overcoming Fear and writes poetry and short stories. Joelle trained at drama school after university where she started to become interested in psychology and how the mind works. She trained in mindfulness with Learn Mindfulness and also meditates and practises yoga regularly. Joelle has coached people to help them overcome anxiety or stressful situations by mindful listening and guiding them through different styles of meditation.

Email Jo at jomarshall2@hotmail.com, or follow her on Twitter: www.twitter.com/jomarshall2.

Dedication

I would like to dedicate this book to you, dear reader, especially if you are going through difficulties at this time. I genuinely hope that our words and meditations help to relieve sorrow and lead you to find peace of mind.

SA

This book is dedicated to my mother, Stephanie Anne Marshall, and my uncle, Peter Bromley Scheldt. May you both rest peacefully.

JJM

Authors' Acknowledgments

Firstly, I (Shamash) would like to sincerely thank my co-author, Joelle. Without her suggestion to help me write this book, I would not have undertaken the mammoth task in the first place. She was patient, encouraging, offered brilliant ideas and was far more efficient than I ever was! Most importantly, she has been a supportive and positive friend – I am so grateful for that.

I'd like to thank the whole team at Wiley who continue to be such a wonderful organisation to work with. Kerry Laundon was instrumental in commissioning the book – truly a delight to work with. I'd like to really thank Rachael Chilvers – a highly experienced and hugely talented editor. She was regularly in touch with me and forgiving of my many mistakes and requests! Without her patience and ability to edit skilfully, this book would not be anywhere near as good. I'd also like to equally thank Andy Finch for his key role in editing this book – he did a great job.

A big thank you to scientific director and author, Dr Shanida Nataraja, who kindly agreed to write the foreword to this book at relatively short notice, despite her busy travel and work schedule. She has written a beautiful foreword, and I'm truly grateful for her generosity.

I'd like to thank my family for their continued support of my work. They are: Amisha, Amy, Aneesh, Ashok, Fateh, Manju, Nikhil, Nirupa, Parul, Shona and Vijay. They're always enthusiastic and accepting of my unusual career path, which is nice!

I'm fortunate in that my friends are very supportive of my work too and offer great tips. I'd like to thank Garry (yoga and philosophy expert), Maneesh (expert on using technology to improve healthcare) as well as my good friends in Singapore who have hosted and encouraged me to bring mindfulness to the Far East – Manoj and Khyati. I'd like to thank my friends from my old practical philosophy class for the inspiration they offered – Jo, Marc, Ying and Marie. I'd like to thank my creative, generous web director and colleague, Paul. I always respect his opinion and look forward to working with him in the future on our online mindfulness training.

I continue to have a lot of meaningful support from my online groups, particularly on Facebook and Twitter. Thank you so much for your encouraging and interesting words. A big thanks to my wonderful Facebook page volunteers – currently they are Gudrun, Lisa and Roisin.

I've played a very small part in the making of this book. Although I've written down my ideas and observations from experience, most of what I've learnt has come from a range of mindfulness giants. People like Thich Nhat Hanh, Jon Kabat-Zinn, Mark Williams and the Dalai Lama have been inspirational to me.

Finally, last but certainly not least, I'd like to thank you, dear reader. Without your support, none of this work would be able to continue.

SA

Firstly I would like to thank Shamash Alidina, my co-writer and mentor, for introducing me to the mindfulness journey and his unwavering support along the way. Secondly, I'd like to thank Kerry Laundon for her editorial advice and guidance in writing my first book. Louisa, thank you for anecdotes from using mindfulness in your day-to-day living. To my friends and family across the world near and far, thank you for your encouragement and positivity and I feel very grateful to be able to share this with you.

Lastly, to my late mother, the ultimate mindfulness teacher without even realising it; thank you.

JJM

Publisher's Acknowledgments

We're proud of this book; please send us your comments at http://dummies.custhelp.com. For other comments, please contact our Customer Care Department within the U.S. at 877-762-2974, outside the U.S. at (001) 317-572-3993, or fax 317-572-4002.

Some of the people who helped bring this book to market include the following:

Acquisitions, Editorial, and Vertical Websites

Commissioning Editor: Kerry Laundon

Project Editor: Rachael Chilvers

Assistant Editor: Ben Kemble

Development Editors: Rachael Chilvers, Andy Finch

Proofreader: Kelly Cattermole

Production Manager: Daniel Mersey

Publisher: Miles Kendall

Cover Photo: © FreezeFrameStudio / iStock

Audio Production: Heavy Entertainment

Vertical Website: Rich Graves

Composition Services

Senior Project Coordinator: Kristie Rees

Layout and Graphics: Carl Byers, Carrie A. Cesavice, Joyce Haughey

Indexer: Potomac Indexing, LLC

Index

FOR DUMMIES®

NESS

...okkeeping
FOR DUMMIES

...8-1-118-34689-1

Pop Up
Business
FOR DUMMIES

Dan Thompson

978-1-118-44349-1

Starting & Running
a Business
ALL-IN-ONE
FOR DUMMIES

6 BOOKS IN 1

Colin Barrow

978-1-119-97527-4

IC

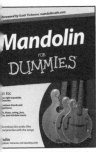

Mandolin
FOR DUMMIES

...8-1-119-94276-4

Ukulele
FOR DUMMIES

Alistair Wood

978-0-470-97799-6

DJing
FOR DUMMIES

John Steventon

978-0-470-66372-1

...BIES

Stargazing
FOR DUMMIES

Steve Owens

...8-1-118-41156-8

Keeping Chickens
FOR DUMMIES

Pammy Riggs
Kimberly Willis
Rob Ludlow

978-1-119-99417-6

Beekeeping
FOR DUMMIES

David Wiscombe
Howland Blackiston

978-1-119-97250-1

Asperger's Syndrome For Dummies
978-0-470-66087-4

Basic Maths For Dummies
978-1-119-97452-9

Body Language For Dummies, 2nd Edition
978-1-119-95351-7

Boosting Self-Esteem For Dummies
978-0-470-74193-1

Business Continuity For Dummies
978-1-118-32683-1

Cricket For Dummies
978-0-470-03454-5

Diabetes For Dummies, 3rd Edition
978-0-470-97711-8

eBay For Dummies, 3rd Edition
978-1-119-94122-4

English Grammar For Dummies
978-0-470-05752-0

Flirting For Dummies
978-0-470-74259-4

IBS For Dummies
978-0-470-51737-6

ITIL For Dummies
978-1-119-95013-4

Management For Dummies, 2nd Edition
978-0-470-97769-9

Managing Anxiety with CBT For Dummies
978-1-118-36606-6

Neuro-linguistic Programming For Dummies, 2nd Edition
978-0-470-66543-5

Nutrition For Dummies, 2nd Edition
978-0-470-97276-2

Organic Gardening For Dummies
978-1-119-97706-3

FOR DUMMIES®

Making Everything Easier!™

UK editions

SELF-HELP

978-0-470-66541-1

978-1-119-99264-6

978-0-470-66086-7

LANGUAGES

978-0-470-68815-1

978-1-119-97959-3

978-0-470-69477-0

HISTORY

978-0-470-68792-5

978-0-470-74783-4

978-0-470-97819-1

Origami Kit For Dummies
978-0-470-75857-1

Overcoming Depression For Dummies
978-0-470-69430-5

Positive Psychology For Dummies
978-0-470-72136-0

PRINCE2 For Dummies, 2009 Edition
978-0-470-71025-8

Project Management For Dummies
978-0-470-71119-4

Psychology Statistics For Dummies
978-1-119-95287-9

Psychometric Tests For Dummies
978-0-470-75366-8

Renting Out Your Property For Dummies, 3rd Edition
978-1-119-97640-0

Rugby Union For Dummies, 3rd Edition
978-1-119-99092-5

Sage One For Dummies
978-1-119-95236-7

Self-Hypnosis For Dummies
978-0-470-66073-7

Storing and Preserving Garden Produce For Dummies
978-1-119-95156-8

Teaching English as a Foreign Language For Dummies
978-0-470-74576-2

Time Management For Dummies
978-0-470-77765-7

Training Your Brain For Dummies
978-0-470-97449-0

Voice and Speaking Skills For Dummies
978-1-119-94512-3

Work-Life Balance For Dummies
978-0-470-71380-8

FOR DUMMIES®

Making Everything Easier! ™

~PUTER BASICS

Laptops For Dummies
978-1-118-11533-6

PCs All-in-One For Dummies
Mark L. Chambers
978-0-470-61454-9

Windows 7 For Dummies
Andy Rathbone
978-0-470-49743-2

~TAL PHOTOGRAPHY

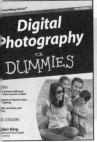
Digital Photography For Dummies
978-1-118-09203-3

Digital SLR Photography All-in-One For Dummies
Robert Correll
978-0-470-76878-5

Nikon D3100 For Dummies
Julie Adair King
978-1-118-00472-2

~NCE AND MATHS

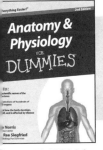
Anatomy & Physiology For Dummies
978-0-470-92326-9

Algebra I For Dummies
Mary Jane Sterling
978-0-470-55964-2

Physics I For Dummies
Steven Holzner, PhD
978-0-470-90324-7

Art For Dummies
978-0-7645-5104-8

Computers For Seniors For Dummies, 3rd Edition
978-1-118-11553-4

Criminology For Dummies
978-0-470-39696-4

Currency Trading For Dummies, 2nd Edition
978-0-470-01851-4

Drawing For Dummies, 2nd Edition
978-0-470-61842-4

Forensics For Dummies
978-0-7645-5580-0

French For Dummies, 2nd Edition
978-1-118-00464-7

Guitar For Dummies, 2nd Edition
978-0-7645-9904-0

Hinduism For Dummies
978-0-470-87858-3

Index Investing For Dummies
978-0-470-29406-2

Islamic Finance For Dummies
978-0-470-43069-9

Knitting For Dummies, 2nd Edition
978-0-470-28747-7

Music Theory For Dummies, 2nd Edition
978-1-118-09550-8

Office 2010 For Dummies
978-0-470-48998-7

Piano For Dummies, 2nd Edition
978-0-470-49644-2

Photoshop CS6 For Dummies
978-1-118-17457-9

Schizophrenia For Dummies
978-0-470-25927-6

WordPress For Dummies, 5th Edition
978-1-118-38318-6

12-47776 – 210.8x274.3mm

Think you can't learn it in a day? Think again

The In a Day e-book series from For Dummies gives you quick and easy access to learn a new skill, brush up on a hobby, or enhance your personal or professional life — all in a day. Easy!

Football Rules & Positions FOR DUMMIES in a day
Howie Long with John Czarnecki

Improving Your Golf Swing FOR DUMMIES in a day
Gary McCord

Buying & Serving Wine FOR DUMMIES in a day
Ed McCarthy Mary Ewing-Mulligan

Getting Started with Crowdfund Investing FOR DUMMIES in a day
Sherwood Neiss Jason W. Best Zak Cassady-Dorion

Boost Your Confidence FOR DUMMIES in a day
Kate Burton Brinley Platts

Giving Presenta FOR DUMMIES
Malcolm Kushner

Knitting a Scarf FOR DUMMIES in a day
Pam Allen, Tracy L. Barr, Shannon Okey, and Kristi Porter

Launch a WordPress.com Blog FOR DUMMIES in a day
Lisa Sabin-Wilson

Rugby Union Basics FOR DUMMIES in a day
Nick Cain Greg Growden

Cricket Rules FOR DUMMIES in a day
Julian Knight

Become More Mindful FOR DUMMIES in a day
Shamash Alidina

Running Grea Meeti FOR DUMMIES
Bob Nelson, PhD Peter Economy Mark H. McCormack Dirk Zeller

Planning a PRINCE2 Project FOR DUMMIES in a day
Nick Graham

Building Rapport with NLP FOR DUMMIES in a day
Romilla Ready Kate Burton

Ukulele FOR DUMMIES in a day
Alistair Wood

Become More Relaxed FOR DUMMIES in a day
Shamash Alidina

Available as PDF, eMobi and Kindle